MIRACLES, MILESTONES, & MEMORIES

# MIRACLES, MILESTONES, & MEMORIES

## A 269-YEAR REFLECTION, 1735-2004

### FRED VOSS

Including his translation of his late
brother Ed Voss's memories of his own life
in Germany

A portion of royalties donated to
organizations dedicated to
preserving the memory of the Holocaust
through living actions

SEAVOSS ASSOCIATES PUBLISHING
ITHACA, NY

USA

Cover photo: for caption, see p. 166.

*Comments on the sixth edition:*
The title has been kept (though it implies an end-date of 2004),
but minor changes and additions have been made to update the book
through 2016.  The major textual change in the second edition was an
expansion of the chapter on joining the Army that begins on p. 129.
For the third edition, substantial revisions were made to the family
trees that begin on p. 116.  A Postscript was added to the fourth edition, the fifth edition brought the story to 2014, and this edition brings
the story to 2016.

First edition published 2005 under the title, *Milestones and Memories, 1735-2004,
A 269 Year Reflection,* by Ed and Fred Voss, ISBN 0-9773137-0-0

Revised edition, Copyright © 2006 by Fred Voss, published by Seavoss Associates
Inc., Ithaca, NY 14850 USA, through Lulu.com

Second edition, copyright © 2009 by Fred Voss, published by Seavoss Associates
Inc., Ithaca NY 14850 USA, through Lulu.com, ISBN 978-0-557-14180-7

Third and fourth editions, copyright © 2011 by Fred Voss, published by Seavoss
Associates Inc., Ithaca NY 14850 USA, through, CreateSpace.com, ISBN 978-
1463551964

Fifth edition, copyright © 2014 by Fred Voss, published by Seavoss Associates
Inc., Ithaca NY 14850 USA, through CreateSpace.com, ISBN 978-1463551964

Sixth edition, copyright © 2016 by Fred Voss, published by Seavoss Associates
Publishing, Ithaca NY 14850 USA, through CreateSpace.com, ISBN 978-1463551964

This book is dedicated
to our children, grandchildren, and to those
who will follow them.

"Once there was a faithful soldier, who loved his girl an entire year,
an entire year and still much more; their love never ended for ever
more"

Translated from a famous German love song:

*Es war einmal ein treuer Husar,*
*der liebte sein Maedel*
*ein ganzes Jahr, ein ganzes Jahr*
*und noch viel mehr*
*die Liebe nahm kein Ende mehr.*

# PREFACE

This book was a long time in the making and it is dedicated to those of the Voss and Machauf families who lived before us, and to those who live currently, and to those who will be born in the future. It is a family story of at least four generations of Vosses who lived before me and two generations of the Machauf side before Ilse. Future generations are urged to continue writing their stories so that they never will be forgotten and will go on from generation to generation. For a long time I had the desire to write this book, but never had the time. When I left Lewisburg, PA in August of 2002, I finally decided to start writing. It is now October 2004, and I am still writing and correcting, adding and deleting.

My late brother Emil, known as Ed, had started writing in the German language about our family's history. He never completed telling his story and ended it with his departure from Germany in 1936. I am ever so thankful to my sister-in-law Diane who gave me the manuscript after Ed passed away in San Francisco in 1991. I translated his manuscript into English, and Diane edited it. I combined it with my memoirs. In this way, I could summarize the stories of the four generations.

I wish to thank the love of my life, Ilse, for her patience watching me type and spend countless hours on the computer instead of being with her. She encouraged me to keep on writing when I had lost the enthusiasm to do so. I wish to thank my severest critic, my daughter Claudia, for all her editing and the time she has spent away from her family asking me questions and correcting my lousy English to where it is acceptable. I wish to thank my son-in-law Bruce Lewenstein for his help in getting my computer straightened out again and again and again after I messed it up and lost pages and pages, "of course, through no fault of my own —." I wish to say thank you to my son Clifford and my daughter-in-law Maj-Lis for their contributions and their urging me to continue writing my memoirs. Finally, I wish to thank Kim A.K.Hassinger, a devoted English teacher at the Selinsgrove Area Middle School in PA for not only urging me to write my memoirs but also for her outstanding work correcting the many pages of this book.

Without the help of everyone concerned, this book would never have been written or printed. So, thank you one and all. I hope that you will enjoy reading this book as much as I have enjoyed writing it.

Fred Voss

# Contents

# Emil (Ed) Voss's Memories

# Our Life in Germany

First of all, we were Germans. Secondly, and thirdly, we were Germans. In our living room, we had two large pictures of the German Emperors, Emperor Wilhelm the First, and Emperor Friedrich the Second. In our dining room were two other pictures, one of the German Secretary of State, Bismarck, and one of President Von Hindenburg.

Although I was still a little boy about four years of age, in 1917 the German Emperor Wilhelm the First came to visit Aachen, the town where I was born and where we lived. That was during World War I. My maternal grandmother took me to see the Emperor who was speaking in front of City Hall in Aachen. I do not remember much of what he said that day, but I remember one sentence very well. He said the time has come to stop talking about Pralines and nonsense. These words left an ever lasting impression on me.

We considered ourselves Germans. After all, our forefathers had always lived in Germany. My grandfather Jakob Voss had volunteered to fight with the Prussian army in 1870-1871 against France and served during the battle of Sedan in France. He was a proud member of the local Wuerselner War Veterans. (Wuerselen, a suburb of Aachen, was the town where he lived and where he was buried in 1932.)

My father Julius Voss and his brothers Leopold and Alfred served in the German army during World War I. My father's cousin who was also named Leopold Voss died as a German soldier during the battle of Verdun in France. My mother's brother-in-law Isidor Voss was already serving in the German Army before World War I. He was a member of the Emperor's Special Guard, and he served with his unit in Berlin all during the war. He was very proud of that fact and would never let anyone forget it. He still spoke about it even when he finally went into exile after Kristall Night in November of 1938. I don't think my family ever

*In their Army uniforms, World War II. Uncle Alfred, Uncle Leopold, my Dad*

thought much about religion. Of course we always knew that we were Jewish as others who were Christians. At that time religion didn't make any difference to us.

*(Comment: After my brother's Bar Mitzvah in November of 1926, my father insisted, in order to please his father, that every Friday night after dinner my brother would recite the blessings after the meal in Hebrew. He also had to recite the blessings over the Torah, so that he would never forget either one. After the Friday night meal, it was the tradition that my parents, and my maternal grandmother who lived with us would bless both my brother and me. Of course, if my grandfather was with us, he too would say a blessing for us. My paternal grandmother had passed away a year after Ed's Bar Mitzvah, in December of 1927.)*

There were a number of mixed marriages in our family. My mother's aunt Amalie (Malchen) Kaufmann was married to a Catholic. My father's brother Alfred also married a Catholic who was from Belgium. With the exception of his parents, it didn't make a difference to his brothers and sister. On the other hand, his parents observing the orthodox Jewish tradition were sitting "Shiva" (sitting on a low stool when mourning) that their son got married to a non-Jew. As far as his parents were concerned, he was dead. That his wife was from Belgium unfortunately cost him his life. He and his wife fled

*Aunt May*

Germany for Belgium shortly before Kristall Night. The story has it that during the war, while my uncle and aunt were living in Belgium, his Christian wife knew and befriended several German Army Officers who were stationed in Brussels. Consequently, the officers protected both my aunt as well as her Jewish husband from a possible deportation to Auschwitz. After the liberation of Belgium, a number of Belgians who knew about the "Protection" during the German occupation were convinced that my uncle and aunt had worked together with the Nazis. They took "revenge" on him and clubbed him to death.

For a long time and long before Hitler, Uncle Alfred and Aunt May had lived in Duesseldorf about 80 miles west of Aachen. Aunt May was my favorite aunt. She had three nieces. The oldest Judith was married to a very nice man, Willie Butterman. The second niece was Maria, and the youngest of the three was Anna. Neither Maria nor Anna was married at that time. I really loved that family. As a little boy, both at Christmas and at vacation time, I was always invited to come to Duesseldorf and spent that time with the family. Aunt May waited for me to come for Christmas. It was my joy and pleasure to go Christmas tree shopping with her. She allowed me to help her decorate the Christmas tree. Christmas morning there were presents for everyone under the tree. On Christmas Eve, we all went to the midnight services. On Christmas day, Aunt May's three nieces came, and both Uncle Alfred and Aunt May distributed the presents. The Christmas goose with all the seasoning and everything else was cooked by Aunt May. I can still smell it and taste it. I was always allowed to stay with these people that I loved.

Our lives were not much different from the lives of the Christian people. All my friends at that time were Christians. Hans Bong, for example, was a great friend of mine whose parents had a little grocery store next door to our home.

Returning home to Aachen, I met with my friends, and we compared notes on what they had gotten for Christmas and what I got for Chanukah. Christmas was not observed at my parents' home. They frowned upon my traveling to Duesseldorf but never objected to it. My mother, too, loved Uncle Alfred and Aunt May.

*(Comment: After Kristall Nacht in 1938, when Jews were no longer allowed to go food shopping except on certain days and hours, it was Hans Bong's family, among a few others, who secretly brought food in the middle of the night to my parents.)*

Then there were Fifi Wienands and Kurt Kraus whose father was killed in World War I who lived with his widowed mother. There were the three Burhalter boys, all about a year apart in age—Hans, Kurt and Rolf. As far as I know, all three served and died in the German army during the war. However, I never found out what happened to Fifi Wienands. Rolf and I were the same age and were the very best of friends. We walked to school together every day for years. Then, one day after Hitler came into power, Rolf came to me and told me that he was so sorry, but it was not in his best interest for him or his family to be a friend of mine any longer. I was a Jew and felt betrayed.

At about the same time (1935) I was friendly with a young lady Johanna (Hanni) Neukamp who was at that time 20 years old. Her father according to the new Nazi Racial laws was considered a Half Jew, since his mother was Jewish. However, Hanni lived with her mother who was a Christian. Hanni and I were very good friends, although it was a strictly platonic relationship. Shortly after the Nuremberg Nazi Racial laws in 1935, my Uncle Isi received a telephone call from a "so called" friend of his with whom he had served at the Emperor Guards during the World War I, and whom he considered a good friend. However, this man was by then a high ranking Gestapo official. He told my uncle to warn me that he had seen Gestapo orders and that I was about to be arrested for violating the new Nuremberg Racial laws which forbade sexual relationships between Jews and non-Jews.

Although I knew that Hanni and I had never had a sexual relationship, my parents did not believe me. At that time my father had a little branch store of our textile wholesale store in a little Dutch suburb of Aachen called Vaals. Without any further ado or questions asked, and without my consent, my father drove me to Vaals which was in Holland with the "Order" to take care of that store and not to return to Aachen until the Nazi time was over, which he was sure would be soon. As far as I was concerned, this was a lot of nonsense because as I had assured my parents, I was not guilty as charged. With the courage of a 20-year-old idiot, as soon as my father left, I left too. I took the streetcar from Vaals to Aachen, about a 10-minute ride, and immediately went to the Gestapo Headquarters located at the Theaterplatz in Aachen. Being more of an idiot than courageous, and not realizing the danger, I told the Gestapo officer on duty that I had heard that an arrest warrant was out for me for violating the Nuremberg Racial laws. This man was totally surprised. He kept looking at me and suddenly he became very friendly. He told me to sit down, offered me a cigarette, and told me to wait. A short while later, he came back with another Gestapo agent in the black SS uniform. They then interrogated me for several hours. Finally, he shook his head and told me to go home, and that the Gestapo had no records at all that I had done anything wrong. (So much for Uncle Isi's good friend who had enjoyed scaring a Jewish boy and his family.)

From the Gestapo headquarters, I walked home to my parents. My mother almost fainted because she believed that now I would really be in a great danger. Several days later I met with Hanna again, and she told me that she too had to appear before the Gestapo and had been cross examined for several hours. She denied that we ever had sex and even offered the Gestapo to have her examined by a Gestapo physician to prove that she was still a virgin. The Gestapo told her to go home and not to worry about it anymore. She was scared to death that somehow the Gestapo would find out that under the Nuremberg laws she was considered one quarter Jewish. We both decided not to see each other again until after the Nazi era. We never met again.

We were Germans. We were also Jews. We were assimilated, and being Jewish was our religion. It was not our nationality or race.

One day long before the Nazi time, my father came home and told us "an unbelievable" story while we ate dinner. He said that during the course of the day, he had met a man with the name of Pakula who spoke bad German. My father asked Mr. Pakula if he were Polish. Mr. Pakula became upset that my father would ask him that question and said no, that he was Jewish. The man said, "I know what you mean. I am Jewish and that is my nationality." We were amused about Mr. Pakula's identification. To the best of my knowledge that was the first time that I had ever heard a man identify himself as a Jew and that to be Jewish could be something other than a religion. We made fun of this man until Adolf Hitler, some years later, told us that Jews were not Germans but a people onto themselves, a different race. When Hitler said that, we laughed once again, and we were sure that the German people would laugh at him as well for making such a ridiculous statement.

My father and thousands of other German Jews had been combat soldiers during World War I. My father was decorated with the Iron Cross Second Class, the same as Hitler was. *(The Iron Cross second class was equivalent to the United States Bronze combat medal.)* My father was decorated with the equivalent of the US Purple Heart. He was promoted to a Corporal, the same as Herr Hitler; he served in France, the same as Hitler had. Ironically, Hitler was not born in Germany, had no German ancestors, and was not a German citizen. My father could never understand how a "foreigner" like Hitler could openly declare that the Jews were not Germans. His father before him as well as his three brothers all served in the German Army. Sufficient proof was that over 3000 German Jews died on the battle field. If that were not enough, how could Hitler say the German Jews were not Germans, when during the Coupe of the Separatist in the Rheinland in 1923, the Jews in Aachen fought the German Separatist? For example, my Uncle Isi who lived in Aachen around the corner from City Hall permitted the German police and the German Firefighters to take refuge in his house, endangering his very own life and that of his immediate family. He was not the only Jew in Aachen with whose help the Separatists were beaten and defeated. All of my parents' Jewish friends as well as my parents were somehow or other involved to protect the Rheinland from the Separatists who wanted to make the Rheinland a separate but not a German State.

We no longer laughed about Hitler or the Nazis, since they came to power. To us it appeared, or so we thought, that the entire German nation was either in love with Hitler or plain nuts. When the anti-Jewish laws became the German laws of the land, we didn't smile or laugh any longer. However, at this point we were still convinced that sooner or later the German people would come to realize that we Jews were not their enemies as they were told by the Nazis, but true friends of Germany, and that they, the German people, would convince the Nazis of this. We were sure that it would not take that much longer anymore. All we had to do was to be patient until that day would come.

All this was really our own fault. It took a very long time for us to remember that it was really only a short time ago that the Jews in Germany felt so assimilated. After all, we had a Judenstrasse (Jew Street) in Aachen. A reminder of the days only two hundred years ago when the Jews in Aachen lived in a Ghetto. The Jews were by German law not allowed to have German names and were limited as to how they were permitted to earn their living. In addition, the Jews in Aachen and in many other German cities as well were forced to wear the "three corner hats" which were refereed to as "Jew hats" based on the Bible story of the Jewish deliverance from Haman who at that time sought to annihilate the Jews from Persia and made the Jews wear the three cornered hats. (Hence, the custom of eating "Hamantashen," three-cornered pastry filled with jam on the festival of Purim.)

The Jews had to pay a higher tax than the German population in Aachen and were considered the personal property of the then Duke of Juelich. I believe that in the period of 1865-1933, most Jews in Aachen and maybe even in all of Germany had forgotten about their history and did not wish to be reminded of it. My family was no exception. Only as I got older and read a lot about Germany and the Jews, I learned of the Jewish past in Aachen specifically, and in Germany in general. At the time when I lived in Germany, that subject was never ever talked about; it was long ago history.  This was after all a different new and liberal Germany, a new German generation.

There were those Jews in Germany who refused to forget that they were Jews, and they refused to become assimilated at all. Even though they lived in Germany, they did not always feel at home. For them, all their ancestors came from the Holy Land, the land of Palestine. But these Jews were at that time very few and most certainly in the minority. They were true Zionists and true followers of Theodore Herzl, the father of Zionism. Again, the majority felt pro-German, and therefore either denied or were not interested in what had happened a few hundred years ago to the Jews in Aachen and in Germany.

Now we were forced to think about who we were. At that time I read a story which I never forgot and which I always related to this situation. The story was about a horse that was raised with cows and lived happily together with the cows in the same barn. The horse always believed that it too was a cow. However, one day the horse realized that it could not give any milk to the farmers and found out the hard way that it really never was a cow.

This story is applicable to the German Jews. We were the horse in the cow shed, and as much as we wanted to be Germans, we could never make it.

Two possibilities remained for us, to wait and see what would happen, or to leave Germany. We had no idea how far Hitler would go to destroy us, and to kill us by the millions. This thought had never entered our minds.

Luckily, I had decided to leave Germany since I did not want to wait to see what might or might not happen to us.

*(Comment: I would like to write a few lines about the Jews in Aachen, their history and prior to Hitler. In 1905 the city had 145,000 inhabitants of which 1600 were Jews, a little over one percent of the population. Jews had lived in Aachen as far back as the days of Charlemagne. In 629 the Jews were expelled from Aachen and residence in the city was forbidden to Jews. The Jewish community of the early twentieth century in Aachen was only about a hundred years old at the time of the French Revolution and in the Napoleonic period. At that time Aachen was part of France, and its Jewish citizens were treated as Frenchmen. There were no Eastern Jews in Aachen at the time. In 1905 Jews in Aachen were only 1.16 % of the people but paid 7.79 % of all taxes. The main industry in Aachen was the textile industry, wool weaving mills and the manufacture of needles. Jews were not in the needle manufacturing business. The Jews were represented in many professions. Of some thirty lawyers in the city, three were Jewish. There were also six physicians. However, the number of Jewish patrons of the theater, concerts, and lectures was far out of proportion to their number in the city. There always was one token Jew on the City Council. The Vice President of the Chamber of Commerce was also traditionally a Jew. However, Jews were never permitted to be members of any private clubs. The Jewish community was liberal in comparison to the rest of the population. The synagogue had an organ. The members of the choir were mostly Christians. Men and women were not seated together. The women were seated on the right side, and men on the left side, separated by a wide aisle. The prayers were mostly in Hebrew and were only read by the Rabbi, not the congregation. The sermon was in German. Over the entrance were two large tablets in Hebrew and in German. One read "For my house shall be called a home of prayer for all nations." The other tablet read "To do justice, to love kindness, and to walk humbly with thy God." Services*

*were every Friday night and Saturday morning. However, the majority of the Jewish population only came to services for the High Holidays. The Jewish community maintained a Jewish public school consisting of two classes with two teachers. Boys and girls were separated, girls on the right side and boys on the left side of the classroom. The study was limited to reading a few selected prayers. The translation was word for word only. The Bible as such was not taught at all. In its place Jewish history was taught, which was specially prepared for all Jewish schools in Germany. There was a special course for those Jewish boys who wanted to be Bar Mitzvah. This was not a compulsory course. Bar Mitzvah Services were strictly held at the Synagogues. There was no celebration in any public place. Some families had some celebrations after the services at their homes where only the closest family were invited. Presents were mostly Jewish related items such as prayer books, books by Jewish authors, and the Bible. Of course some children got a watch, a "fountain pen," or some very personal items. Never money! The disaster that overtook the Jews in Europe engulfed also the Jewish community in Aachen. Of the 1500 Jews living in Aachen before Hitler, over forty percent died at the various concentration camps. After the war, a total of 15 former old Jewish residents returned to Aachen. Since 2003 Aachen has a new Synagogue which the city of Aachen rebuilt and paid for in full. There are approximately 1500 Russian and Eastern Jews, including many Israelis, living in Aachen again.)*

# The Voss Family and Relatives in Germany

Aachen was a town of 160,000 people at the time of my youth. After World War II the town grew, and by 1985 it had a population of close to 250,000 people. During World War II over two thirds of the town was destroyed by both the Allied air raids and the advancing American armed forces. The house in which my brother Fred and I were born was hit by a bomb and destroyed. Everyone inside was killed. During the war my brother Fred who was then a Sergeant with an American Combat Engineer Unit visited Aachen. He gave us his first-hand eyewitness and detailed report, sending us many photos of the destruction of the city, as well as what was left of the house where he and I, as well as my mother, her sister and brother, and her father before that, were all born.

The Romans originally built Aachen long before the time that Jesus was born. The Romans gave it the name of Aqueous Garner, the Great Water. The Romans discovered the hot sulfur wells which were all over town. They quickly built bathhouses wherever they found a well and used them as spas and rest-places for their soldiers. During the nineteenth century, the Emperor Karl The Great, Emperor of the Holy Roman Empire, changed the name of the town from Aqueous Garnet to Aix-La-Chapele. He built his Cathedral and his Castle in Aix-La-Chapele and made it the capital of his entire Empire. Aix-La-Chapele is French, translated as "Cathedral by the Water." During his reign, 52 French and German Kings were crowned at the Cathedral in Aachen. The Cathedral, or as it is called in German, "Der Dom," still stands and is one of the highlights to be seen by tourists from all over the world. Today in 1988, Aachen is a border town bordering on Holland and Belgium. There is a spot in Aachen called the "Three country lookout." From this spot one can clearly see to the north, east Germany, to the west Holland, and south, west Belgium. Aachen is part of the Rheinland with Bonn the capital only 40 miles to the north. Aachen as a city changed hands numerous times in its history. Since its over two thousand year old history, it was first a part of the Roman Empire.

Among others, it became part of France, Prussia, and Belgium. The citizens of Aachen never really considered themselves as Germans. They were a mixture of many nations. Before Hitler, French was spoken freely as well as German. They never spoke a first class German and most Germans from other cities made fun of the German being spoken in Aachen.

The people in Aachen developed their own "jargon," a kind of pigeon German called "Ocher Platt." Over the centuries it became a mixture of German, Dutch, Flemish, and French. For example, they used only French words; for a fork it was fourchette, luggage was baggage, a street car was a tram, and so on.

About eight miles north of Aachen is the little town of Wuerselen. There my father was born in 1884; also his father (Jakob Voss) was born there, but his grandfather Jonas Voss was born in a little village called Muentz about 12 miles north of Wuerselen. An historian who did some research for me established in 1986 that my great-great-grandfather's name was Leib Voss, born in 1791 in Muentz. His father was Natan Voss, and Leib Voss' grandfather was also named Natan, born 1735 in Muentz. All were born and lived in Muentz. Not too much of their personal life is known except for some of the stories my grandfather used to tell his grandchildren.

I still remember the many stories which my grandfather told us as children about his parents and ancestors. Levy/Leib Voss (pick either name, it was the same person), like so many Jews at his time, was a cattle dealer, one of the professions which Jews were permitted to do in order to earn a living. Leib had two wives. His first wife was Henriette Keller. We don't know if they had any children. After Henriette passed away, he married a much younger woman. She was Balbina VOHS, my great-grandmother. Balbina, also called "Binchen," had five children during her marriage with Leib, two sons and three daughters. The oldest boy was my grandfather Jakob Voss. My father remembered his grandmother "Binchen" very well. He often talked about his grandmother. He always said that even as an old lady, she was a beautiful lady, tall and very religious. She was very strict in raising her five children. Even as an old lady she still had control over all of them. My grandfather said that this was very necessary because his father died very young, and his mother Binchen had to raise her five children all alone. Since my grandfather (Jakob) was the oldest, his mother took him out of school at the age of 12, and made him help her with her business as a cattle dealer. At the time it was totally unthinkable that a woman, yet a widow, would be a cattle dealer. She did it mostly to be independent and to show her strength. As her second son Gottschalk grew up, at the age of 12, he too "joined the business." The two brothers took over the business and took care of their aging mother and their three sisters.

My great-grandfather Leib Voss lived in Wuerselen as well which was then a tiny village, and the population was predominantly Jewish. However, at Leib's time, there was a still smaller little village called

Bissen where most of the people were also Jews. Later on Bissen was incorporated with Wuerselen. It was in Bissen where my father was born in 1884. The house in Wuerselen where they lived was at the corner of Klostergasse and Kaiserstrasse. It was a little house and was still standing when I left Germany at the end of 1935. On the ground floor was the butcher shop, and behind the store was a kitchen which also served as the family room, the living room, and dining room. A tight, circular staircase went up one floor to the bedrooms. Jacob's younger brother Gottschalk bought his parents' house, lived there with his first wife Sophia, and after her death with his second wife Hilda. They had two children, Erich and a daughter named Billa. I remember them very well. Billa and her mother still lived in the same little house when I left Germany. After Gottschalk's death, Hilda changed the store from a butcher store to a variety store, selling everything from mostly candies to groceries and textiles, a little bit of everything. This house too was totally destroyed during the second World War.

*Grandfather Jakob Voss*

After my grandfather's three sisters got married, he built a house at number 12 Bahnhof Strasse in Wuerselen. His sister Louise Voss married Mathias Hoeflich who owned a little butcher shop in a town called Bedburg which is near Aachen. His sister Johanna married a Leopold Myer who had a little cigar factory in Essen. After her marriage to Leopold Myer, she moved with him to Essen.

*(Comment: Louise, like her sister Johanna, during the Holocaust in 1942, together with her husband, both in their mid 80's, were deported to Auschwitz from which they never returned.)*

The youngest of his sisters Emma married a man with the last name of Kaufmann (no relation with my mother) and moved to Aachen. The only two left were the two brothers Jakob and Gottschalk who remained in Wuerselen. (Both brothers died before the Nazis came into power.)

In his newly built house in Wuerselen, Bahnhof Strasse 12, my grandfather Jakob started a butcher shop. The house was built of heavy stones so that it would last for many generations to come. On the ground floor of the house was the butcher shop, in the back were two separate kitchens, a large living room and five bedrooms, just in case the three sons and the one daughter wanted to come visit and stay with them. Behind the house he built a slaughter house; behind that was a large lawn with many pear and apple trees. He built a chicken coop at the very end of the lawn. The two kitchens were absolutely important to him and my grandmother Clementine because both of them were very religious, and they both observed all the kosher rituals to the letter. One kitchen was for meat and meat products, the other kitchen for milk and milk products. Each kitchen had its own stove, china ware, and eating utensils. My grandmother was very strict that none of these items were ever mixed up. I do remember as a child that when we had a meat dinner, we had to wait for hours before we were allowed to have a milk dessert.

As time went by, for reasons not known to me, and of which my grandfather never spoke and even my parents claimed that they did not know, my grandfather had suddenly built another house next door to Bahnhof Strasse 12 where he owned the property. That new house was at the time considered a very large house, two floors, no longer a butcher shop. The ground floor was rented out, and my grandparents moved upstairs. My grandfather had now retired. The new house had only one kitchen (which was a major change in their lives and unheard of among the Jewish families in Wuerselen), one living room and two bedrooms. These were their new living quarters. Although his brother and sisters had remained strictly orthodox, my grandfather began to question the laws. His philosophy was, "It is not a sin what goes into one's mouth, but one had to be careful that not a sin would ever come out of one's mouth," and with that statement came his kosher lifestyle to a very sudden end.

*(Comment: This even surprised his children who had kept kosher only for their parents' sake in case they would come and eat at their homes. Why and what brought this on, we never found out, since my grandfather refused to speak about it, not even to his children. As far as he was concerned, it was not to be discussed.)*

Opa, as we called our grandfather, was a tall man, about 6'1." He was extremely strong and very muscular, broad shouldered and extremely lovable and gentle. He had such a friendly face; his dark black eyes were beautiful, and there was always a smile on his face. I do remember him only with a long gray beard, never a white beard. He was very good-natured, but at the same time, like his mother before him, very strict. He ruled over his entire family to his very end and was loved and appreciated by his children, grandchildren and everyone who ever knew him. He had established his own code of ethics to which he often referred. "The name Voss," said he, "is a good name. Always honor that name because through the generations no Voss ever got into trouble with the law. Don't be the first one." Then, there was this quote of wisdom. "Always behave yourself, so that you have nothing to fear should the police ring your door bell at night."

Then there was this one, which he always told us. "A promise or a handshake is something one has to keep no matter what, if one is to be considered honest." The one I used to love was, "When we are young, we think that we know everything, but when we are getting old, we realize that we don't know anything." Or this: "Never, ever swindle someone out of their money. You would not want anyone to do this to you." "Don't accuse others of the mistake that you made. Live by that." And finally, he used to tell us all the time, "Don't ever fear God. You must love him with all your heart." Those were some of his immortal quotes which often were quoted by the next generations and repeated by his grandchildren. I must say that they all lived by his quotes, his ethics, and his memory.

Oma is what we called my father's mother. Oma Clementine. In many respects she was just the opposite of my grandfather. She was a little woman, about 5 feet tall, and at the most weighed about 100 pounds, very petite. She had beautiful dreamy blue eyes and a heart of gold. In her entire life, she was never angry with anyone and never said a nasty word about anyone either. Just the contrary, she believed that all humans were good and never saw any faults in anyone. If anyone in the neighborhood got sick, she went there to help. It did not matter to her if she knew the person or not, or if they were Jewish or not. She cooked for them,

*Oma Clementine,*
*our grandmother*

and brought the meals to their home. She always visited them and talked to them, trying to calm them and gave them hope. Everyone in the little town of Wuerselen knew her, and she knew everyone. It has been said that when she passed away on December 7, 1927, that almost two thirds of the village turned out for her funeral. Like Opa, she had her very own philosophy, and again I would like to quote some of her immortal sayings. "Help the poor; that is your duty." Her favorite expression was, "All illnesses come galloping like a horse, and crawl back like a turtle." And then there was this saying, "Anything good that you do and everything bad that you do comes back to you at one time or another." And finally, the one which I do remember most is, "We are all God's children, and therefore we are all siblings." Those quotes, like my grandfather's are still being used within the family until this very day.

Both Opa and Oma did not only preach those words, they both lived by them. Here is an example of my grandfather's character, his way of life, his honesty, and his ethics by which he lived. Shortly after the First

World War in 1919, a man came to him, whose name I do not remember, and reminded my grandfather of a promise which my grandfather had made to him shortly after the war broke out in 1914. Opa had promised this man that when the war was over, he could buy his house for a certain amount of money. In the meantime, four war years had passed, and Germany had experienced one of its biggest inflations in history. The man said, "Jakob, you promised to sell your old house to me for such and such an amount. Now I would like to take you up on that promise and buy your house." Even though due to inflation, the house was worth 2000 times as much, if not more, my grandfather said, "A promise is a promise, and you can buy the house for the amount which I told you years ago." With all the inflationary money he got for his house, he could barely buy a dozen eggs. None of his three sons or his daughter ever dared to discuss that with him. They knew better. A promise is a promise; a handshake is a handshake, and that was all to it. And so it was. There was no deviation.

Oma Clementine was born on March 27, 1847, in the little village of Schornsheim on the Rhine river near Mainz. Her parents had a small vineyard which was their livelihood. When she was only two years old, her father had a terrible accident. Their horse hit him on his head with its hoof. This accident caused him to lose his left eye, but worse than that, he also suffered a bad concussion from which he never recovered.

*Part of the little town of Schornsheim, near Mainz, Germany, where my grandmother Clementine (Michel) was born and met my grandfather Jakob Voss. Photo courtesy Clifford Voss, 2003*

In 1849, there was no cure for a concussion. He passed away shortly after that accident. Her mother died only a few years later. This left her, my grandmother, an orphan. Her older sisters and brothers raised her and cared for her. Her schooling was strictly for a few years only. At that time in history, Jewish children in her little village were not allowed to attend a public school. She went, like her siblings, to a Jewish day school for four years. There she learned to write and read but only in the Hebrew alphabet. She would write in German with Hebrew letters only. She often told us that her school consisted of only one room and one teacher, and the few Jewish children spent all four years with the same teacher in the same classroom.

Somehow or other, Opa met the oldest brother of Clementine, Michel, who had taken over the vineyard his parents had owned. He told my grandfather a lot about his little sister Clementine. On another occasion, my grandfather took some cattle for sale and found himself in the vicinity of Schornsheim where the Michels lived. He used that opportunity to visit the young vineyard man Michel, and there he met his youngest sister Clementine. He fell in love with her. At the time Clementine was only 16 years old, and Opa thought that this was a good age for a young girl to get married. So he came back to Wuerselen with his wife Clementine. They lived happily together for 64 years until her sudden death parted them. They had six children together, but two of them, both girls, died very shortly after they were born. The other four who survived were three sons and one daughter, the oldest Leopold, then Alfred, Berta and our father, Julius.

For many years Oma Clementine had a "weak heart problem," as it was diagnosed in those days. As if she had a premonition that her death was imminent, she started very suddenly to collect all her personal belongings, like dresses, underwear, and so on, packed it up, and gave it to the poor. Very shortly after that, my grandfather found her in the early morning hours in December of 1927, dead, sitting in her favorite arm chair next to the kitchen stove. They had talked to each other only moments before.

After her sudden death, Opa could no longer stand to be alone in his house. He moved to his oldest son Leopold and his wife Bella who lived at 188 Bismark Strasse in Aachen. At the age of 87 he passed away from the complications of a prostate surgery. Even at his age of close to 90 years, he had only gray hair and so his beard was never white. Up to the day when he was admitted to the hospital for surgery, he still walked as straight as "a Prussian soldier." He was as alert, strong, and bright as he always was during his entire life. He was still the same man as he was when he was in his 70's, when one day he came to visit us at our home with one hundred pounds of potatoes carried over his shoulder. He had walked that way from his home in Wuerselen. When my father asked him why he didn't use the streetcar, his answer was for him a simple one. "The streetcar had raised its fare, and he refused to pay the higher fare. It was as simple as that."

*(Comment: I still remember when around 1931 a year before his death and two years before Hitler, a man came to our house to see my*

*father for which reason I don't remember anymore. Opa was standing next to my father. Suddenly this man made an anti-Semitic remark to my father. Before my father knew it, Opa grabbed this man by his collar and literally kicked him in his behind and threw him out of the house. He looked at my father and said, "That takes care of him for today.")*

It was in the year 1932, shortly before his death, and only four months before Hitler came to power in Germany that I had my last conversations with him. Like me, he loved to talk about politics.

*(Comment: My late brother Emil, or Ed, as he was known, and my grandfather had a lot in common. Their political views were very much liberal; my brother's more so than our grandfather's.)*

He asked me if I really believed that Hitler would come into power. I told him that I was very much afraid that he would. His comment which I will never forget was, "Well, he will have the surprise of his life; he will not last. The German people are too liberal and too smart to fall for his politics of anti-Semitism, unless Hitler would change his politics. Christians would never let this happen." He then reasoned, "After all, Jesus Christ was a Jew too, and that the Christian religion was based on his teachings, of 'Love Thy neighbor as you love yourself.'" He ended that in ancient days, in many countries, the leaders tried to destroy the Jews and chase them from their land, yet the Jews always survived. After all, he said, "Nothing can be eaten as hot as it is being cooked." This is an old German saying.

At that time I, of course, had no idea how wrong his reasoning would turn out. I certainly had no idea that this would have been our last conversation. Only few weeks later, we buried him in the Jewish Cemetery in Wuerselen next to his beloved Clementine. At the time of his funeral all stores in Wuerselen were closed. The Wuerselner War Veterans escorted his flag-covered casket and the funeral cortege with military music and honor from the home where he once lived to the cemetery for his final resting place.

*(Comment: This is the story of his "final resting place." During or shortly after Kristall Night, the Nazis not only destroyed our Temples throughout Germany in their hate against the Jews, they destroyed our homes and stooped as low as to destroy our cemeteries. Our grandparents' gravestone was torn off its foundation. As on many other Jewish cemeteries, they destroyed what ever they could. Gravestones were smashed up and used for road construction. I know that in Haaren, outside of Aachen and close to Wuerselen, for instance, the Jewish gravestones were used by the head of the local SS as ornaments in his back yard, where after the war they were found.)*

About Opa and Oma's siblings I don't know too much. His brother Gottschalk Voss died in 1915. At the time I was only 2 years old and of course, do not remember him at all. However, I do remember a story which my grandfather always would tell us. Opa and his brother Gottschalk were together one day at the slaughterhouse in Aachen. One of my mother's uncles who was also a cattle dealer had taken me along to the slaughterhouse. He must have carried me in his arms. Opa and his brother didn't know this man too well. To come to the slaughter house with a toddler in his arms caused them to take a good look at the man and the little boy. "Look," Opa said to his brother Gottschalk, "that little boy looks just like my little grandson, Julius's son Emil." "Of course," answered Gottschalk, "it is your grandson Emil." Gottschalk, like his brother Jakob, also was a cattle dealer and butcher. Many years before the two brothers had made an agreement in order for Jakob to learn the butchering of cattle. The agreement was made that he (Jakob) would become a kosher butcher only. The kosher meat which Gottschalk sold at his butcher store was killed in accordance with the proper Jewish rituals and laws. Opa did this as a "Mitzvah," a good deed and was not paid for it.

Gottschalk's first wife's name was Sophia. They had four children together. I only knew two of them, Selma and Berta. Their oldest son, also named Leopold, was killed during the first world war during the battle of Verdun in France. I knew his widow Regine Voss very well. Later in her life Regine got married again to a very nice man, a Hermann Kahn.

*(Comment: Hermann Kahn had left Germany after the first World War for America. Regine Voss came on her own to visit New York in the early 1930's. During her visit, she met Hermann Kahn. Hermann proposed to her, and after her return back to Germany, she decided in 1933 right after the Nazis came into power, to accept his proposal and moved to New York. They had no children. It was Uncle Hermann and Aunt Regine, as we called them, who welcomed us when we arrived in New York in May of 1940. They took us under their wings and helped us to find an apartment. Uncle Hermann helped me to find my first job in America. He knew a man who owned a hand weaving-mill consisting only of four looms. This man hired me for $10 a week, working 6 days —10 hours a day, which at that time was a nice salary.)*

Gottschalk's and Sophia's son Heinrich was killed as the result of an accident at the age of 12 years. I never knew him. Their daughter Berta had moved to Essen where she married Heinz Heineman. They had one daughter Gerda. Later on, Gerda's parents escaped Germany for Chile.

Gerda married Otto Tobias. They had no children. Gerda died in Santiago, Chile in 1982. After Gerda's death, Otto Tobias married Gerda's cousin, but the marriage ended in a divorce. I didn't know this part of the family too well. I knew their oldest daughter Selma very well. She married a Leopold Rosenthal, called Leo. He too was a butcher and owned his own slaughterhouse behind their residence in Wuerselen. I recall him very well. He made the best "Liverwurst," and every time I visited them, he would cut a big piece of Liverwurst for me to eat. Leo and Selma had two children. The oldest was named Sofie, a pretty girl about three years younger than I. Her younger brother Alex was the same age as my brother Fred. The entire family escaped during the Nazi time to Chile. Alex died at the young age of 38 years in Chile. He had one daughter named Eva who to the best of my knowledge lives in the USA.

My grandfather's brother Gottschalk remarried after his first wife Sophia passed away. He married Hilda Strauss and had two children with her. His son was named Erich. His daughter's name was Billa. Both resided at their parents' house. After Erich had done his apprenticeship as a butcher, he too followed the family tradition and became a butcher. He opened his own non-kosher butcher shop in Wuerselen. However, sport was his love, and he devoted most of his life to Germany's favorite sport, soccer. In time, he became a well-known German soccer player. When Erich got older, he became a referee and as such was well known throughout Germany's sport world. He married Luise Levi who came from a little village called Langerwehe.

*(Comment: Luise Levy was related to a Herta Levy who later on married Uncle Leopold's oldest son Kurt. They moved to Johannesburg, South Africa. Kurt was a well-known Social Democrat in Aachen and at one time tried to run for the German Reichtstag but lost the election. Because of his anti-Nazi activities, he was on the Nazis' hit list and left Germany shortly after the Nazi takeover.)*

Anyhow, Erich, together with his wife and his mother Hilda, his sister Billa, and her husband Paul Weis, left early during the Nazi Regime for Rio de Janeiro, Brazil. There Erich opened a butcher store. Erich and his wife Luise had one son and one daughter. Both their children were married in Brazil. They have children and are grandparents. Both Erich's and Billa's children, as well as their grandchildren went into the medical profession; all of them are physicians in Brazil. As long as my parents were still alive, they were in touch with all of them, but now we only get a card from them for the Jewish Holidays without any comments.

*(Comment: Good friends of Ilse's and mine Michael and Lilian Freemont, on a cruise to Brazil, visited the family in Copacabana out-*

*side of Rio several years ago. The Freemonts reported back that they met with everyone and that everyone seemed to be doing well and were well established physicians.)*

Now, to Opa's other siblings. The oldest of them was Johanna who married Leopold Meyer who came from Essen. There he had a cigar factory. They had one daughter Bertha. I only met Johanna, Leopold, and Berta once or twice in my life and have no idea what happened to the family. I contacted other family members who likewise have no idea what happened to them either.

*(Comment: Several years ago I met some people who came from the city of Essen. They told me a story which was very sad. The entire family committed suicide just before the Gestapo came to deport them to Poland.)*

Opa's other sister Louise whom I knew very well, married a Mathias Hoeflich and moved with him to Bedburg, not too far from Aachen. Like most Jews at that time, he too was a butcher. They had two sons, Julius and Heinrich. Julius married Claire and they lived in Nuerenberg (Bavaria). They had two daughters. Julius was an inventor in Nuerenberg. He owned a little motorcycle plant. His motorcycles sold under the trade name of "JUHO." They were able to move to the United States and lived until their deaths in Baltimore, MD. I have no knowledge what happened to their two daughters. The oldest of them was Ilse, and she was about my age.

The other one was Liselotte and was my brother's age. I do remember her very well. She and my brother Fred played together as children. I was told once that they both lived somewhere here in the States and were married. Anyhow, we found out that Louise and her husband died at the Theresienstadt Nazi Concentration camp.

*(Comment: Liselotte Hoeflich, whom I knew very well, and her husband were able to get out of Germany and lived in southern France where they were married. When the Nazis invaded France in 1940, they went into hiding but in 1942 were caught by the Nazis when a Frenchman who worked for the then Vichy Government reported them to the Gestapo. They were deported and never heard from again. Her sister Ilse and husband moved to Phoenix, AZ, where, as far as I know, they still live. The saddest story is what happened to their grandparents Luise and Mathias Hoeflich. Luise was our grandfather's sister. Luise was born on July 22, 1858, in Wuerselen. I have a copy of her wedding and birth certificate in front of me. The Nazis were so organized; they made a number of entries on a lot of Jewish birth and wedding certificates. Her wedding certificate shows that on August 12, 1942, she was deported*

*at the age of 84 years, together with her then 92-year-old husband to the Theriesenstadt Concentration Camp. A further entry is made dated August 17, 1938, stating that according to a new Nazi law the name Sarah, as a Jewish female, was added to her name. The next entry is made by the Sonderstandesamt (a division of the SS) that she died in Theresienstadt on October 8, 1942, which was less than two months after she was deported. The next entry made on December 17, 1948 (after the war), states that the name Sarah was rescinded as of that date. The final and last entry made was on January 13, 1953. This one reads that according to the research done by the authorities in Cologne in October of 1952, the couple Mathias and Luise Hoeflich (nee Voss) are declared deceased. The date established by the German government as to their official death is 31 December 1945.)*

Opa's sister Emma, like all her siblings, lived in Wuerselen where she was born. She met a man whose last name was Kaufmann, but he was not related to my mother. He died very young. I never knew him. They had two children together, a son named Alfred and a daughter named Dina. Alfred was an artist painter, well known in the Rheinland for his paintings. When my parents got married in 1912, as a wedding present he painted a wall in their bedroom. The painting was wonderful, and I still remember it. It was a scene with angels overlooking and blessing my parents' bed. Until my parents left Germany in 1939, 27 years later, this wall was never repainted and looked as beautiful as ever. Alfred was a member of the Communist party in Aachen and participated against many political Nazi rallies. An SA man shot him to death shortly before the Nazis came to power. He was the first victim in our family, killed by the Nazis as early as 1932 (many untold others followed him in their death). He was never married. He was a very nice, sweet, and generous man who was known all over town for always helping the poor.

*(Comment: When Hitler came into power, the SA man who had killed Alfred Kaufmann, Klaus Butterfeld became a "Nazi hero" in Aachen. In his "honor" the Nazis named the street where he had killed Alfred Kaufmann "Butterfeld Strasse." That street name was still there until 1949, when the street name was finally changed back to its former name. Butterfeld was killed during an air attack in 1943 in Aachen.)*

Alfred Kaufmann's sister Dina had a little variety store in Aachen. She got married very late in life to Benno Sachs an American Jew who lived in Aachen and was an English teacher. He was born and raised in New York City. Shortly after their marriage, and long before Hitler came to power, they moved back to New York. Both died in New York City shortly after World War II.

Dina's mother Emma who was my father's aunt and my grandfather's other sister had a`stroke shortly after the end of the first war which had left her partially paralyzed. She was a resident at the Jewish Nursing home in Aachen where my father and grandfather visited her weekly. Often I was allowed to go along with my father to visit her. I do remember her very well. She passed away in 1927 and is buried in the Jewish cemetery in Aachen.

*Leopold Voss*

Of my grandmother Clementine's siblings, I only knew her brother Max Michel. Max and his wife Eva lived in Aachen. Max suffered from diabetes and eventually lost his sight. He passed away shortly thereafter. Max and Eva had no children. One of Oma's nephews Salomon Weil lived in another little village called Weiden. Weiden was a few miles from Wuerselen. I saw Salomon here and there but do not remember him at all.

Now to the offsprings of Jakob and Clementine Voss, my grandparents. The oldest son was Leopold, born in Wuerselen in 1873. He completed his apprenticeship at a textile store, the same as my uncle Alfred, and later on my Dad. After he completed his apprenticeship, he worked as a salesman in a textile store. There he met a Billa Stiel who was born in Eschweiler and whom he later married. At that time it was customary when a girl got married that the girl's father would give their future son-in-law a dowry. He gave his son-in-law a dowry that was large enough for Leopold to start his own textile store on Kaiser Strasse in Wuerselen. The business was very successful, and after my Dad had finished his apprenticeship, his oldest brother Leopold took him into his business. The business continued to do well and grew. They worked together until my Dad married my mother and decided to move to Aachen. I remember Uncle Leopold's store very well. Behind his store was a lovely and very comfort-

*Cousin Kurt Voss*

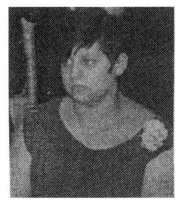

*Cousin Else Voss*

able living room, very nicely furnished. The bedrooms were on the first floor. They had three children. Their daughter Else was the oldest, and then Kurt, and the youngest of the trio was Walter. Walter was exactly eight months older than I, and so we had a lot in common, both the good and the bad things we did together.

When we came to Wuerselen which was very often, we always played together. Very often we got ourselves into trouble for which our parents punished us. Sometimes Opa had to discipline us himself. For example, one fine day we found an acorn, took a straw and made a pipe out of it. Then we stole one of Opa's cigars, cut it into pieces, and smoked it. I believe we were about six or seven years old at the time. Opa discovered that one of his cigars was missing. It didn't take him long to figure out what happened to it. Confronted with our adventure and confessing to it caused us to get a tough licking from Opa and a sermon about stealing. We never forgot that episode. Even when Walter and I were married, we still wrote and laughed about it. When Uncle Leopold was drafted for military duty in 1914, Aunt Bella took over the business. She had no experience in running a business and besides had three little children to take care of. Consequently, the

*Cousin Walter Voss*

business went down. After Uncle Leopold returned from the war in 1918, he tried to sell the business, however, to sell a business during those years was impossible. In 1924 he finally moved his home and business to Aachen. He found a good location for his store and living quarters at 188 Bismarck Strasse. There he lived with Aunt Bella and my cousin Walter until they had to leave Germany. In the meantime, his daughter Else got married to a Josef Stock who under the Nuerenberg laws was considered a half Jew. Else and Josef had two children, Ruth and Heribert. Unfortunately, the marriage ended in a divorce. Josef had a nice sized textile store in the town of Dueren which was half way between Aachen and Cologne. After the divorce Else moved back with her parents and later married Kurt Frank. Together they left for Argentine where he had cousins. They had no children. Ruth and Heribert stayed with their father in Dueren. During Kristallnacht in November 1938, Josef Stock, like thousands of other Jews, was rounded up and shipped to the Sachsenhausen Concentration Camp. Once released from the Camp, he returned home to Dueren and took both children to be safe from the Nazis to London, where he had cousins. Unfortunately, he returned back to Dueren to liquidate his business with the intention to leave shortly for London himself.

However, as fate wanted it, he was no longer able to leave Germany and became another of the six million Jews killed. His daughter Ruth was only 18 years old, and his son Heribert about 15 or 16 years old. Ruth married in London a Hans Presh, and they had a son together, Richard Winston. Shortly after the baby was born, Hans Presh died very suddenly. Ruth got remarried to Reginald Arbiter who adopted the baby Richard Winston. Unfortunately, this marriage did not last long. After that Ruth married an Englishman Asher Bernstein who lived in Bulawayo, Rhodesia, which is known today as Zimbabwe. Ruth moved to Bulawayo. Asher

*Cousin Ruth Bernstein at 18*

Bernstein passed away several years ago, and her son Richard, known as Dickie Arbiter, lives in London, England. There he became the personal secretary to the late Princess Diana until she was killed in a car accident. Ruth visited me in our home in San Rafael, California about five years ago. Of course we had not seen each other in many years and had a lot to talk about. Ruth's son married Rosemary Brook, and they have a daughter named Victoria. Victoria became an actress and moved to New York where she got married.

Ruth's only brother Heribert, in order to become a British subject, joined the British Army after the war. At the time there was a lot of fighting going on between the British Army occupying Palestine and the Jewish Freedom fighters. Heribert was sent to Palestine as a British soldier and was killed in 1947 by the Jewish freedom fighters in Haifa.

He was not married. Because he was a British soldier at the wrong place at the wrong time, he is buried on the British Army Cemetery in Haifa, Israel. The son of my uncle Leopold and aunt Bella, Kurt, as I mentioned earlier, had left Germany for South Africa. His wife's sister was married to a man named Karsebom who somehow and the other had connections with South Africa. Through the connections it was possible for them to leave Germany and move to Johannesburg, South Africa. Kurt was able to bring both his parents to Johannesburg. Aunt Bella died of cancer shortly after they were in Johannesburg. Several years later Uncle Leopold at the age of 81 married a widow by the name of Lenchen Goldschmidt. Both lived until his death in Johannesburg. Uncle Leopold died shortly after his 90th birthday as a result of a massive and sudden heart attack.

The youngest son of Uncle Leopold and Aunt Bella, Walter, married a Lilo Willner from Krefeld, Germany. They got married in 1936 and moved to Rhodesia, today Zimbabwe. Walter and Lilo opened a dog kennel and started dog breeding. Walter was busy and very successful with his part of the business, while Lilo, who was by trade a dressmaker, opened a dress store in Bulawayo. Walter was drafted during the war into the British Army and served in Egypt. In 1957, Walter died suddenly at the age of 44 of a massive heart attack like his father did. Lilo died five years later from cancer. Neither Walter nor his brother Kurt had any children.

*(Comment: The Willner family was very close to our family. Tilly Willner's maiden name was Kaufmann. She was a second cousin of my mother, the daughter of my mother's cousin, Hugo Kaufmann. They had three daughters, Lilo, Edith and Ilse. We called their parents Uncle Herman and Aunt Tilly. Lilo had two other sisters Edith and Ilse. Edith was a few years older than I. Edith was married in mid-1938 at the age of 21 to an Erich Kahn who was also from Aachen. I always considered Lilo, Edith, and Ilse as cousins and was very close to them. During the infamous Kristall Nacht, November 9, 1938, I was visiting with the family in Krefeld. I was staying with Edith and Erich because I liked them the best. Besides, they had a large apartment. Unfortunately, that was also the last time that I saw both in my life. The night of November 8-9, Erich was arrested by the Gestapo at their home. He was removed in his night clothes and taken away. That was the last his wife Edith ever saw of him. At the time he was only 24 years old. They were married that young because Edith's sister Lilo had arranged for both of them to come and live with them in Bulawayo. After the arrest of her young husband, Edith refused to leave Germany because she was convinced*

*that Erich would return. Edith, her sister Ilse, and their parents all died in Auschwitz.)*

Now comes Uncle Alfred, as my grandparents' next child. I wrote about him previously in detail. The only additional comment I would like to mention is that Uncle Alfred had his own Real Estate agency in Duesseldorf and later on in Brussels as well. He always earned a comfortable living. Before I was born, they had a little boy named Hans who unfortunately died shortly before his second birthday. They had no other children.

This brings me now to Aunt Berta, the only surviving daughter my grandparents had. At the time when she grew up, it was customary in Jewish families to contact a matchmaker before the daughter got too old. Berta was born in 1879. Of course, following the old Jewish tradition, my grandfather looked for and found a matchmaker, of course for a price. The matchmaker found a man who would fit the "requirements." The man's name was Emil Hirsch. Emil Hirsch came from a good Jewish family in Germany. He was foreign sales-manager for a large German company headquarters in Brussels. Of course, Aunt Berta had no other choice but to marry this man in 1904 at the age of 25. A little over a year later they had a baby girl named Estelle. Aunt Berta was very unhappy with this man. She discovered that he had a number of affairs. When she told her father about it, he went to Brussels immediately and brought Aunt Berta and little Estelle home to Wuerselen with him. During the years from 1905 until about 1919, Aunt Berta and Estelle lived in Wuerselen.

Aunt Berta's oldest brother Leopold who was married to Aunt Bella (nee Stiel) managed to bring Aunt Bella's oldest brother Albert Stiel and Aunt Berta together. They got married about a year later. By coincidence, Albert Stiel was offered a position as a manager of a large silk fabric wholesale business in, of all places, Brussels. They moved to Brussels, and Estelle was back again where she was born. The company for which Albert worked was sold a few years later to a cousin of Albert Stiel. His name was Benno Rotschild and related to the very wealthy Rotschild family who were well known bankers in Europe at the time. The business went very well and was enlarged several times. They opened stores in Cologne and Bad Homburg in Germany, in France, in Lyon, and in Milan, Italy. Uncle Albert's cousin Benno Rotschild made him a partner in the business, and Uncle Albert was now in charge of the Brussels, Lyon, and Milan wholesale business. In the meantime, Uncle Albert too became very wealthy, and besides their beautiful house, at 50 Rue de l'Ermitage in Brussels, they bought a gorgeous villa on the Bel-

*Uncle Alfred Voss*

gium seashore in Le Zoute. My cousin Walter and I would always spend a part of our summer vacation there.

*(Comment: The summer vacations were always split between my brother and Walter. The other half was my turn, Estelle's daughters Sonja, and Estelle's niece, Friedel Stiel, from Eschweiler. Both girls were one year younger than I, and Friedel's younger brother Hans was about three years younger than we were. Here, I would like to make the sad remark that both Friedel Stiel, her younger brother, and their parents all perished in Auschwitz. They had escaped to Belgium at the same time we did, but had no way to get out of Belgium and were caught by the Nazis when they invaded Belgium.)*

Estelle married her stepfather Albert Stiel's youngest brother Julius. They had two children, Sonja, a year younger than my brother Fred, and Nadia, three years younger than her sister Sonja. Both girls were born

*Aunt Berta Voss Stiel*

in Cologne, Germany. Shortly after the Nazi takeover in Germany, Uncle Albert brought his brother Julius to Brussels to manage the Brussels store. As time got worse for the Jews in Germany, the boycott by the Nazis against Jewish owned business led to the two store closings in Cologne and Bad Homburg.

Emil Hirsch, Estelle's father, after the first World War moved to Brazil where again he represented the same German company as he had in Brussels. He got married again in Brazil. He always kept in touch with his daughter Estelle and was a good and loving father to her and her children even after the divorce from Aunt Berta. He was well established in Brazil, and he too had a very comfortable life there. When World War II started, and when the Nazis first invaded Belgium, Estelle, her husband Julius, the two girls, Aunt Berta, and Uncle Albert, all fled from Brussels to the south of France. Estelle managed from there with the help of her father to be allowed a legitimate entry into Brazil. As a matter of fact, Emil Hirsch had offered to bring Uncle Albert and Aunt Berta to Brazil as well. They refused the offer and finally had to hide in a Catholic monastery.

While in Brazil, and through friends of Emil Hirsch, Julius Stiel met a man with whom he started manufacturing ladies blouses. As luck had it, they became very successful, and when the war ended they had a new life in Brazil. Their daughter, Sonja, now 25 years old, married a Brazilian Jew, and they had two children together. Their marriage ended in a divorce.

*(Comment: Sonja's son Charles stayed in Brazil after his parents' divorce. Later on he left Brazil for Israel where he joined the Air Force and became a decorated fighter pilot. He remained with the Israeli Airforce. I have no idea what happened to him later on. I was told that he got married and had children and lived on a Kibbutz in the Negev. His sister stayed with their father in Brazil where she, too, eventually married. I have no further knowledge about her fate.)*

Uncle Albert and Aunt Berta returned to Brussels after the war. To his greatest amazement and with the fortunate streak of luck which he always had, he found his businesses in Belgium, France, and Italy had not only survived the war, but had grown and were larger than before the war. The German Gestapo had confiscated both businesses and had put a German manager in charge. As it turned out, he was the former manager of their business in Cologne to whom uncle Albert had sold the store when he could no longer operate the Cologne store due to the Nazi boycott of Jewish owned business. This man had become a big shot in the Nazi party which had led him to run both the Belgium and Italy business. The profit the stores made during his leadership went to Germany. After the war, the Belgium and the government in Italy restored full ownership to uncle Albert and his cousin Benno Rotschild. The so-called Nazi-German manager was arrested in Belgium after the war. After a court trial, he was sentenced to five years in jail and when released was deported back to Germany.

Julius and Estelle returned after the war to Belgium where Julius resumed his job as manager of the Brussels store. Julius died several years later after suffering a stroke.

Sonja eventually also went back to Brussels where she too married again. She and her husband came to visit my wife Diane and me several years ago.

Nadia married a diamond dealer from Antwerp, Belgium, with the last name of Epstein. Uncle Albert, his brother Julius, Aunt Berta, and Estelle passed away many years after the war and are buried in Brussels.

The youngest of my grandparents' children was my father, Julius Voss.

# The Closest Family

June 22, 1936, is a day I will never forget. It was a rainy spring day. I stood in front of the house where I was born, and as far as I knew, I was standing there for the last time. This was the house in which my mother's grandfather was born and where he had grown up. It was the house that my maternal great-grandfather had built about one hundred years ago, the home where four generations of my family had lived, including my brother Fred and me. This was the Kaufmann homestead, a part of our family history and our heritage. If the walls of this house could only talk, what stories they would tell. Every room brings back memories of the lives of all those people who once lived there. Here was the room in which my grandfather died on May 31, 1901. I regret that I never knew him, but I can identify with him. He

*My mother and my brother Emil, 1914*

was my mother's father, Emil Kaufmann after whom I was named. He was the son of Hermann Kaufmann and Caroline Compri who was born in Mastricht, Holland. Her cousin was Adolf Sutro, born in Aachen as well. Later on he became a mayor of San Francisco. Both his parents are buried at the Jewish cemetery in Aachen. A park was named after Adolf Sutro in San Francisco and still is in existence.

This was the day when I was leaving my home in Aachen to start a new life in San Francisco. I thought of all the things that had happened to me here in the house where I was born, good things and bad things. I remember my parents telling me that in the late fall of 1914, when I was a toddler, my father held me in his arms in my parents' bedroom on the second floor of our house. My father was in the uniform of the German army. He was on his way to the battlefield in France. As my mother said good-bye to him, she burst into tears, and when I saw her crying with tears running down her cheeks, I said, "Don't cry, Mommy. Daddy has such nice gold buttons."

My very first memories have to do with World War I. I remember the garden in the back of our house and the railroad tracks leading to Belgium. A small wall separated our garden from the tracks. One day, like little boys do, I climbed up the wall and looked down the tracks. I saw rows of military boots besides the tracks with gray blankets covering the bodies of dead German soldiers who had been returned from the front. I will never ever forget this sight as long as I live.

I will never forget the nights when British war planes flew over Aachen, when my mother and my grandmother would come and wake me up and take me into the cellar to be better protected if a bomb hit the house. I have been told that during World War II one bomb hit the same house where I was born, and twenty people lost their lives in the same cellar during an air raid by allied planes bombing Aachen.

Very little food was available. Our evening meals consisted only of boiled potatoes, and even they were hard to find. When ever possible my father's father, my grandfather whom I called Opa Jakob, would come from Wuerselen when ever he could and brought us meat and eggs. Still clear in my mind is the day that my mother, my grandmother, and I were walking in the forest looking for mushrooms to add to our evening meal. Suddenly the earth shook. We could hear the big cannons, "Big Berta" in action in Verdun. Later, we received news that my father had been wounded in that battle.

All of these memories flooded my mind on this, the most important day in my young life. The time had come for me to say good-bye to everyone I knew. My parents and my brother would go along with me to the ship in Rotterdam which would take me to San Francisco. I was in tears as I said good-bye to my 77-year-old grandmother. I loved her so much, and I was sure that I would never see her again. We cried. I am sure that it brought back to her the day twenty-five years earlier when she said good-bye to her only son, seventeen-year old-Heinrich, when he too left Aachen for San Francisco to find a better future in America. She never saw him again.

My mother's mother, Oma Tilly (Otilie), really raised my brother Fred and me. Our mother worked with our father in their business, taking care of the books and of all of the correspondence. She had very little free time to raise us. Oma came from a large family in Brilon, Westphalia. She was the second youngest of thirteen children, ten brothers and three girls. Her father Aaron Elsbach remarried after the death of his first wife. There were six children from the first marriage and seven from the second marriage. His second wife, Oma's mother, was Julie Schoenholz. From that marriage, Oma had two more sisters, Berta and Jetchen, who married two brothers named Reinsberg. Berta and Robert Reinsberg moved to Ostend on the Belgium seacoast where they opened a restaurant. They took Oma with them to work in the kitchen and later on she became the chef. Oma Otilie was an excellent gourmet cook capable of cooking in the finest restaurants. Six of her brothers left America where four of them died without ever having been married. The oldest brother Hermann was the only brother who married. They had all left during 1860 - 1870 to avoid serving in the Prussian army.

*(Comment: Politically there was a huge difference in the 1860 - 1870 period between the State of Prussia and the State of Westphalia. Each was a totally independent state within Germany, and Westphalia resented being associated with Prussia. However, everyone had to serve their military duty under the Prussian military authorities.)*

Hermann Elsbach was married to Emma, also from Westphalia. They had three sons. The oldest was Hermann Jr.; the middle son was Edwin, and the youngest was John. None of the three brothers had children. Late in life Edwin married a women named Violet. They adopted a little girl whom they named Mary. Oma's youngest brother Albert Elsbach who also left for America later on in life, never married either and died in San Francisco in 1930.

Oma, "Tilly" as she was known to all, never knew her father. He died when she was only two years old. Her mother died when Oma was twenty years old. I remember her telling us that before she died, her mother made her promise that she would never kiss a man until she was married to him. Oma claimed that she kept that promise that she made to her dying mother. Her mother came from a strict orthodox Jewish family from the village of Luetgendortmund in Westphalia, a suburb about twelve miles west of Bochum and Dortmund. Oma's maternal grandfather Hertz Schoenholtz had ten children. He was born in Luetgendortmund in 1744. He was a rag peddler and lived in poverty his entire life. Oma's parents were not any better off. Her father too was a rag peddler, and he and his family also lived in poverty. Perhaps this was the real reason why all of Oma's brothers left for America. After Hermann left his home in Brilon for San Francisco, he and my grandmother wrote to each other every month until he passed away in 1936. Hermann had become a successful merchant in San Francisco, but his piece goods fabric business was destroyed in 1906 when a strong earthquake destroyed a large part of the city. Oma sent all of her money, 30,000 German Marks, about $7,500 to her brother. Hermann never forgot her help when he needed it most. As soon as he was financially able, he paid back all of the money. After World War I, when food was still hard

*Grandfather Emil Kaufmann*

to get in Germany, he sent a case of food with instructions to share the fruit, especially with the children. It was only natural that Oma asked Hermann to help me to come to America and escape the Nazis in Germany.

When Oma was thirty years old, she worked as a cook in the restaurant of her sister's hotel in Ostend, Belgium. That is where she met a guest called Emil Kaufmann with whom she fell in love and married. Opa Emil, after whom I was named, had a butcher shop at the Klostergasse in Aachen. His father, Herman Kaufmann, also a butcher, built the house in Aachen at Burtscheider Strasse 32, which became the family's homestead.

*(Comment: I too remember Oma's stories as well as Ed (Emil) did. Ed failed to write that Oma always told us her husband's family on both of his mother's sides came during the Inquisition from Spain to Holland. Hence, the names Compri and Sutro which are of Spanish origin. They were all Sephardic Jews.)*

*Our grandmother Oma Tilly Kaufmann (Elsbach)*

Oma and Opa had two daughters Irma and Else and one son Heinrich (I wrote about him before). Our mother Else Kaufmann was three years younger than Irma, and Heinrich was five years younger than my mother. My grandfather Opa Emil died of pneumonia at the age of 45. At the time of his death, my mother was only twelve years old. Oma Tilly told us the story how he died and she always blamed him. According to her story, it was a very cold and rainy day in Aachen. Opa got out of a sick bed suffering from a nasty cold and a bad cough to be among the first people in Aachen to ride on a new electric street car. Opa's cold developed into pneumonia. In 1901 there was no cure for pneumonia, and he died within a week. My mother loved her Papa, as she called him, dearly and his early death left her mourning for a long time. After his father's death, Opa Emil bought the house in the Burtscheider Strasse from his siblings and continued the butcher shop at the same location. After Opa Emil's death, Oma Tilly continued to run the shop even though she had no previous experiences.

*Aunt Irma Voss (Kaufmann), 1940*

Both our grandmother and our mother have always told us that on May 31, 1901, when they came home from my grandfather's funeral, there was a terrible thunderstorm in Aachen. As we grew up, mysteriously every year thereafter on May 31, there has been a thunderstorm in Aachen.

*(Comment: For many years I have encountered these thunderstorms on May 31, both when we were in exile in Belgium and England as well as later on here in the United States.*

*According to Ed, Oma Tilly continued to run the butcher shop. However, she had hired two experienced butchers to do all the actual work. She had hoped that her son Heinrich would have been able to take over. Unfortunately, the butchers whom she had hired were a bad influence on young Heinrich. Heinrich dropped out of school, started smoking, gambling, drinking, and did all the wrong things. His mother in despair contacted her brother Hermann in San Francisco asking him for his advice.*

*Hermann told her to send Heinrich who was then 17 years old to him in San Francisco, and he would try his best with him. By that time it was already too late. Heinrich was wild and totally out of control. He was psychologically badly hurt because his mother had sent him so far away from home, and his sisters had not stopped their mother from doing that to him. He broke off all relationship with his mother and his sisters. None of them heard from him ever again. In World War I, when America joined the war against Germany, he volunteered to serve in the American army, and he*

*Our mother, Else Voss (Kaufmann), 1937*

*stayed on with the army of occupation in Germany. At that time he was seen in Aachen by a number of people who had known him well before he had left for America. They told his mother and sisters about it. He did not see nor visit his mother and sisters while visiting Aachen as an American soldier. After he was discharged he met and married a native American Indian girl who at that time was living with her family on an Indian reservation in Arizona. Nobody knows what happened after that, except that during Prohibition, he got into serious trouble with the law and served time at Alcatraz. When he was discharged, he changed his name to "Henry Carlson Sr." That was the last that any family member ever found out about him. Some years later he changed his name again, but nobody ever found out what that name was.)*

*Heinrich Kaufmann, their only son, at the age of 14 shortly before he left for San Francisco in 1905*

My father married Else, the daughter of Oma Tilly, on May 5, 1912. My parents closed the butcher shop, and together started a textile business. Both my brother Fred and I were born in this house. My mother's older sister Irma married a man whose last name was also Voss. His first name was Isidor, known as Isi. His father Markus Voss was born in Hoegen, a suburb of Aachen, but we have never been able to establish a family relationship between the two Voss families.

Aunt Irma and her husband Isi had two children: a son, Hans, born on April 6, 1906, and a daughter, Edith, born on June 30, 1914. Edith and I were always close friends. Hans was an honor student and graduated from the finest school in Aachen even though he had a speech defect. He worked for his father who had a textile store at number 8 Marktplatz in the center of Aachen. The store was on the ground floor of their home. Behind the store was the kitchen, and one flight up was the living room. One floor up was one bedroom and another room behind the bedroom. That room had no window. It was Edith's bedroom. The house was over 120 years old and belonged to the city of Aachen. Uncle Isi had rented the house from the city when he was married. Uncle Isi had an older sister Mathilde who worked in her brother's business as a sales lady and lived with Uncle Isi. She had her own bedroom in a house across the street. Hans had a bedroom as well in the same house where Mathilde lived.

*Our parents' engagement photo, taken around January 1912*

*(Comment: In mid 1938, the city of Aachen dispossessed Uncle Isi and Aunt Irma after living there for 43 years from their rented house at 8 Markt-platz because they were Jews. When that happened, their son Hans fled to Brussels as an ille-gal alien. During the November 9, 1938, Nazi pogrom in Ger-many, and of course in Aachen as well, Uncle Isi and Aunt Irma, like their son Hans had previously done, fled during the night, walked through the woods and finally got to Belgium. Aunt Mathilde remained in Aachen. When the Germans invaded Belgium on May 8, 1940, Hans was taken prisoner by the Gestapo and died in Auschwitz. Uncle Isi and Aunt Irma were likewise arrested by the Gestapo, and both were shipped to a con-centration camp, first in Belgium and then to the south of France called Gurs. Both were liberated by the British army. However, Uncle Isi had contracted bladder cancer and died shortly after his liberation. While I was with the US Army in Europe, I was fortunate to visit them both in Brussels only a few days after their liberation. They both looked like skeletons. In 1948, Aunt Irma moved from Brussels to New York and moved in with my parents. Her daughter Edith married a man named Alfred Melzer in Tel Aviv. Melzer was originally from Berlin. They had two children, a son David and a daughter Sonja. The four of them left Israel for America in 1950 and also moved into the same apartment with my parents. Aunt Mathilde was deported from Aachen in April 1942 and sent to the Thersienstadt Concentration Camp where she died.)*

I was almost five years old when the first World War ended and almost seven years old when my brother Alfred, called Fred, was born on April 12, 1920. On that day my father woke me up early in the morning and told me to dress quickly. He wanted to take me to Aunt Irma and Uncle Isi's house because the stork had just knocked on the window and as soon as we were gone, the stork would bring me a little sister or a little brother. I wanted to stay and see the stork. My father told me that if the stork saw that my parents already had a little boy, he would take the new baby to some other family. I finally left after I had told my father to make sure that the stork would know that we already had a boy and that we wanted him to leave a baby girl. Later that morning Aunt Irma told me that my father had just called to tell Aunt Irma to bring me home  so I could meet my new little brother. I objected and said that I didn't want a new little brother. I told Aunt Irma that I would rather stay with her than go back home. Finally she convinced me to go home and welcome my new little brother. But I agreed to see the baby only after a lot of coaxing from my Oma Tilly.

Several months after my brother Fred was born, I came down with a horrible cough and a high temperature. I had polyps in my throat and had to have my tonsils removed. However, neither my cough nor my temperature improved after the surgery. The doctor informed my parents that it was the climate that caused my problem, and he recommended that they take me to a children's hospital in Wyk of For on the North Sea where there were many other children with similar symptoms. I spent the next six months at that place which was far away from Aachen. But instead of getting better, I got much worse. A new doctor was consulted, and after taking a series of x-rays, he advised my parents that at best, I had only a year to live. He suggested that since the sea air hadn't helped me, they might try the mountains. My parents took me to a children's hospital in a town called Bad Duerheim in the Black Forest region of Germany. There I spent the next two years. Even though it was a long way from Aachen, my parents visited me regularly. Suddenly I improved so much that the hospital discharged me. I was so happy to be home again! I know now that my so-called illness was not physical at all, but psychological, dealing with my feelings about the birth of my brother.

In 1920, the year that my brother Fred was born, I was accepted at the pre-school of the Realgymnasium, one of the finest schools in Aachen. I was a good student, but because of my so-called "illness" I had to drop out, and I spent the next two and one half years attending classes at the children's hospital in Bad Duerheim. The classroom was one very beautiful large room. Children of all ages were taught by the same teacher. The education was not the best. When I returned to Aachen, my father took me back to the Regalgymnasium. After testing me, I was admitted to the school provided that my parents saw to it that I had tutors in all my subjects. I was graduated from this school with honors. I will never forget my last teacher, Otto Buttfass. He was an excellent teacher, and it was he who recommended that I should address the graduating class. I no longer remember what I said, except that I closed with a little poem that I wrote for the occasion, called "The Future."

*(Comment: It is impossible to translate this poem into English.)*

It was my intention to go on to the University in Cologne for an MBA. My father suggested, however, that I should get some experience in merchandising before I started at the university. I was able to get an internship at Kaufmann Brothers (no relation), a large Jewish-owned department store in Aachen. I enjoyed my internship there very much and learned a lot about merchandising. By 1933, the Nazis had begun to boycott Jewish-owned stores including my parents,' and the owners were forced to sell their establishment to non-Jews. Thus my internship was over. I could still return to the university because my father had served in the war. I was sure that my attendance there would have been short-lived because I was after all, a Jew. I decided to leave Nazi Germany and go to America.

At that time, it was not easy to obtain a visa for entering the United States. Since Hitler came to power, the applicants for immigration to the United States had drastically increased and the 20,000 quota was filled within days. Each applicant received a waiting number which was based on a first come first served basis. Even when an applicant's number came up, there was no guarantee that he or she would be granted a visa. The applicant had to appear in person before the US Consulate and undergo a physical examination before he or she was interviewed by three members of the US Consulate. At that time, the assistant US Secretary of State was Brekenridge Long, a known anti-Semite. He had full jurisdiction over all immigration and had instructed all US embassies around the world to delay as long as possible all applications by Jews for entry into the United States. One of the three interviewers was the Consul himself. The second was the First Secretary of the Consul, and the third was an intelligence officer of the US State Department. They asked me why I wanted to go to the United States, if someone in the States had offered me a job, and whether I was, or had ever been, a member of the fascist or the communist party. The applicant had to know an American citizen who would swear to take full financial responsibility for the applicant. As proof, the sponsor had to submit certified copies of his income tax returns. Once the sponsor was able to prove that he had sufficient funds to carry out this responsibility, and once the applicant had passed the interrogations, a visa to enter the United States was granted. My concern was to find an American citizen who would give me the required notarized declaration that he or she would be financially responsible for me.

The only person I knew who might assume such a responsibility for me was Oma's brother Hermann in San Francisco.

I wrote him a long letter explaining my desire to leave Germany and come to the United States. I asked him for the notarized letter I needed from him about assuming responsibility for me financially, and at the same time I promised that I would never ask him for financial support. Oma Tilly included a letter of her own assuring Hermann that he would never have to support me. By return mail, I received a letter from Uncle Hermann saying that he would send the documents that I had requested. Several months later, however, I received a letter from the American Consulate advising me that Uncle Hermann's request to sponsor me was denied because of his advanced age. Needless to say, I was very much upset and depressed. After a few days I pulled myself together again and informed Uncle Hermann of the bad news from the American Consulate. To my great surprise and relief, I received another letter from Uncle Hermann informing me that his son Hermann Jr. would supply all the documentation that was required. As soon as I received this letter, I went to the American Consulate in Rotterdam with the documentation from Hermann Jr.

Several months later I received a letter from the American Consulate in Rotterdam, requesting that I go to Rotterdam for a complete medical exam and a further interview. Before I left home in Aachen, my parents bought me a new gray suit and according to the German fashion of the time, a black silk shirt and a red tie. Surely, my parents and I thought that I would make a good impression at the Consulate. But the Consulate believed that I was a member of some kind of a black shirt fascist movement, and my request for entry into the United States was denied. The US Consul was just looking for a reason to deny me entry. This is how unfair and how difficult it was for a Jew to emigrate from Germany to the United States during the Hitler period.

About a month or so later, I received a letter from the American Consul in Rotterdam explaining that my records had been reviewed, and I was eligible for a visa to enter the USA. I was somewhat confused but very happy that I could leave Germany and live in the United States as a free human being.

Many years later, when I was living in San Francisco, Hermann Elsbach Jr. told me that he showed a friend of his from his college days both letters that I had received from the American Consulate in Rotterdam, the letter denying me entrance to the US and the one granting me an entrance visa. This friend was the son of the then American Secretary of State in Washington, DC. Totally unknown to me, he had forwarded the first letter to his father in Washington, DC. I can only assume that this is how I was finally granted permission to come to America and was able to escape from Nazi Germany.

*Photo taken on board ship in Rotterdam in 1936 before Ed left for America. Left to right: Aunt Berta, Ed, and me. Front: Our parents.*

# Epitaph

𝕴 would like the reader to know that my brother Emil, later called Edward or Ed, passed away in San Francisco, California on October 10, 1991 at the age of 78 years. He had been seriously ill for a number of years. I believe that at the time of his death, he was writing his memoirs. He wrote the last chapter in 1988. I don't know if he intentionally stopped or passed away before he could complete his memoirs. The other interesting point is that he mastered the English language rather well, yet he chose to write his memoirs in German. I have no idea and cannot think of any reason why he chose to do that. It was my privilege and honor to have translated his memoirs from German into English.

In his memory I have taken the liberty to fill in the highlights of his life which he never completed in his memoirs.

In 1942, Ed married Lore Donner in New York City. Lore was born and raised in Hamburg, Germany. They both returned to San Francisco in April of 1943, where Lore's parents and brother lived. Ed found a job in the accounting office at the Kaiser Shipyard in San Francisco where he worked until 1946. In November 1943, their son Robert Jacob Voss was born. Their second son, Kenneth Steven was born in June 1951. Robert (Bob) married Barbara Birnbaum whose parents were born and raised in Poland. They have two daughters, Michelle, born in 1967, and Renee, born in 1969. Kenneth (Ken) married Madeline Konig, born and raised in San Francisco. They have two sons, Ryan, born in 1977, and Michael, born in 1981. Unfortunately, Lore and Ed got divorced in 1972.

When his brother-in-law Curt Donner returned home after his discharge from the Navy in 1946, Ed and Curt together formed their own accounting office. However, prior to 1959, Ed and Curt Donner split up their business relationship. Ed then started Associated Business Services, Inc. Hal Braun became an officer of ABS and died around 1971 while working for ABS. Ed remained the president of ABS until his death in 1991. The corporation was dissolved shortly after Ed's death.

In 1973, Ed married Diane LaVoi, born and raised in San Francisco. At the time of Ed's death, they were married for eighteen years.

*This is the last photo taken in 1983 of us
together, myself, Diane, Ed, and Ilse*

*My parents' silver anniversary, 1937*

# Fred Voss's Memories

# Early Childhood in Aachen

*A achen, April 12, 1920*

I was born at eight o'clock on a beautiful sunny spring morning on Monday April 12, 1920 at the Kaufmann homestead. Kaufmann was my mother's maiden name. The homestead was located at 32 Burtscheider Strasse in Aachen, Germany. At the time I was born, Aachen had a population of about 150,000 people. Less than one percent were Jewish. Aachen was a very picturesque town bordering on Holland and Belgium. Most of the people in Aachen spoke French (as well as German) because of the city's closeness to Belgium.

My father was Julius Voss who was born on April 19, 1884, in a small community called Bissen. Bissen was part of a little village called Wuerselen located about 10 miles north of Aachen. He was the youngest of four children, Leopold, Alfred, and a sister named Berta.

My mother Else was born on November 21, 1888 in Aachen. She was the middle child with an older sister Irma and a younger brother Heinrich. Her father passed away when she was only 12 years old.

Since my parents already had one boy Emil who was born on November 12, 1913, they and he wanted a baby girl. To their disappointment, they now had two boys when I was born. At the time of my birth I was named Alfred after my father's brother Alfred Voss. He was my mother's favorite brother-in-law. Had I been a girl, my name would have been Karolla after my grandmother's mother-in-law whom she loved very much.

I have always been told that while I was actually being born my father assisted the midwife on the upper floor in their bedroom. During that time, a young lady whom my parents knew well was taking care of the customers at the downstairs store. She was too excited to notice

*Dad as a peddler, around 1910*

that two young men had come into store and helped themselves to merchandise and walked out without paying.

The house in which I was born was built by my great-grandfather Hermann Kaufmann about one hundred years before my birth. The house at 32 Burtscheider Strasse stood at the top of a steep hill. To the left was a bakery. I can still smell the cakes. The actual bakery faced our back yard. To the right of the house was a store selling men's clothing.

As children we always played in the back yard. At the west end of the yard was a stone wall, and behind the wall were the railroad tracks leading from Belgium into the main railroad station "Der Hauptbahnhof" in Aachen. The garden was my grandmother's pride and greatest joy. There were several lilac trees in the garden which her father-in-law had planted. Omi Tillie, as we called our grandmother, raised vegetables and flowers in this garden, and as children, we loved to help her.

*Sales help at my parents' store*

Before my parents moved into this house, my maternal grandparents had a butcher shop there. My grandfather Emil Kaufmann after whom my brother was named, was a butcher like lots of Jews at that time. He passed away in 1901 at the age of 45 years. My grandmother who had three children, Irma, Else (my mother), and a son named Heinrich, continued operating the butcher store until 1912, when my mother and my Dad got married. At that time, my Dad had in mind to start a textile store at this location. However, he had to postpone his ambition because of the outbreak of the First World War.

My Dad was drafted into the German army only weeks before the war broke out in 1914. He served in the German army and was finally discharged after Germany had lost the war in November of 1918. During his military service, he was wounded by the French troops at Verdun. For this he received the German version of the Purple Heart. Previously he had been decorated with the Iron Cross, Second Class, for bravery under fire and was promoted to Corporal. When my Dad had recuperated from his wounds, he was shipped to Russia to face the Russian front. He was still in Russia when the war ended. After his war experiences, he was a changed man - very nervous and quickly agitated. The story I was told as a child was that during the battle of Verdun, he and some of his army buddies were in a trench. A grenade hit the trench and while his two buddies were killed, my Dad was trapped under several feet of dirt for many hours until he could be rescued.

As soon as my Dad was discharged and came home again, he had the butcher shop remodeled to open up a textile store. Several years later he changed from a retail textile store to a textile wholesale establishment. His customers were peddlers who went into the farm region and distant districts from house to house selling textile goods. Years before the war, my Dad had been a peddler also, selling from house to house to the farmers. Eventually he worked his way up from being a peddler to having a good-sized wholesale textile business. My mother was always involved with the family business too, doing at first all the selling at the store,

*My father's office, 1937*

the secretarial work, and the bookkeeping. As the business grew and employees were hired, she took over as the supervisor and was involved in every phase of the business until the business was closed after the infamous Kristall Nacht on November 9, 1938.

At the time that my parents had the butcher store converted, first to a textile store, and then to the wholesale business, they removed the storefront windows, and in their place they put two large windows about 10 feet high and 7 feet wide. I still remember those new windows. They had my father's name in gold letters on a black background. The words on the windows were "Julius Voss, Textile Wholesale Only." Both windows looked the same. To the left of the windows was the entrance door to the business as well as to the family living quarters. Above the windows on the building in very large letters, again was my Dad's name, "Julius Voss." The first floor had three windows on which the word "Wholesale" in gold letters on a black background was inscribed.

It was common at this time in Aachen for business people to have their own business and living quarters at the same location. Over time, the house was remodeled and more changes were made. My father made his and my mother's office in the area that the butcher shop used to occupy. Later on, they hired a young lady Fraeulein Bruelles as the secretary, and she worked in this office. At one time the business had as many as eight or nine employees which even included a chauffeur, Herr Hubert Kerchgens.

Behind the office was our living room. The furniture in our living room was antique. It was handed down to my mother's parents and came even from her grandparents. They were mostly the antique "rococo style" furniture. The upholstery was dark red velvet and with long fringes at the bottom.

A number of beautiful and valuable oil paintings hung in this room, too. All of them had been in the family for one or two generations. There was one old and beautiful painting called "Judith." According to the Bible, Judith was a pious, wealthy, courageous, and patriotic woman who delivered Jerusalem from the assault of Holofernes. The painting was a rather grisly one. It showed Judith cutting Holofernes' head off. During Kristall Nacht, on November 9, 1938, a very "courageous" SS officer took out his bayonet and cut the picture to pieces. He must have known the story of Judith. I have no idea who the painter was, but I was always told that it was of some value. The other paintings, as far as I can remember, were some landscapes. Of course there were lots of family photographs as well; most of them were of the parents and grandparents on both sides.

*Ms. Bruelles, the secretary*

To the left of the living room and still on the ground floor was the kitchen. In the kitchen stood the same coal-fired stove that my grandmother Tillie had used when she first got married. The kitchen was about 20 feet long and 9 feet wide. On the 20-foot wall stood a beautiful oak cupboard which came from my great-grandparents' home. It contained all our dishes, the ones we used daily and those which we used for special occasions only. In addition, the Passover dishes and lots of crystal glasses, as well as the silverware, were all stored in it. Against the other wall stood a large oak table which also was from my grandmother's parents. This table was used for the preparation of food. When I was a child, the icebox or refrigerator was not known in Aachen. People used the cellars of their house to store perishable foods. Pasteurized milk, although by that time available at very high prices, was not used by the average family. We used to go to the "milkstore" with a little pan and would purchase a pan full of milk. The milk was delivered daily directly by farmers to the milk stores. The milk had to be boiled at home before it could be used. This left a skin on top of the milk which was a delicacy to put on top of a cup of coffee instead of milk.

From the kitchen a door led to the backyard of the house. Outside, between the door and the entry to the yard, stood the outhouse. We all used this outhouse until about 1928. This outhouse was built at the time that the house was built around 1820. The original structure was about 4 X 7 feet, made out of wood. The outhouse was built above a hole dug into the ground which had to be cleaned out from time to time. However,

*Our family room in Aachen, 1937*

shortly before his death in 1901, my grandfather had the hole hooked up to a cesspool which had just been built and at the time was considered a great, new civic improvement.

I remember that the outhouse always had a very horrible odor. Toilet paper (as we know it today) was commercially available, but people had better things to spend their meager cash on than this totally new unnecessary stuff. Since there were always lots of stories still to be read in the old magazines and old newspapers, these usually would be taken along to the outhouses to be read there and then were cut or ripped into a usable size.

Our outhouse was about 50 yards away from our house. It was terrible to use it in the middle of the night or during the winter months. That is why we, like other families, had chamber pots under our beds. These were used exclusively for #1 and NEVER for #2. When someone had to do that, then they still needed to run to the outhouse.

Years later my parents had a flush toilet installed at the outhouse which replaced the old system. This was a major construction and the absolute envy of many other people in our neighborhood who still were using the outhouses at that time in Aachen's history. This was something new for all of us.

One floor above the office was what might be called today a "family room." In the family room was a large book case with many wonderful books and the encyclopedia. There we would read, talk, write and relax.

Across from the "family room" were three very large rooms which were used to store all merchandise and to serve the customers. On the next floor up were both my parent's and my grandmother's bedrooms. A staircase led to the attic of the house which my parents had built out to make more living space available.

The attic had two bedrooms. One was shared by my brother and me until he left for the United States. The other bedroom was used by the housekeeper or maid whom my parents employed. From my bedroom I had a most beautiful view over the magnificent Aachener forest and of the town of Aachen itself. The other bedroom faced the Burtscheider Strasse.

In the early part of my life, there was only one coal stove in the house, used for heating the living room and the family room. There was no other heat in any other room. The climate in Aachen was generally mild both in summer as well as in the winter. However, on cold winter nights we used to take either a hot water bottle or a hot brick to bed with us to keep warm. Around 1928-1929, my parents had central, hot-water heat installed in all rooms, except in the attic where my brother's and my bedroom and the housekeeper's bedroom were located, so our rooms were still cold.

In the early days, we had no running water inside the house except in the kitchen. There was a well pump next to the outhouse which we would pump by hand to get the water from the well. This water tasted of sulfur, as did all water in Aachen and could not be used for drinking. We had to buy bottled water at the grocery store which was very expensive.

Since Aachen was in the Rheinland, and the wine from the Rheinland area was well known all over Europe, people in Aachen drank more wine than water. Ever since I can remember, there was always wine on our table at mealtime. As a matter of fact, it was really much less expensive than water. From early childhood on, we children would drink wine with our meals as well. There was a saying, "Water was for the cows, and wine was for the people."

Since by now we had running city water and city sewers, each person had a water basin and a pitcher in the bedroom. The pitcher was filled with fresh water by the maid daily, so that we could wash ourselves. The water in the basin was emptied after each use in the morning.

In the basement we had a large bathtub, home made, out of zinc. Next to the bathtub was a stove which would be lit early in the afternoon so that it could warm the water enough to take a quick bath at night. Usually two people would have to use the same water for their bath but not at the same time. Of course it was a luxury to take a bath this way. We took a bath about once a week and mostly on Friday nights before Sabbath. I guess that this was a leftover tradition in my home from the time when my parents were little children, and their very religious parents had them always take a bath before Sabbath. It was still a custom in our family always to take a bath on Friday before sundown so that we were clean for the weekend. At that time, there were public bath houses all over town which used the sulfur water for which Aachen is still famous today all over the world. The water was pumped into the bathhouses from the underground wells. Sometimes my grandmother would take us children there for our bath. This was considered a special treat for us because it was so much nicer than the bathtub we had at home.

Shortly before Hitler came into power in 1933, my parents had the old zinc bathtub removed and had it replaced with a ceramic one which was a novelty. However, the water situation in all other rooms remained as it was before.

It was a tradition in every German home that Mondays were designated as "laundry days." It took the domestic, the maid, all day Monday to wash our clothes. First of all, the same stove and the same bucket which were used for heating the bathtub water were used for the laundry as well. The washing machine had yet to be invented. Those days people used a wooden board on which a corrugated piece of galvanized sheetmetal was screwed.

The maid would then rub the clothes over this board until she thought that the clothes were clean. After that, a squeeze-type of a gadget was used to squeeze the wet laundry through to remove all the water. Once this was done, if it was summer the laundry was hung outside until dry. In the wintertime the laundry was hung on lines in the cellar until it would eventually dry. As with the washing machine, the dryer was not yet invented.

# Growing Up

There were not too many children my age in the neighborhood. A girl Inge lived a few houses from us who was about my age. When I was about 3 or 4 years old, my brother Emil used to tease me because I played with girls rather than with boys. The only boy my age who lived across the street from us was Kurt Rosendahl. He was related to me; his mother "Aunt Erna" was a second cousin on my father's mother's side. Aunt Erna's maiden name was Weil; my father's cousin and Aunt Erna were sisters.

Kurt and I were inseparable; we were often called "Max and Moritz" after the two Wilhelm Bush characters in German children's books who were always up to something that would get them into trouble. I remember that one day Kurt and I were playing and found a can of green paint. At the time my family had a little brown dog Mirtza that was very playful, and we could do anything with that little dog. Well, like mischievous little boys, we decided that neither we nor anyone else had ever seen a green dog before. It did not take us too long to use the green paint on poor little Mirtza. We now had produced the first green dog! Needless to say, when my father saw what we had done, Kurt was sent home, and I got some spanking which I can still feel. Poor little Mirtza was taken to a veterinarian who removed the paint. Other than his pride, Mirtza was not hurt.

Then there was the story of the cute little cat we had. It was a plain old alley cat but very sweet. Again, one day Kurt and I were playing with the cat. We decided that the cat was sick and needed medicine. We located a bottle of "Schnapps," which is like whiskey. Somehow or the other we were able to push a teaspoon of whiskey down the cat's throat to make her "feel better." My grandmother caught us, gave me a spanking, and poor Kurt was sent home again. The cat must have enjoyed the medicine or needed it. It never complained about it and was very happy for a long time.

At around the same time, when I was five years old, my parents sent me to a Catholic Kindergarten. It was like a Montessori school but run by the Catholic nuns. The reason I was sent to a Catholic school was because there was no Jewish kindergarten in town. My parents had become friendly with the Mother Superior of the school, and I am sure that my parents paid them a good amount to take in a Jewish child. The nuns were really very nice to me. I can still remember that every morning all the children had to recite the Lord's Prayer before school began. Of course, I recited it too, but had no idea what it was all about. One day I must have told my grandmother about it, and she told me that I should listen to the other children praying but that I should not pray with them and that I should keep silent. The next morning I told the nun what my grandmother had told me. The nun who as I remember was very sweet to me said that this was all right with her as long as I would bow my head with the other children. I stayed at this school until I was six years old and entered the Jewish school system as a first grader in 1926.

In Aachen the usual practice was for all children to go to a parochial school of their religious choice for the first four years. We had a Jewish day school in Aachen for grades 1-4. We shared the same classroom and the same teacher. Boys and girls would sit separately based on their grades. Some thirty years earlier, my mother had the same teacher, Herr Lehrer Wallach. He was a little man, very sweet, very strict, and a real good teacher. The school was about a 35 minute walk from our house; by street car it took about 15 minutes. My parents did not have a car at that time; in 1926, few people we knew had a car. The first and maybe the second year my mother or my grandmother used to alternate with Kurt Rosendahl's parents to walk us to school and pick us up again. Only when the weather was bad would they take us by street car. But by the time we were eight years old, we either had to walk alone or again rode by street car in bad weather. The curriculum was the same as in a secular school but with a little bit of Bible history, the basic Hebrew alphabet, and the basic Jewish prayers added. That was what we learned.

# Aachen 1930 - 1933

In 1930, I passed the entrance examination for the 5th grade at the Mittel Schule, the same school my brother had entered years earlier. He, however, had been fortunate to matriculate from this school with high honors before Hitler's days in Germany. The German school system, then as well as now, is totally different from the American school system. In Germany by law, school was only required for eight years or until the student's 14th birthday, whichever came first. If a student planned on getting only an eighth grade education, the student would enter a "Volks Schule," the grammar school. However, for a higher education there were two different types of schooling. One was the Mittel Schule, and the other one was the Gymnasium. The Mittel Schule went up to the age of 17 and the Gymnasium up to the age of 19. My parents opted for me to enter the Mittel Schule because the entrance exam was so much easier than the Gymnasium, and the school was also much less expensive. Neither Mittel Schule nor Gymnasium was free. Only at the Volks Schule was an education free. I went to the Mittel Schule until 1935. When I was 15 years old., I had to leave the school at that time because Jewish children were no longer allowed to attend the German schools. School was held daily from 8:00 AM to 4:30 PM with a 30 minute lunch break. On Saturdays school was from 8:00 AM to 12 noon. In addition, we had at least two hours of homework every day.

When I think of these years, I remember that my parents could not afford to spend a lot of time with my brother and me. In my early childhood, I remember that they usually got up at about 6:00 AM every day and went to bed very late, almost at midnight. They both were very hard working people who would spend all their available time building up their business. As I said earlier, it was our grandmother Omi Tillie who raised us as children.

She was such a sweet woman, born in Brilon, Wesphalia, on February 3, 1857. She was so understanding; both my brother and I loved her so much. There wasn't a thing that she would not do for us, doing it with all her love and kindness. In the early years of our lives, she would read us all the fairy tales, the ones which the Brothers Grimm had written. She read them to us over and over again. She especially liked to tell us stories from her youth when she was a little girl. She often told us that her parents were very poor, that her older brother and sister would make their own toys to play with, and that the toys were handed down from one child to another. She never had her own new dress until she was about 13 years old. Her sister would make her dress as she got older, and when she was 13 years old, she helped her to make her own dress. Because she was the youngest of her siblings, they all spoiled her. She cried her heart out when her eleven brothers left for San Francisco when they were 18 years old because they refused to serve in the Prussian army. She knew that she would never see any one of them alive again, and she never did.

During the summer my parents would always take time off from work, one or two weeks, usually in August. They loved the Belgium sea-shore and always stayed at the same Hotel (Memling) in Blankenbergh, right across the boardwalk from the ocean. Of course, they would take us children along. Sometimes only our grandmother and our mother would go with us because my Dad had to be at the business, but he always made sure that my mother was able to take the two weeks off from work.

When I was about four years old we went to Bad Kreutznach, a pop-ular resort, on a large lake near Mainz and Kobelenz. That time my mother, her sister Irma, my Aunt Bella, and all five cousins of mine went along. I had lots of fun being together with my brother and cousins who lived in Aachen at the time. I remember that trip like it was yesterday; it is about the earliest I can remember from my childhood.

On Sundays the Voss business was closed. In the mornings my par-ents would spend a little time in their office, and in the afternoon we would take walks into town. We would usually go to a movie and very rarely would we go for a bite to eat. However, that was considered a very special treat. The movies, when I was a child, were still the black and white silent movies with the dialogue written across the bottom of the screen. You had to be a fast reader to catch it all. When I was maybe eleven or twelve years old, "The Jazz Singer" had just been released; that was the first "talking picture" as people used to call it. The movie was with Al Jolson, a very famous singer in Europe at the time. It was the story of a Jewish family in which the father was a Cantor. The son, played by Al Jolson, didn't want to follow in his father's footsteps as a Cantor. Then one year on Kol Nidre night (the evening of the day of Atonement prayer), while chanting the opening prayer, his father had a heart attack and died. The son Al Jolson went to the Bima (Altar) and finished the Kol Nidre Nidre prayer.

In Aachen the movie houses did not yet have the equipment for this new invention, the talking movie. But we knew it was showing in Brus-sels, Belgium. Since Brussels was not that far away from Aachen, and since my father's sister and her family lived there, we all went by train to Brussels to see this new wonder, the talking movie, and visit with the family at the same time.

When my parents had time, we took many walks through the woods outside the city of Aachen. These walks were always so enjoyable. My mother would pack sandwiches, and I was always designated to wear the back pack in which were the sandwiches. The woods in Aachen were beautiful, especially for long

*Bad Kreutznach. From left: Aunt Bella, Walter, Emil, Edith, and me. Behind Edith stands Aunt Irma. My mother is behind me. Taken in 1924, I am 4 years old.*

hikes. There were many trails and many rivers. We enjoyed watching the many species of birds and animals all roaming through the woods. We always had stale bread with us to feed the animals.

Around 1929, my parents bought their first car, a brand new Opel. It was a little green car which my brother and I named "The Frog." It had room for four people provided that they didn't weigh too much and most of all were not too tall. The car did not have an automatic starter like we have on today's cars. One had to go and crank up the engine of the car in order to drive. There was a turn handle in the front, and somebody had to turn it until the car would start up. Dad had bought the car in order to increase the business and to see more of his customers. He now could see more customers each week than he had before he had the car. This way, when his customers ordered merchandise, he could deliver it to them the following week. This really made the business grow larger.

The car was our parents' pride and joy. But Dad would not drive it. Even though Dad had taken driving lessons and had passed the test, he was afraid that he might hit a tree or another car. So he hired a chauffeur to drive the car which allowed my Dad to see all his customers personally by car.

The car was parked a block away from where we lived. There was a large grocery store; Lontzen was the name. On their lot Mr. Lontzen had built the first garages in our neighborhood. They also had a gasoline pump on their premises which was operated by hand only. Again, the motorized gasoline pump had not yet been invented. "The Frog" was never used for pleasure just for business. About two years later, Dad bought a larger car, a six passenger Chevrolet. This was one of the first cars that had an automatic starter inside the car. There were two rings around the steering wheel. Once we had this car, Dad took driving lessons again but still was scared that he would hit another car or a person. So he never drove this car either.

Our chauffeur Herr Hubert Kerchgens was a young man of about 25 and being single, was always happy to join our family, my grandmother, my parents, my brother and me for outings with the car. All six of us in the six passenger car would drive into the countryside for day trips. Everyone loved it so much that for a long time, especially in the summer, we would drive into the country every Sunday. There were beautiful little mountain ranges called "Die Eifel" all around us. Nearby were also the very nice, picturesque - like small hamlets of Monschau and Vossonack. (These little hamlets became famous during World War II, as the first places on German soil which the American forces occupied on their march to enter Aachen at the end of October 1944.)

In late 1932, when I was twelve years old, there were already signs that the German Weimar Republic was slowly fading into history as the Hitler Nazi movement gained more and more power in Germany. The Nazi Party had gained a small majority of the German votes in the German Parliament, "The Reichstag."

On January 30, 1933, Hitler was appointed by the then German President Von Hindenburg as the new Chancellor of Germany.

For the Jews in Germany a new era had started, an era of hate and destruction where friends suddenly turned on us and became enemies.

It certainly was the end of my childhood at the age of twelve years. I was still so innocent and so young.

# My Six Years Under the Swastika, 1933 - 1939

*April 1, 1933*

Today was the day of my bar mitzvah (when a Jewish boy reaches his 13th birthday). All my relatives had come from Duesseldorf and from Brussels to hear me chant (sing) the Torah (from the five books of Moses). My grandmother, my Omi Tilli on my mother's side, was the only living grandparent I had. After the temple services were over, the members of the congregation were served a light snack which consisted mostly of herring, eggs, chicken liver, and bread. My parents had invited the family to come to our house for a hot dinner which customarily was always served in Europe at lunch time. In the evening a light meal was served. That was

*My 13th birthday photo, 1933*

the custom those days, and that also was the entire celebration. The bar mitzvah boy usually got either religious presents, such as prayer books, the Bible, or personal gifts, books, etc. but never any money. Usually from the parents he would get his first watch and from relatives little items like a wallet, a briefcase, or a "fountain pen." The pen as we know it today was not yet invented. There was not very much money spent on presents. It was an extended birthday party, but that was it. No big bands, nor big affairs, it was strictly a close family affair.

When we came home from the temple, the Nazis had started their very first anti-Jewish boycott of all Jewish stores throughout Germany. They pasted large black posters with a yellow circle on the Jewish store windows. In front of the stores, armed SA men dressed in their brown shirts were standing guard to prevent any customers from entering the Jewish owned stores. Since our home was in the same house where the store was located, we had some minor problems entering our house. Two armed SA men were blocking our entrance. My father talked to them. One of them was familiar to my father, and finally he let us into our home. Of course that was the end of my bar mitzvah celebration. Unfortunately it was also the beginning of what was yet to happen to us.

From then on, our aspirations, our hopes were gone. We lived in tense homes with our families who were always on edge and so fearful. At the time in 1933 when the Nazis came to power, I was 13 years old and a student in the public school system. Because as children we spent 5 1/2 days weekly in school, unprotected by our parents and family, we had to deal all alone with the blatant repercussions of Nazism at school.

My next encounter was with the Hitler youth in the spring of 1935. I was beaten up by the members of my own class, boys who were my "friends" before Hitler came into power but who by then were all active members of the Hitler Youth. All the boys involved knew me well; we often played together. On orders of their leaders, they beat me up because I was a Jew, and in their already brain washed mind, I was responsible for all of Germany's problems.

In 1935 I joined first the Jewish sports group Macabee. I did not particularly like their sports activities, and after a while I joined another Jewish sport group, "Blue-White." There I first learned and then played soccer. It was a great team. Soon I became the goalie and enjoyed the sport a lot. But around the end of the year, the Gestapo had forbidden us to get together any longer to play soccer. They considered Blue-White as "an anti Nazi sport activity." Then, I joined a pro-Zionist Youth group called "Kameraden," but when most of the kids had left for then-Palestine to work on the Hachsharah (farm programs), the rest of the group dissolved. The only Jewish youth group left was an ultra pro-Zionist group, Brit Trumpeldor. I enjoyed the group of kids and especially those who were in charge. We did a lot of reading on Palestestine. We learned a lot of Hebrew songs, but most of all we collected a lot of money to be sent to the Kibbutzim in Palestine. By mid-1936, this Youth group was also closed down by the Gestapo.

Before we were finally expelled from the German public schools, we had lost our rights as German citizens. We had to sit apart from our Christian classmates because we were Jews. No matter how well an essay was written, a Jewish child never received a good, never mind a top grade. In my school, we were only 7 or 8 Jewish students including my friend Kurt Rosendahl, yet not one single Christian child wanted to sit near us or play with us during recess. They were all too scared of the repercussions they would have had from the Hitler Youth.

Some of our teachers wore their brown SA or their black SS uniforms to school, while other teachers just simply enjoyed harassing us Jewish children in class before our schoolmates. It was obvious that the teachers were afraid to be reported by the Hitler Youth to their leaders if they were too friendly to the Jewish students. Other teachers were just plain Nazis and enjoyed hurting us.

I remember only too well when one of the teachers told me in class one day that I should stand up in front of the class so that the students would see what a Jew looks like. Then, there was our music teacher, a highly educated person, who always was in his SS uniform. It was his sick pleasure to have us Jewish students stand up at attention while he ordered the rest of the class to sing the infamous Hitler Youth song "When Jewish blood gushes from our knives, then Germany will be better off."

I remember another time when a man who knew me well, ever since I was a little boy, dressed in his notorious Nazi uniform, angrily yelled at me while I was on a bus on my way to school, "You Jew boy, get off this bus when I am on the bus." Most people on that bus started smiling and laughing. You cannot imagine how humiliating this is for a young boy. There were literally hundreds upon hundreds of those anti-Semitic incidents in our daily young lives. We often trembled for fear when we left our homes for school. I could no longer face the daily insults. I was too young to cope with them, and yet the law was that we had to attend school.

When we were finally expelled from the German school system at the end of 1935, I was only 15 years old. The job training programs and jobs were very limited and almost impossible to get. The Jewish-owned business and factories were closing down. The Christians would not let us on their premises for fear of Nazi reprisals.

I cannot tell or even recount the number of times when I was stopped on the streets by the Gestapo agents or by members of the SS and frisked for weapons or anti-Hitler material. Especially as youngsters, we were liable to such body searches, male and female alike, which provided free entertainment for the German spectators.

I don't remember the exact month or even the year, but I believe it was in mid or late 1936 when my brother Emil who would later change his name legally to Edward, left Aachen for San Francisco. I remember that my parents and I accompanied him by train from Aachen to Rotterdam in Holland. There he got on a freighter which had only twelve passengers; the rest was all cargo. The ship stopped at many ports before it finally arrived in San Francisco. The sailing took over six weeks. Why he traveled on this particular ship, I don't know.

*From left: My Dad, Kurt Rosendahl's Dad, Uncle Isi, in 1936*

*Irma Hartog, Aunt Irma, Kurt's mother, my mother, in 1936*

*The last family group picture taken, in the summer of 1936. Back row: Heinz Hartog, Kurt Rosendahl, Irma Hartog, Ed, my mother, me. Second row: My grandmother, Kurt's mother, Erma Hartog\*, Uncle Isi\*, my Dad, Kurt's father\*, Kurt's brother Heinz, Aunt Irma, Aunt Matilda\*. Standing up in front of my Dad is Kurt's sister Lore.*
*\* Four family members and friends who were killed by the Nazis*

In March of 1936, Hitler had ordered his troops of the German armed forces to march into the demilitarized Rheinland. Aachen of course is a city in the Rheinland. This step by the Nazis constituted open breaches of the Versailles Treaty between the defeated Germany of World War I and France, Belgium, and England. Under that treaty, Germany was not allowed to occupy the Rheinland. Now, when the German Nazi army did indeed march into Aachen and the rest of the Rheinland, we Jews were filled with hope and prayers that the French and British would move right in as well, and that would have ended Hitler's conquests of the world. The British had already mobilized, but at the last moment the French backed out. The rest is now history. This of course was the final blow for us Jews, and now any hope we had slowly faded away.

From then on, my parents always looked so sad, so worried, and bewildered to me. During the years from late 1935 until the final end, my parents tried so hard to protect me by always telling me that life would get better. Somehow or other, I had realized that the outlook for my future and physical survival was very bad indeed.

After the German army had moved into the Rheinland my mother insisted, over my father's objections, that the family should be registered with the American Consulate in Stuttgart, Germany to be put on a waiting list to file for a visa application to be permitted entry to the United States of America. In 1934, a year after Hitler came into power in Germany, the United States enforced a quota ruling which permitted only 20,000 German nationals to enter the United States per year. As Jews under this law we were considered German nationals. German nationals applied to people who were actually born in Germany and whose parents were born in Germany. Needless to say that by 1936, over 200,000 of the 500,000 German Jews had already registered at the American Consulate. The applicants were given a number and would be called to submit all the necessary paper work to the Consulate. An American citizen was needed to sponsor the applicant in the United States. This person had to submit to the American Consulate certified copies of their tax returns and of all their assets to prove his/her ability to take care of the emigrant. In our case we had to travel to the nearest American Consulate which was in Stuttgart about a 10 hour train ride from Aachen which meant that we had to secure a hotel that would permit Jews to stay there. We were fortunate we found a Jewish owned hotel. Every applicant regardless of his or her age or physical condition had to line up in person at the American Consulate. By 5:00 AM there were lines already over two blocks long. The Consulate would close at 3:00 PM. Whoever was still waiting outside had to line up again the next morning and start all over again. Again, we had to line up with my 82-year-old grandmother. We were very fortunate that on the second day we were able to get inside the Consulate. While waiting in line, we were of course always the entertainment of the German people who would walk by smiling, laughing, and spitting at us. Once inside, we had to fill out forms again, and then we were assigned only a waiting number. I must say again that my father was totally opposed to all this. He was such on optimist that he was sure that Hitler's Germany would not last much longer. On the other hand, my mother was determined to get that American waiting number.

My parents' talk frightened me even more, although they tried so hard to keep all the bad news from me. I felt so insecure, so scared. The conversations between them and their friends were always the same. How could they pack up and leave the country where they and their parents, their grandparents and even their great-grandparents were born and had lived for uncountable generations? How could they start a new life, a new business or find a job in a strange country whose language they did not speak or understand? Which country was even willing to let them immigrate? Uppermost in my mother's mind was that she never could or would leave her old widowed and almost blind mother behind.

In June of 1938 in my home town of Aachen the Gestapo arrested some of what they called "Anti Social" Jewish men, sending them to the Buchenwald concentration camp. They all had been arrested for traffic violations at some previous time in their lives. The Nazis now considered this for Jews, a major criminal offense. Of the maybe 15-20 men arrested on that day, within two weeks, five of them at the Buchenwald concentration camp had been killed. Their families and friends exerted major efforts to have them freed. This action kept many if not all of the Jews in my hometown from driving their cars for fear of being stopped on trumped up charge of a traffic violation.

By now, we Jews were required by a new Nazi Law to have the red letter J stamped on all our personal records. The J was for Jude or Jew. This was the forerunner of the yellow stars which Jews had to wear on their outer clothing later on. Caught without openly displaying the Yellow Star was considered a major crime and a cause for arrest and deportation to a concentration camp.

As Jews we had to have and carry with us at all times what the Nazis called a "Kennkarte," a personal ID card. When stopped by any SS Officer or a Gestapo agent, this ID card had to be shown. This ID had a big yellow J for Jew. At the same time the Nazis changed all our first names in addition to our given names, all Jewish men had to add 'Israel' as their first name, and all Jewish women had to add 'Sarah' to their first

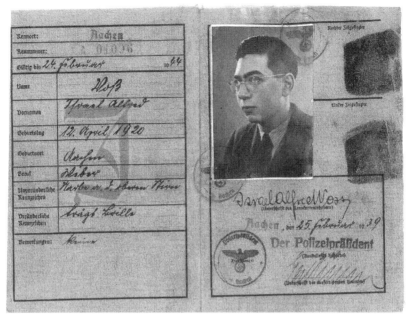

*This is my ID card which every Jew above the age of five years old had to carry with him at all times. The penalty for not carrying this ID card was arrest and the concentration camps. Note in early 1938, the Germans forced all males to have the name of Israel as the first name and all females the name of Sarah.*

name. From then on we could not use our previous first names, and all documents showed the new names. Failure to carry this card was again considered a major crime and cause for arrest and deportation to a concentration camp.

Our lives were made tougher and tougher from day to day. The Nazis were determined to break us mentally now, and physically later on. Daily, there were new laws and insults added against the Jews. At our local swimming pool the Nazis posted a sign one day that said "Jews and dogs were no longer allowed at the pool." An eleven year old Jewish boy got caught writing on that sign, "What if dogs can't read this?" The Hitler Youth caught him, and he was mercilessly beaten up until he was unconscious. As a Jew, he was not allowed to be treated at the hospital. Consequently, he died at home one week later from internal bleedings. Our daily newspaper which of course was controlled and censored by the Nazis commented on this incident: "The Jewish boy's penalties against the German society was properly deserved and dealt with." The German people in Aachen did nothing to stop these atrocities. For them the reprisals were just too great.

Julius Streicher the notorious Nazi Jew baiter who was later hanged after the Nuremberg trials became the editor of a Nazi weekly newspaper called the "Stuermer" (The Fighter). Every week this paper was displayed in large red colored glass frames throughout Germany and later on throughout Austria as well. In Aachen alone, we must have had at least ten of the displayed show cases. They were one hundred percent pure lies about the Jews, just anti-Semitic propaganda to arouse the German public to violence against us.

Since I had to leave school in March of 1935, my father knew one of the Jewish owners of a large woolen weaving mill in Aachen. The company's name was "Meyerfeld and Hertz." Bernard Tisch was the gentlemen my Dad knew well. I also knew him. My Dad called Mr. Tisch and asked him if I could learn the textile weaving business at his mill. Mr. Tisch was agreeable and promised to keep me until he too would be forced to sell out to a so-called "Aryan." I started learning the weaving business at their plant on April 1, 1935.

In July of 1938, "Meyerfeld und Hertz" was forced to sell out to Aryan owners, and I was discharged from one day to the next because I was a Jew. Before that time it was still possible for Jews living in Aachen to cross the border into Holland for which we did not need a passport, just a local ID verifying that we lived in Aachen. My parents enrolled me at textile school there in 1935 already. The Dutch border town which we reached by streetcar was called Vaals and was about one mile inside Holland from Aachen. Both my good friend Kurt Rosendahl, whose fate was the same as mine, and I attended the "M. Mockel School of Textiles" four nights a week from 5 - 9 PM and on Saturdays from 9 AM - 1 PM. The school was geared strictly to textiles like any vocational school. But by early 1938, the Nazis took from all Jews in Aachen our border crossing passes. This of course made it impossible for us to follow up on our education further.

My mother had a second cousin living in the town of Krefeld which was about 100 miles north of Aachen. Their names were Tilly and Herman Willner. Herman Willner owned a tie factory in Krefeld. He too had been forced to sell his business to an Aryan. My parents thought that in addition to having learned the weaving business, I should also learn how to cut and sew ties so that I might become employable in a foreign country. Since Jews had to get the permission from the Gestapo if they wanted to stay over night away from their homes, I got the permission from the Gestapo to leave Aachen in April of 1938 for four months to live in Krefeld with the Willner family. During the four months I did really learn how to cut patterns for ties and also learned how to sew them together. I wanted to stay longer in Krefeld but did not get an extension from the Gestapo office in Krefeld which forced me to go back home to Aachen in August of 1938. By that time my parents' business was already mostly ruined due to all the Nazi laws against Jews. They had drastically lost their help who were too afraid to work for Jews. Herr Kerschgens, the chauffeur, got married in the meantime, and he too had left my parents' employment. I became useful to my parents in the last stages of the business by running errands and helping out wherever I could until November 9, 1938. The pogrom against all Jews in Germany forced the closure of my parents' business. During the night of November 9-10 in 1938, the Nazis (SS officers and Gestapo) ransacked and destroyed much of the interior as well as some of the store windows of my parents' business.

In the early days of November 1938, I asked my parents for their permission to spend a few days in Krefeld. I wanted to visit Erich and Edith Kahn. Edith was the Willners' daughter and was two years older than I was. I always considered Edith and her sisters Lilo and Ilse as cousins. My parents agreed that I could go for a week to Krefeld, and the Gestapo in Aachen, to my greatest surprise, gave me permission for a visit to Krefeld from November 7-17.

In the summer of 1938, the Nazis started deportation of all Jews of Polish descendants who lived in Germany. They rounded up about 17,000 people during the night, put them on trains and literally shoved them across the Polish border. There was one family with the name of Grynspan with those who were deported. The Grynspans had a 17-year-old son named Herschel. The Grynspans were held by the Polish Government in a refugee camp. The conditions at that camp were horrible. The Grynspans needed help. They needed food, and they needed money.

On November 1, 1938, in their desperation, the Grynspans wrote a letter for help to their son Herschel who had previously fled to Paris and worked there as a dish-washer at a restaurant. Young Herschel got his parents' letter on November 7, 1938, and not knowing how to help his parents, he went to a pawn shop in Paris to pawn what earthly goods he had. With the money, he went to a gun shop and purchased a handgun. Armed, he decided to call the world's attention to his parents' sufferings. He went to the German Embassy in Paris. He asked to see the German ambassador, was denied seeing the ambassador, but was allowed to see the third secretary of the embassy, a man named Ernst von Rat. As soon as Herschel met Ernst von Rat, he pumped three bullets into him. Mortally wounded, Ernst von Rat was taken to a French hospital where he died in the early morning hours of November 9, 1938.

*This newspaper photo taken on November 10, 1938, shows the Jewish men taken by the SS to the railroad station in Aachen to be transported to the Buchenwald concentration camp. My father is one of the men in this group.*

The Germans had looked for a long time for an incident of this kind to happen so they could find an excuse to start their "Final Solution against the Jews." This incident gave them what they were looking for. During the night of November 9-10, the now infamous Kristall Nacht, the pogrom called "the night of broken glass" against the Jews in Germany and Austria was carried out.

Consequently, I was in Krefeld visiting with my cousins on the night of November 9, 1938. We had a nice evening together. They were newlyweds. They were making plans to escape from the Nazis and to leave for South Africa to join her sister Lilo within the next few months. At the time they had a little apartment which was located closely to the synagogue in Krefeld. We were still up around midnight when suddenly we heard a lot of strange noises and a lot of commotion. I decided against their will that I would go outside to see what was going on. As soon as I stepped outside, I saw in the sky high flames and lots of people running towards the synagogue. Using my instinct, which told me that something terrible was going on, I walked slowly to the synagogue and saw the fire and the temple in flames. There were hundreds of people watching. The SA and SS as well as the Gestapo cars were all over. They were making sure that the fire department would not extinguish the fire. I watched this horror for a few minutes and went back to my cousins. As soon as I walked inside, I saw that my cousin Edith was hysterical. She was screaming for me to get out of the house as quickly as I could because the Gestapo who knew that I was in Krefeld had just been there looking for me and her young husband. They had arrested her husband who was in his night clothes, did not permit him to get dressed, shoved him into the Gestapo car, and sped off in the dark of the night. We never found out what happened to her husband Erich; he never came home again. I was a survivor of that night.

Not knowing what to do and not experienced in such terrible emergencies, I had to make some very quick decisions. Scared to death that the Gestapo would catch me, I walked to the railroad station. I purchased a one way fare to Aachen. After what seemed to me to be hours and hours, a train finally came into the Krefeld station around 4 or 5 o'clock on the morning of November 10, 1938. As the train traveled through the German countryside, wherever there was Jewish life, I could see in the dark of the night the fires burning. When I finally got to Aachen around 6 or 7 o'clock in the morning, I called my mother from the railroad station to let her know that I had come home. She told me not to come home, that I should hide because the SS and Gestapo were looking all over town for Jewish boys and men. She also whispered to me that during the night the Nazis had smashed in the store windows of our house and had thrown some stones through the windows of the first floor.

Not knowing what to do, terribly frightened and scared to fall into the hands of the Gestapo, I went back on another train to Krefeld. When I got back to Krefeld, I was too scared to leave the railroad station, and so I took the next train back to Aachen. I finally got back to Aachen around 1 or 2 o'clock in the afternoon. By now I was running away from the Gestapo for the past 14 hours. Since I was scared, alone, hungry and tired, I decided I would go home. As soon as I got home, my parents told me that the mayor of the town who was also the head of the Gestapo had issued a warning to all Jews to stay inside their homes and not to be seen outside.

At around 10 o'clock that same night of November 10, 1938, our doorbell rang. There was no doubt—but mortal fear in our hearts, because we knew that this was either the SS or the Gestapo or both of them. The fear I just cannot describe in any words. It was a fear of being killed immediately. We were so scared that we could not move. My poor Dad, shaking, went to open the door. There were four black uniformed SS men standing there. The leader of them asked my father how many guns he had hidden in the house. Of course we had no guns because as a Jew we were not allowed to have any kind of a weapon. My Dad told him that we didn't have any guns. He then looked at my Dad and said, "We know that you are lying; all Jews lie. We will search for weapons, and may God have mercy on your soul if we find any." The great danger was that many times the Nazis would claim, "We found this gun in your room." When they pulled that one, it was like an automatic death sentence. As Jews, having a gun was a one-way ticket to a concentration camp.

These SS men ordered that my parents, my 82-year-old and almost blind grandmother, as well as I had to stay in the living room and not make any moves. One of the SS men, armed of course, stayed guard over us. In the meantime the other three went from room to room ransacking and destroying everything they saw. With their bayonets they cut the mattresses and pillows open which allowed the feathers to fly all through the house. That is when they destroyed the oil painting of Judith about which I wrote before, and they finally went into the kitchen to pull the dishes out of the cupboards and have them smashed to the floor. Within about one half hour they left our house for the next Jewish home to destroy there as well.

About an hour after they had left, we were still in a deep state of shock. The door bell rang again. My Mom opened the door, and there were two Gestapo agents facing her. They demanded to see my Dad. When he came in, shaking and scared to death, they told him that they had to take him for his "own security into protective custody." He was handcuffed and shoved into a police car. It was a cold rainy and misty November night. I remember that my Dad asked them if they would allow him to take his overcoat along. The answer he got in front of us was, "Where you will go, you don't need an overcoat anymore." The Gestapo car sped away with my Dad into the dark of the night. It was the night when we were sure that by daylight none of us would be still alive and would have met our maker.

My mother, grandmother and I would just look at each other, waiting at any moment for the Gestapo or the SS to come and kill us. We were too scared to move or even to talk. I can still hear my grandmother leading us to recite the Kaddish, the Jewish prayer for the dead. The night never seemed to end for us, we never thought that we would ever see daylight ever again. I was a survivor once again. The Gestapo did not have my name on their arrest list, since they thought that I was arrested in Krefeld by their fellow hoodlums already.

We had no idea where they had taken my Dad. Weeks went by, until one morning my mother received a telephone call from the Gestapo to come to their office because they wanted to talk to her. My mother was shaking and frightened. I insisted on going along with her, but she did not want to hear about that. She was afraid the Gestapo would arrest her and me, and then none of us would be there to look after my old grandmother.

She went on her own into the lion's den, the Gestapo. When she got there, she was led into an office where several Gestapo agents were sitting. They offered her a chair to sit down and then proceeded to tell her that my Dad was in the Buchenwald concentration camp. They told her that they were willing to discharge my Dad if she would be "kind enough" to sign the papers which they would give her for signature. When my mother saw the papers, she almost fainted. The first paper which she signed stated that she would turn all the property including all the money, bankbooks, and so on, over to the Nazi party immediately. The second paper she had to sign was that she would offer our house for sale to a buyer whom the Nazi party would send to buy the house, that she would accept the money the buyer was paying and turn that money over to the Nazi government. Finally, the third paper stated that my mother understood the content of the two papers she just signed and

*Uncle Albert and Aunt Berta around 1938, when they helped us to escape from Germany.*

would comply with them immediately. Then, the Gestapo told her that once the papers were signed, my Dad would be discharged. Of course my mother signed all the papers without daring to ask a single question. Another document she signed also stated that once my Dad came home, we would have to leave Germany. However, before they would discharge my Dad, my mother had to prove to them that we had legal documentation to enter another country which of course my mother signed as well.

Dad's older sister Berta who was married to Albert Stiel had moved to Belgium right after the first World War. Somehow Aunt Berta and Uncle Albert were involved with a Belgium underground group helping Jews to escape from Germany and Austria. They knew lots of influential people in that group. One of them was a Secretary of the Cuban Embassy in Brussels, and another one was the Chief of Police at the Belgium seashore town of Le Zoute. My mother contacted Aunt Berta and Uncle Albert for help. The next day, Aunt Berta came to Aachen and picked up our German passports. She took them back to Brussels to her sources at the Cuban embassy who issued tourist visas for Cuba, and within about

*This is a copy of my Dad's discharge paper from the Buchenwald Concentra-
tion Camp, which was near Weimar, in Germany. Please note the various
dates. My Dad was arrested by the Gestapo on November 10, 1938. The
discharge paper states that he was discharged from the Concentration Camp
on November 27, 1938. However, they actually released him on January
13, 1939, after my mother had signed all pertinent papers for his release as
requested by the Gestapo. He returned home on January 15, 1939, which was
seven weeks later. This was another of many Nazi tricks, to show an earlier
discharge date than the actual date the prisoners were released.*

2 or 3 days she was back again. Of course these were forged visas and
not approved by the Cuban government. The Cubans would have never
allowed entrance into their country with the forged visas. We had no
intentions of going to Cuba; we simply required the visas to convince
the Gestapo that we had a country to which to go.

The next morning my mother went to the Gestapo and presented
them with our "visas." The Gestapo did not question my mother on how
quickly and suddenly we had obtained these visas. They now told my
mother to go to the Hamburg-America Line and purchase four one-way
tickets for Havana. Since the Gestapo controlled my parents' money,
they told her that they would approve the costs for these tickets, leaving
from Hamburg, Germany. My mother pleaded with the agent, whom she

described as being reasonably decent to her, to please let us leave from Antwerp in Belgium. Since Antwerp was only a two-hour train ride from Aachen, and Hamburg was about a twelve hour train ride from Aachen, Antwerp would be much easier on my 82-year-old grandmother. This argument convinced the agent, and he approved her request. But now we had another problem. We needed a transit visa in order to travel from Aachen through Belgium to get to Antwerp. Again Aunt Berta was contacted. She was able to have the Belgian

*Photo taken 1939 shortly before I left Germany*

consulate in Aachen issue us transit visas based on our forged Cuban visas, and again a forged document was produced that showed that we had four berths booked on a ship for us leaving from Antwerp to Cuba.

On January 15, 1939, ten weeks after he was arrested, my Dad was discharged from the Buchenwald Concentration Camp and came back home. He had aged terribly. He had lost half his weight since they were fed only one bowl of soup at night, and a cup of artificial coffee, and one slice of stale bread in the mornings. He was too frightened to tell us anything that had happened to him at the camp. At his discharge he was told by the Nazis that he was forbidden (verboten) to talk about anything. Later on, as time passed by, he didn't want to talk about it. The only thing he ever told me was that from the time he and the others were arrested until they arrived three days later in Buchenwald, they had neither solid food nor anything to drink. They were transported in very old German railroad cars. The cars had lights on day and night during the three days of traveling; they had to look at the lights all the time. They were not allowed to speak to each other, and only every six hours they were allowed to go to the bathroom. At all times they were guarded by the SS.

By the time my Dad finally came home, the house had been sold for almost nothing, which didn't matter anyway because the money was turned over to the NASDAP, the Nazi Party. The car which was parked at the Lontzens garage for the longest time had suddenly disappeared and was never seen again. When my mother told this to the Gestapo, she was told, "You people don't need cars anymore."

My father still refused to believe that the Nazis really meant what they said, and refused to leave Germany. After all, he had served in the German Army during the first World War, and he was wounded in France. All his brothers had served in the German army, and even his father had volunteered during the Prussian-French war in 1870.

About two months after Dad was home again, our door bell rang in the morning at six o'clock, and two other Gestapo agents were standing at the door. They showed my parents the letter which my mother had signed that said we would leave Germany immediately after my father's discharge. The Gestapo told us, me included, that they would give us 30 days to get out of Germany or the four of us would be shipped together to the Buchenwald Concentration Camp on a one-way ticket. Finally, my Dad believed what he heard, and that there was only one way to save our and his life which was to leave Germany. But now the question was, where to? Almost all countries had closed their doors for the Jews to flee to. The United States under the Franklin Roosevelt administration had it made almost impossible for Jews to enter the USA. Roosevelt did almost nothing to come to our aid even though the American public had put a lot of pressure on him to do so.

The Gestapo gave us a deadline—we had to leave Germany no later than April 30, 1939. My parents called a moving company which would pack all our belongings that had survived Kristall Nacht in a large wooden crate to be shipped to Antwerp for further disposition. The moving company picked the loading date of April 19, 1939, my father's 54th birthday. The crate was packed under the supervision of the Gestapo who checked each item very carefully to make sure that nothing of any value, mostly money or jewelry, was loaded. When all this was done, the Gestapo took all the pertinent documents with them. My father was given a copy. The agreement was that once we had notified the Gestapo of our residence in Havana, they would then release the crate for shipping either to Havana or any other country of my parents' choice.

Years later after the war, we found out from the forwarding company that the crate was delivered directly from our house in Aachen to the Nazi headquarters in Aachen. The items inside this crate were distributed to Nazi officials. I am sure that the Nazis must have been sorry that they had previously destroyed so much and now found so few valuable leftovers.

We spent the night of April 19 in our totally empty house. We did not sleep for one second. We were scared of what would happen next to us and felt depressed.

Our train for Belgium was leaving at ten o'clock in the morning from Aachen to Brussels. April 20, 1939 was Hitler's 50 th birthday. The German populace was ordered to fly the Nazi swastika from every house. As we walked from our house, each with one suitcase, to the railroad station, we saw the red swastikas flying from every house. We hoped that we would never see a swastika again. That one suitcase was all that we were allowed to take with us. We were allowed to take only 10 German marks per person with us which at that time was equal to only US $2.50. Once we had arrived at the railroad station, each one of us was frisked by the SS once more to make sure that we had no "contraband" on us.

We, who were eventually lucky enough to escape Germany, faced very painful farewells with our friends and our relatives who were trapped and had no way to escape. We were all so worried about those whom we had to leave behind. We knew, but the world didn't believe it or didn't care that those left behind would face increasing torment and maybe even death. On the day that we escaped from Nazi Germany, together with my 82-year-old grandmother, Omi Tilly, the few friends and relatives still there met us at the railroad station to say their last good bye which we all knew was for all eternity to come. The train rolled into the railroad station. Somebody yelled, "All on board." We went to our seats; the train began to move westward towards freedom and safety. We waved, took our last looks at them, and with tears in our eyes looked at them through the window. Trying not to think, not to talk, our minds totally blank, vacant, depressed. I can still see my parents, worn out from all the sufferings and worries, middle-aged, their faces very serious, gazing with total disbelief out of the windows into the unknown to come. Germany, their home for generations, where they had experienced both happiness and suffering, the land in whose armies they had served, whose country they had defended with their lives, the land whose only language they spoke, betrayed them and forced them into an unknown exile.

We were the survivors of six years of daily Nazi terrors and laws aimed against us. We were the survivors of Kristall Night, the beginning of the end that followed. If it would not have been for my Aunt Berta in Belgium and her association with the Belgian underground movement, we would have been illed as well. I know that I carry an emotional scar that will never heal, as did my parents, and every other survivor, until our death from the dredful life we haad uner the Nazi Swastika.

# Our Life in Exile

*April 20, 1939*

We spent the first few days in exile in Belgium at the home of Uncle Albert and Aunt Berta. Various other relatives had taken this route out of Germany before us. My father's brother Alfred and his wife Aunt May had left Germany two years earlier and lived in Brussels. My mother's sister Aunt Irma and her husband had left during Kristall Night by escaping through the woods into Belgium and were now living illegally in Brussels, together with their son Hans who had escaped shortly before Kristall Nacht. Also my friend Kurt Rosendahl and his father had escaped during Kristall Nacht through the forest into Belgium where they, like thousands of other German and Austrian Jews, were living illegally. Life as an illegal refugee was horrible. These people had to live on a very meager amount of money which the Belgian Jewish community gave them. They lived 6-8 people in a furnished room, sharing a kitchen and bathrooms with many other refugees. Their lives were a miserable way of existence, but their hopes of a better tomorrow kept them alive. That was the reason my father refused to leave Germany illegally or to live in Belgium illegally. Most of the illegal refugees stayed "at home" most of the time for fear of getting caught by the Belgian police. If they were caught, they were sent back to Germany.

Aunt Berta and Uncle Albert had a little summer house at the Belgian seashore town of Le Zoute. They made this house available to us. As soon as we arrived in Le Zoute, Aunt Berta took us to the Chief of Police whom she knew very well. He had the authority to extend our transit visa for an additional four months and did so. We were relieved and grateful for the extention of our visas.

Since there had been uncertainty that our Belgium transit visa would be extended further after the four months had expired, my parents had contacted my grandmother's nephews Herman and Edwin Elsbach in San Francisco to help us get transit visas for England until such time that our quota number at the American Consulate in London would be called for us to enter to the USA.

Again, a lot of red tape was involved in getting the transit visas for England. The British government demanded a security deposit of several thousand British pounds as a guarantee that we would never become a public burden in England. Consequently, Herman and Edwin Elsbach deposited the requested amount with the Barclays Bank in England. The British were now assured of their requirements. On June 6, 1939, we received from the British Consulate in Ostende, Belgium, a one-year transit visa for our stay in England. Herman and Edwin Elsbach promised their father on his death bed that come what may, they would always take care of his sister, my grandmother, and us.

We left Belgium early morning on the 28th of June, 1939, for Dover, England, where we arrived some time in the afternoon after a very rough crossing of the English channel. I remember that when we got off the boat in Dover, we were standing there, totally lost, not speaking a word of English. Fortunately, we met another German Jewish family on the boat who like us were going to London. Somebody in that family spoke a little English, and they helped us through the British Customs and Immigration to clear our way to the train station for our train ride into London. With their help, we got on the right train. As I mentioned before, our luggage consisted of one suitcase each, which was all the Nazis had permitted us to take out of Germany. These were all our worldly possessions. Uncle Leopold's wife, Aunt Bella's sister, had lived in England since after the first World War. Their names were Leo and Berta Hess. They had one daughter Annelise who was born in England. When we arrived in London, we had to take a taxi to their home. Fortunately for us, Aunt Berta and Uncle Albert in Brussels had "loaned" my parents money to cover all the immediate expenses. The Hesses had rented for us two furnished rooms. One room was my parents' bedroom, and the other room I shared with my grandmother. We had kitchen and bathroom privileges, but we had to share them with several other refugees living in the same building, 75 Lansdowne Road, London W 11, close to Holland Park, the Portobello Market, and Marble Arch. Our family in San Francisco gave us a loan again, so that my parents could cover all our expenses. This loan, which my parents eventually paid off in full, allowed us to maintain a very meager existence while living in exile in England.

As soon as we were settled into our two rooms, my old grandmother, my parents and I went to the Jewish Relief organization at the Bloomsbury House in London and started to learn English. They had free courses, but the class size was about 50-60 people. The course was two hours, three times a week. The age group ranged from 16-85 years of age. Our instructor was a Dr. Immergut, who like us, had fled the Nazis. He was an English teacher at a high school in Vienna. After taking lessons for about two months, my Dad decided to have Dr. Immergut come to our room at the Lansdown Road address and give us private lessons.

This worked out much better, and we started to learn more. He insisted that we should listen to the radio, read the newspapers, and go to the movies to learn more. However, there was no way on our limited budget we could afford the tickets for a movie. And so we did the best we could. I tried to get a job, but since I had only a transit visa, I was not allowed to work in England. There was just no way to earn a bit of money to supplement the spendable money. We lived a very idle life, mostly eating, studying English, going for walks to either Holland Park or Hyde Park, and sleeping, which was depressing for all of us, especially my parents.

Around August 15, 1939, my German passport expired. In order to get an American visa, I had to have a valid German passport. There was only one way to get it, and that was to go to the German consulate in London to have my passport renewed. In the process of renewing, they also added the name "Israel" to my name. There were already rumors flying about the possibility of a war between Germany and England. A few days after my passport was renewed, I received a registered letter from the German consulate, which stated that I was to return to Germany without fail. I thought that this was really funny, and I wrote them a letter back, over my parents' objections, that they should "start the war without me" and that I would see them later on, which I did as an American soldier wearing my American army uniform in 1944-1946.

On September 1, 1939, the German army marched into Poland. At that time the French and British governments issued an ultimatum to Hitler to get out of Poland at once, or the Allies would come to Poland's aid. Since Hitler ignored this ultimatum, England declared war on Nazi Germany on September 3, 1939, even though the British were not prepared for it. Two days later the first air raid alarm sirens sounded in London, but no enemy planes were seen. The war proceeded slowly, neither side was fully prepared for what was called "The sit-down war." After the Germans overran Poland they had exhausted their supply lines, and the French and the British who were totally unprepared did nothing. They now started to build up their armed forces. As aliens we had to go to a tribunal, and since we were all holders of German passports, even though the large red J for Jews was stamped on the passport identifying us as Jews, the British authorities declared all of us as "Enemy Aliens." This of course was not only frustrating but also scary for us. Now both the Germans and the British considered us enemies.

We shared our London "boarding house" with some other interesting families. There was an Egyptian journalist and his wife, Mr. and Mrs. Noel. He did the war-time cartoons for the London Evening Standard. Since I did a lot of cartooning in those days myself, I became kind of friendly with him. Then there was a Viennese couple, the Kruh family. They had one married son, one single son Herbert who got married while he lived in London, and two daughters. The oldest daughter Ruth was married. The younger daughter Edith was my age. Edith was a very nice girl and lived with her parents at the time. Edith and I became very friendly because neither one of us had anything to do. She was working illegally as a cleaning lady to make a few shillings. Then there was a single fellow Erich Liffmann living there as well. He was a few years older than I was. The only thing we all did was listen to the London BBC news, hoping to hear of the end of Hitler.

# Meeting Ilse in London

*December 31, 1939*

Very suddenly, within one minute, my life changed forever. New people had moved into the house where we lived, a mother and her daughter from Vienna. The mother had been working as a cook and the daughter as an au pair for a doctor and his family in Sudbury, England. Since Sudbury was a very quiet and isolated place to live, they had left their employment and moved to London. The mother's name was Olga Machauf, about my mother's age, and the daughter name was Ilse Machauf, about a year younger than I was.

On the same day that they moved in, the daughter knocked on our door. My Dad opened the door, and there stood this most beautiful, gorgeous blond girl with the most fantastic blue eyes I had ever seen. She asked my Dad if he could change a one

*Photo of Ilse when I met her, December 1939. Ilse was 18 years old, and I was 19 years old.*

pound English bank note. While my father looked for the change, she came into the room, and I had an even better look at her. I was struck by her beauty, her smile, and her milk and honey appearance.

I was smitten. We exchanged a friendly hello. I made it my business to see her later that afternoon. There was a little place in London called the Austrian Center where all the young Austrians and German Jewish kids would always "hang out." Being that it was New Year's Eve, they had planned a New Year's Eve party at the center. I approached Miss Machauf, as I called her, and asked Miss Machauf if she would like to go out that evening with me to the party at the Austrian Center. I got

*Ignatz Machauf, Ilse's father*

the "cold shoulder" and was told that she had already made plans to spend the evening with Walter and Gerti Ungar at the Austrian Center. With that comment she vanished back into her room. A few days later, I saw her again and convinced her to take a walk with me through nearby Holland Park. To my greatest surprise, Miss Machauf agreed. We met later on that day, and we took a long walk through London and through Hyde Park. On our way home, I asked her permission to call her Ilse, and she reluctantly agreed as long as I would not call her Ilse in front of her mother or my parents. I agreed. Since my English was still very poor, we conversed mostly in German. In front of our parents, we would address each other with the German word "Sie" and not "Du." By the time we got back to where we lived, I had decided that Ilse Machauf was the girl who had stolen my heart, and as the song goes, "Once you have found her—never let her go." I never did, and I am writing this on the 19th of May 2004, 64 years later, on our 58th wedding anniversary. I still see her as the most beautiful, sweetest, perfect, charming, most understanding, and loving girl I have ever met.

On our first walk we talked about our families. I was shocked when Ilse told me that she had to leave her father and 12-year-old brother back in Vienna. She and her mother had received working permits to work as a cook and au pair for a doctor and his family in England. The doctor had promised to help her father and brother to come to England as well. They were almost ready to get all the proper documentation when the war between England and Germany broke out on September 1, 1939. After that date there was no more travel permitted between these two countries. Her father and brother were now caught in the Nazi web from which it was impossible to escape. Tears were rolling down her beautiful cheeks as Ilse told me her story. It broke my heart especially since I had been able to escape with my parents and grandmother at about the same time. My brother, Ed, was safe in San Francisco. I didn't want her to feel so hurt and did not pursue our conversation any further on that subject that day.

We exchanged our horrible young experiences in life growing up under the Nazis, what we had gone through within six years from 1933-1939. Ilse and her family had gone through so much in one year from the day the Nazis invaded Austria in March of 1938, until she was able to escape in March of 1939. She told me how she had seen old Jewish people in Vienna being forced by the Nazis to scrub the side-walks with toothbrushes just like the Nazis had done years earlier to the German Jews in Aachen.

*Olga Machauf, Ilse's mother*

During one of the next walks that we took together, holding hands in London's Hyde Park, she told me that she was born on March 16, 1921 in Liesing on the outskirts of Vienna in Austria. Her father's name was Ignatz Machauf who was born on May 18, 1881 in Atzgersdorf which is also on the outskirts of Vienna. Ignatz Machauf's parents were born in Poland. They were merchants in Atzgerdorf. His first name was Nuchem, and her first name was Mina. He passed away before Ilse was born, and she passed away when Ilse was about four years old.

Her mother's maiden name was Olga Beck, and she was born on November 20, 1889 in Vienna. Coincidentally, my mother was born on November 21, in 1888. Her father was born in Hungary, and her mother was born in Poland. His name was Jonas Beck, and his wife was (Franziska) Fanny Eibuschutz. They lived in Vienna where they owned a men's tailor shop. He passed away in 1936 at the age of 74 years, and his wife passed away in 1942, a victim of the Holocaust at the age of 78.

*Kurt Machauf, Ilse's brother*

*Ilse, 1924, 3 years old*

*Ilse, 1925, 4 years old*

*Ilse and her brother Kurt*

*Ilse, 1938*

Ilse's parents were married in May of 1920. Ilse, like me, had only one brother. His name was Kurt, and he was born on August 19, 1926.

Her parents had moved to Liesing, a suburb of Vienna where her father had opened a building supply and electrical appliances store and also had a gasoline pump on the premises. Her father had made an invention and patented it, called "Aridit." This was a paint like application which would prevent damp basement walls and even stop basement walls from leaking. He had received a medal in recognition of his product. Her mother in her younger years had worked in a jewelry store. During the first World War her father had served in the Austrian army and fought like my Dad in Russia. During her youth, Ilse had belonged to the young Jewish Zionist oriented youth groups like I did in Germany. Both of us had a good Jewish education.

We quickly discovered that we came from almost the same identical backgrounds and had a lot in common. The main difference between us was that we were born and raised in two different German speaking European countries which both had similar cultures.

Because the Nazis didn't invade Austria until March of 1938, it was possible for Ilse to stay in school until the "Anschluss," the occupation of Austria. Her closest girl-friend Julie Czerner was the same age as Ilse and lived across the street from her in Liesing. Julie's father was a hat maker and had his own store in the same house where he and his family lived. They grew up together and as little girls always played together. Ilse talked about an episode when she was about four years old, and she was playing in a white dress.She fell into a bucket filled with tar. Her Dad came to her rescue.

Julie left Austria for Boston several months before Ilse was able to leave Austria. Julie married Harold Cohn in Boston. They have two children, Geriann and Andrea.

The Machauf and the Beck families had many brothers and sisters, most of them living in Vienna and some in Hungary. Ilse had a large number of cousins on both her father's and mother's side. On her father's side were two sisters, Anna and Helene, and four brothers. His oldest brother named Joseph was a jeweler, and then came Bernard who also was a jeweler, Moritz, who had a furniture store, and Adolf who died very young. The only ones who survived the Holocaust were Joseph, his wife, and son, Egon. They had fled to Montevideo, Uruguay, where they opened a jewelry store. On Ilse's father's side, only Egon in Montevideo and Ernst (who was Adolf's son) later on in France survived.

On her mother's side there were two sisters, Louise and Else, and a brother named Dori who was a merchant as well.  Only Louise sur-

*Ilse's maternal great-grandparents, Isaac Eibuschutz, born 1830,*
*and Sarah Eibuschutz, born 1830*

vived, her sister and brother died in Auschwitz. All three of her Aunt Louise's children survived—Eva (Suchmann), Hans (Johnny) and Fred. Her sister Else had two children, Erich in Toulon and Luci in Israel. Luci's son is Daniel who lives in Yaffa, Israel, and Erich's children are Jean Claude and Jacqueline in Toulon. On her brother Dori's side was a son Herbert who was as a child a member of the world famous Vienna Boys Choir. He had escaped to England with his mother, and there he joined the Free Czechoslovakia Air Force flying with the RAF as a gunner. His plane was shot down over Germany where he was killed. All the rest of Ilse's cousins, uncles, aunts, and grandmother died during the Holocaust.

As a little girl Ilse went to the Volksschule in Liesing until she was 10 years old. She went to the Gymnasium in Moedling near Vienna, which was a thirty minute train ride from Liesing. She attended this school and graduated when she was fourteen years old. After the Gymnasium she went to an advanced occupational vocational Jewish school in Vienna. She should have been there for four years, but because of the German invasion, she was not able to finish the last year.

It was her dream to become a Montessori school teacher. However, Jews were forbidden from attending schools after the Nazis took control of Austria. She spent her time visiting her grandmother, baby sitting, learning English, and doing all kind of work to keep herself busy. As the Nazis started to destroy Jewish life in Austria, Ilse's parents tried to escape.

*Ilse's paternal grand-
parents, Nuchem
Machauf, 1851-1915, and
Mina Wasser-Machauf,
1855-1924*

*Ilse's maternal grandparents, Fany Beck, born 1866*,
and Jonas Beck, born 1862.
* Fany Beck died during the Holocaust.*

With tears in her eyes, she remembered that her father had often as a child taken her with him on his various business trips through Austria and Hungary.

Ilse's younger brother Kurt started out at the same Volksschule until he was 10 years old and then studied one more year in the Liesing High School. This was the end of his education being a Jewish child living in Nazi-occupied Austria. Kurt finally was assigned to a children's transport from Vienna to England, departing from Vienna on September 1, 1939, the day the war started. This was the end of his escape from the Nazi killers.

Ilse told me her story of Kristallnacht, and she could not stop her tears. Shortly after the Nazis invaded Austria under Nazi pressure, her parents sold their house at Wienerstrasse 14 in Liesing to a Nazi by the name of Geisel. Geisel then rented the house back to her parents. However, several weeks before the pogrom night of November 9, 1938, Geisel who had become a Nazi big shot, came and threw her family out of the house. Their little dog whose name was Lumpi was so frightened at the turmoil of the move that he ran out of the house into the street and was killed instantly by a passing car which was a horrible thing for her and her family at that moment. Since they had no place to go, the Machaufs moved into their temple at the former Rabbi's apartment who had fled to escape the Nazis earlier.

*Ilse's parents, Liesing, August 1937*

*Ilse and her parents and her brother, Liesing, at the Temple
backyard, October 1938*

SERVICE INTERNATIONAL DE RECHERCHES
INTERNATIONAL TRACING SERVICE
INTERNATIONALER SUCHDIENST

D - 3548 AROLSEN
Tel. (05891) 637 — Telegr.-Adr: ITS Arolsen

Ma/N/ej

Arolsen, 17th March 1977

Mrs. Claudia Voss
12/209 Resnick - Mt. Scopus
Hebrew University

JERUSALEM

Our Ref. : T/D - 466 835
1.037 151

Re : MACHAUF Ignatz, born 1885
MACHAUF Kurt, born about 1927

Dear Mrs. Voss,

Reference is made to your letter dated 30th November 1976 and to our acknowledgement of receipt of 4th January 1977.

Please be advised that a check of our records has revealed only the information already known to you, that is:

MACHAUF Ignaz and MACHAUF Kurth, Religion: Jewish, last known place of residence: Vienna 25, Atzgersdorf, Siebenhirtenstrasse 5, were deported to Lodz on 23rd October 1941.

Unfortunately we know nothing regarding the further fate of the aforementioned persons.

We regret very much not to be able to send you a more satisfactory reply.

Yours sincerely,

A. Opitz
Chief of Archives

*The cup that Ilse rescued from the Liesing temple on Kristallnacht*

During Kristallnacht, the Nazis set fire to this temple while the family was inside. They fled from the burning building and just as they were leaving their temple, Ilse spotted in the ashes the silver kiddush (a wine) cup which she grabbed and kept as a reminder of that night when all four of them almost burned to ashes. This cup is still in our possession and has served as the cup from which Ilse and I, Cliff and Maj-Lis, and Claudia and Bruce, drank under the Chuppa, the wedding canopy.

The Machaufs left almost everything behind and finally found another apartment in Atzgersdorf about a ten minute walk from Liesing. Four months later Ilse and her mother managed to leave for England. Unfortunately, it was also from there that her father and brother were deported by the Nazis to Lodz in Poland and from there to Auschwitz from where they never returned.

*[In 2007, our daughter Claudia and I used records now available on the Internet to learn the fate of Ilse's father and brother. We used the Central Database of Shoah Victims' Names maintained by the Yad Vashem memorial center in Israel, the records of the Documentation Centre for Austrian Resistance in Vienna, and the Lodz ghetto list maintained by jewishgen.org.*

*After Ilse and her mother left in 1939, Ignatz and Kurt Machauf lived in Atzgersdorf. They were deported on October 23, 1941, to the Polish town of Lodz (known then by its Nazi-imposed name of Litzmannstadt). In May 1942, the Nazis conducted one of several major "liquidations" of the Lodz ghetto. Ignatz Machauf died in Lodz on May 13, 1942. Kurt Machauf was deported the next day, May 14, 1942, to the Chelmno extermination camp in Poland. No further records exist. We must assume that the Nazis killed him in the special mobile gas chambers at Chelmno shortly after he arrived.]*

A few weeks after we met, Ilse and I knew that we had found each other and that we belonged together forever. We both talked about it, and we both agreed that both of us felt the same about each other. Soon it became very obvious to Ilse's mother, my parents, and my grandmother that we had found each other.

My parents and my grandmother loved Ilse as much as her mother loved me. We spent the next few months together as much as we could. Ilse found a job at a dress factory in London. As a "friendly" alien,

*Photo of our last day together, London, May 1, 1940*

because she was Austrian and not German, the British allowed her to work in England. Every evening when she returned home from work, we met at the "tube" (subway) station at Holland Park and walked home together arm in arm, or holding hands, fantasizing about our future. Ilse knew that I was waiting for our American visas and that once we got them, we would leave for America. Our visas to live in England were valid for one year only.

On March 16, 1940, my mother made a surprise 19th birthday party for Ilse. That was the moment that Ilse and I knew that my parents had accepted her as their future daughter-in- law. About a month later we were notified by the American Consulate that our immigration visa for the United States was approved and that we could leave for the United States. My parents booked a sailing to America leaving from Liverpool, England on May 2, 1940. I would have given anything in the world to stay in England; I did not want to lose Ilse. However, I realized that this was not possible.

I remember our last evening together. With the limited amount of money I had, we went to the Lyons Corner House on Marble Arch in London for tea and cake to say good bye to each other. It was a very sad and a very tearful evening. The next morning Ilse and her mother went with us to the Victoria Station in London to see us off for Liverpool. I had never felt that badly in my life, but I vowed that we would get together again as soon as possible.

I promised Ilse that I would do all that I could to help bring her and her mother to the United States. Of course, at that time we didn't know the world events would affect us that America would get involved in the war with Germany. I would enlist in the American army, and Ilse would be unable to leave England until the war would end five years later.

We had often talked about all the uncertainties, and both agreed what ever happened, we would write to each other every single day. This we did. We still have about 75% of the letters which we wrote to each other, and every once in a while we still sit down and read them.

# Ilse's Years in England

When Ilse moved from Sudbury to London in December 1939 she looked for a job in the garment industry as a sample maker for ladies garments. Her first and only job from 1939 until she left England in 1945 was with a famous dress company in London called "Matita" on Great Portland Street. There she met many women with whom she became close friends. They went dancing and went to theaters together, and she told me that she always had a good time because all the soldiers wanted to dance with her. So, she picked and chose and enjoyed her life even under the war-time conditions.

*Ilse during the "blitz" of London, 1942*

The appearance of the German bombers in skies over London during the afternoon of September 7, 1940 and thereafter did not stop her and her friends from enjoying themselves and making the best of it all. On September 8, 1940 at about 4 o'clock in the afternoon, 348 German bombers blasted London until 6 PM. Several hours later the German bombers returned to London and bombed away until about six o'clock in the morning. For the next 57 days, London was bombed daily either during the day or night. Ilse recorded in her diary as follows. "Shortly

*Photo taken in London, 1940. Top row, left to right: Ilse's mother Olga, Ilse, me, Joyce, my mother. Center row: left to right: My Dad, Mrs. Kruh. Third row, front: Lady is unknown, Mr. Kruh, Mrs. Filer, my grandmother Tilly.*

*Ilse, March 1945, when I was on Army leave in London*

after the sirens wailed we could hear the Germans flying and bombing overhead. In my room, with its black curtains drawn across the window, I could feel the shake from the guns as well as the heavy bombs hitting their target below tearing the buildings apart." Eventually, they first fled into the cellar of their house, and later on she and her mother took refuge at the air raid shelters below in the London Subway system. One bomb hit the Subway Station at Marble Arch while they were inside, and it took them hours to walk underground from the Marble Arch station to the nearest station to come above ground. This happened many times, and she and her mother escaped many close calls.

We started to write letters as we had promised to each other, but the mail was terrible. Those days it took weeks for an airmail letter to reach either one of us. Needless to say, how worried I always was and how disappointed Ilse was not getting my letters as quickly as we hoped for them to arrive.

# The Years Which Followed

In mid-1941 my parents decided that they were convinced Ilse and I would get married. They started all the necessary papers to bring Ilse and her mother Olga to America. They forwarded all the documents to the American Embassy in London. On December 7, 1941, when America got into the war, the American Embassy in England stopped reviewing all requests for people to immigrate to the United States. During my army furlough to England in March of 1945, I went with Ilse to the American Consulate in London. We had a nice meeting with a consular official. I told him that I wanted to marry Ilse as soon as she and I would be together in the US. I told him that my parents had supplied the Consulate with all the necessary documents. As the meeting ended, he told both of us that he would see what he could do to help us. Not too long after that meeting, Ilse and her mother were called to the American Consulate, and they received their immigration papers for the United States.

However, since the war was not over yet, they could not book a passage to sail to America. No passenger ships were sailing at that time. As soon as the war ended in May of 1945, they were able to sail to America on an American troop transport. There were only a few civilians on that ship, and Ilse was the only young woman.

Recently I read a book written by Martin Goldsmith who wrote a true story of his parents' life and their love in Nazi Germany and eventually their escape and coming to America. At the end he quotes the author Rainer Maria Rilke's Letters to a Young Poet.

"Destiny is like a wonderful wide tapestry in which every thread is guided by an unspeakably tender hand, placed beside another thread and held and carried by a hundred others. And it is always my wish that one might find enough patience within oneself to endure, and have innocence to have faith. Believe me, he writes, life is right in all cases."

# From London to New York

*May 11, 1940*

After a rough sea journey from Liverpool, England to New York, we saw the Statue of Liberty standing tall and ever so proud at the entrance to the New York Harbor on Saturday morning, May 11, 1940, around noon. It was one of the most spectacular sights I had ever seen, the dream of every Jew who wanted to escape from the Nazi terror and death. "The land of the free, the home of the brave." The joy and the feeling all of us had, I just cannot describe. I remember that my grandmother was crying that she too was able to come to America

*My 83-year-old grandmother at the time when we arrived in New York, in 1940*

together with us. The dream came true after the nightmare under which we had lived for six long years. As the ship pulled into the New York harbor, we passed all the mighty skyscrapers which we had seen previously only in the movies and on post cards. Our brains could not register the mighty sights of our new land, our new home. We could not believe that America would now be our home for ever, that the time living in exile was over.

We had arrived to be safe from religious persecution, like so many others before us. Free at last—free at last.

**Fast forward:**

Even today after almost 64 years, I can never forget that only five years later in 1945 and almost to the date, I was a Tech Sergeant in the US Army, on temporary duty at a displaced persons' camp in Offenburg near Frankfurt am Main in Germany. A man who looked more like a walking skeleton than a human being came up to me and asked me in perfect German if I spoke German. When I told him that I did, and he heard my accent-free German, for a moment he wasn't sure if he wanted to talk to me or not. He was still afraid of anyone in a uniform especially speaking in his mother tongue. I looked at him and told him that I was a German Jew, serving with the US Armed Forces in Europe. At that moment he broke down, crying and shaking, holding onto me

*My friend Julius Maier in 1943*

tightly embracing me and told me that I was the best sight that he had seen in seven years. Then he looked at me and said, "Now I feel safe again." The feeling upon seeing an American Jewish soldier speaking his mother language was as overwhelming for him as had been my feelings when I saw the Statue of Liberty five years earlier. I, too, had finally felt safe again.

On the family's ocean journey to New York, I met two people, one who became my closest friend, Julius Maier. We were real good friends from 1940 until 1998 when he passed away. Like me, Julius had a rough life behind him living under Nazis in Germany for six years, and he was arrested by the Gestapo during the 9th of November pogrom in 1938. He was shipped by the Nazis to the Dachau Concentration Camp and was there from November 1938 until March 1939, when his sister who lived in New York successfully gained his release. He left Nazi Germany for England and then, like us, came to the United States. Like us, Julius and his wife Ruth got married in May of 1946.

While on the ship an announcement was made on the PA system, that a Ms. Machauf was asked to come to the ship's office. Of course I was stunned to hear the name Ms. Machauf and made every effort to meet her. When I introduced myself to her and asked her if she was related to Ilse Machauf, she just looked at me and asked me why I asked her. As it turned out her name was Helen Machauf. She was traveling with her step brother Rudy Schlesinger to America. Helen Machauf was a step cousin of Ilse. Helen was only a little girl when her father passed away. Her mother remarried; her second husband's name was Bernhard Machauf who was a brother of Ilse's father. This man adopted Helen, and she took the Machauf name. After some years in New York, Helen married a John Loeb. She worked as the manager of a Barton store, makers of famous chocolate candies on 35 Street and Broadway in New York City until she passed away in 1969. Ilse had very little contact with her cousin Helen during their childhood in Vienna. Through me, the two cousins met again in 1946.

When our ship the "SS Britannic" finally docked in the New York harbor, we had to wait for the immigration and custom officers to come on board, as well as the inspectors from the US Department of Health.

After they checked our passports and entry visas as well as the one suitcase that each of us carried, we still had to go for a physical examination. An eye test was taken to check if we had glaucoma. If the test turned out positive, the immigrant was refused entry into the USA. The fear at the time was that glaucoma was contagious, and that it would lead to blindness in which case the Immigrant could become a liability to the American government. Fortunately, the four of us passed the tests and we were free to enter the USA.

As we got off the ship representatives of the HIAS, "The Hebrew Aid Society" were standing at the pier to meet us. They had instructions from Herman and Regine Kahn to call them as soon as we were off the ship. Herman and Regine Kahn were not directly related to us. Regine's first husband, a man named Leopold Voss, was my father's first cousin. Leopold was killed during the First World War fighting with the German Army against France.

Over the years my parents had always remained in touch with the Kahns. They were hard-working, lower-income bracket, middle class people with not much money to spare but had a heart of gold and an urge to help. And they had a heart of kindness. Herman came to the USA right after the First World War and was a leather goods salesman. Regine came to America shortly after the Nazis came into power in Germany and worked as a sales clerk at Macy's Department store in New York. I don't how where and when they met, but they did and got married in New York.

Within a short while after getting the call from HIAS, both Herman and Regine arrived at the pier to welcome us to America. The pier was located at Twelfth Avenue and 42nd Street in New York City. Since the subway station was on Eighth Avenue and 42nd Street, and as neither the Kahns nor we had sufficient money to spend on a taxi, we all walked to the subway, each of us carrying our one suitcase containing all of our worldly possessions. It was a Saturday evening in May, a hot and humid day. That overcrowded subway ride was some experience for us to say the least. We had never seen a subway before and were amazed to see that many people squeezed together at one time. We finally got off the subway at Broadway and 178th Street.

Since the Kahns lived at 167th Street, we had to walk the eleven blocks with our suitcases to their small apartment. The apartment consisted of one bedroom, a living room, and a small room that Herman used as an office. They made their bedroom available for my grandmother and my mother. Regine and Herman slept in the living room on a sleeper couch, and my Dad and I bedded down on the floor in the little office room.

That first Monday morning the Kahns took us to 75 Fort Washington Avenue to look at an available furnished apartment. My Dad immediately rented the apartment which had three bedrooms, one for my parents, one for my grandmother, and one for my brother, Ed, and me. My brother was to come from San Francisco shortly to be living with us.

That would make the family complete again. The one kitchen and the one bathroom was to be shared with about seven other people living in the same apartment on the same floor.

I had been told I would have to understand that when I came to the United States in 1940, that America had just about recuperated from the "Great Depression" which had lasted from the mid 1920s to the end of 1938. In 1940, the total American population was about 132 million people. Unemployment was still very high. Total unemployment had been reduced to about nine percent from an earlier twenty percent in 1930. When we got here many people, including many college graduates, felt lucky to find any job. A popular song at the time was "Brother, Can You Spare a Dime?" which illustrates the nationwide despair at that time. I knew that I would face a tough time to find any kind of a job.

However, the following morning, Tuesday, Uncle Herman took me by subway to see a friend of his a Mr. Field. Mr. Field was the manager of a little hand weaving mill consisting only of six hand looms. When I went to textile school in Vaals, Holland I had learned hand weaving as part of the school curriculum. To my surprise Mr. Fields hired me on the spot, and I started working as a hand weaver the next day, Wednesday, only four days after I had arrived as a "Greenhorn" in America. Greenhorn was the term people used for newcomers to America.

On weekdays work started at 8:00 AM and ended at 6:00 PM with one half hour off for lunch. On Saturdays we worked from 8:00 AM to noon. My wages were $10 a week. After a month I got a one dollar a week raise which was a ten percent unexpected increase for me. That extra dollar covered my travel expenses between home and work for a week and still left me 40 cents. The 40 cents was enough to buy one dozen eggs and one loaf of bread.

Within a month or two, my parents had found a furnished, seven-room apartment that they could buy at 580 West 161st Street which was a corner building on Broadway and 161st Street in an area called Washington Heights in upper Manhattan. It was a six-story apartment house, and our new apartment was on the fourth floor, Apt. number 47. The people who had owned the apartment, like us, were refugees from

Nazi Germany. They had decided to move to St. Louis and had put the apartment up for sale. The purchasing price for four very poorly furnished bedrooms, a shabby living room, and a dilapidated kitchen was $750. At that time $750 was a lot of money, considering that earning $11 a week was common.

My mother's cousin Herman Elsbach advanced the money to my parents. Now, for the first time in over two years, we had our own permanent home.

But still it was not for us to live there alone. The seven-room apartment included the kitchen and a bathroom, one bedroom for my grandmother, one bedroom for my parents, one bedroom for my brother and me, and a fourth bedroom that my parents rented out for extra income. Our renters were Selma Levy and her aging mother. Of course they shared the kitchen and the bathroom with the rest of us. There was a little storage room with a toilet and a very small wash basin. It certainly was a great improvement over living in boarding houses with furnished rooms and sharing bathrooms and kitchen with many strangers. This was the typical life for most of the refugees coming to America after their escape from Nazi Germany.

Our timing in leaving England and coming to the US had been very fortunate for us. About a week after we had left England, around May 8, 1940, Germany suddenly attacked Belgium, Luxembourg, and Holland. But worse yet, they had started the bombing of England and mostly London. This came to be known as the "Blitz," the lightning war against England. Of course for me, this was terrible news. I now started to worry about the physical survival of Ilse and her mother. When I left England, Ilse and I had promised to write letters to each other every day. I could not wait to hear from her from one letter to the next. Telephone calls between Europe and the United States in those days were not that easy to make, and if they were made, they were very expensive. It could cost a week's pay for a one minute phone call. So we relied on letters.

One day I got a letter from Ilse about a new problem arising from the outbreak of fighting between England and Germany. The Red Cross would no longer accept letters mailed from England bound for Austria which was occupied by the Germans. This posed a terrible problem for Ilse, since it broke the communication chain between her and her mother in England and her father and little brother in Austria. Since America was not yet at war with Germany, we worked out an alternative plan. Ilse would send mail to me in New York, and I would forward her mail to her father and brother in Vienna. They would then send the mail to me to be forwarded to England.

*This is the very last letter received from Ilse's father before his deportation to Lodz. It is postmarked in Vienna on July 27, 1941. From Vienna the letter first went to Frankfurt, Germany, to be opened and censored by the German Army Headquarters.*

Of course that gave me a chance to write to her father and brother as well, and for a long time I was able to communicate with them. I tried to get an affidavit to bring them to the United States. Mrs. Zoehrer who lived in New York and was an old friend of theirs, was getting all the papers together, when suddenly on December 7, 1941, the Japanese invaded Hawaii and the United States declared war on Germany. (Austria had been invaded by Nazi Germany in 1938 and had become a part of Germany.) From then on, there was no longer any mail between England or America and Germany or occupied Austria.

The German bombing of London got worse every day. I listened to radio news broadcasts hourly, always fearing the bad news from England. I was so much in love with Ilse and so very worried that a terrible thing might happen to her that would separate us forever. I just didn't want to hear anything bad anymore.

In the 1940s, there was no television; all we had were radio broadcasts from reporters at the scene in London. Most people listened to Edward R. Morrow, a CBS reporter, who would report from London at 9:00 PM nightly. I met him personally in 1945, when I was with the US Army in Paris, and he came to interview some of us. I was not interviewed, but I told him that I had been a faithful listener of his when he was broadcasting nightly from London. And so it went on, I was just plain miserable to be lonely and missing Ilse so much.

When my brother Ed moved to New York, he left his girl friend Lore Donner behind in San Francisco. The depression in 1940 was far from over; the unemployment rate was still about ten percent, and jobs were hard to find.

I was able to get him a job as a shipping and office clerk at the same place that I worked at Handcraft Weavers for $10 a week. After almost a year with Handcraft Weavers, I found a new job as a weaver which doubled my income with A. Kosoff and Son located in an old factory building on the lower East Side in New York at 119 Prince Street. The Kosoffs had come from Russia to America in the early 1930s and had started this little weaving mill making men's scarves. Both Mr. and Mrs. Kosoff and their son Al worked in the mill from 8:00 AM in the morning until after midnight. They had their living quarters somewhere in the same building. My wages were based on piece work; the more yards of fabrics I could weave in a fifty four hour work week, the more money I would make. I worked there from 4:00 PM until 1:00 AM, six days a week. Sunday was the only day off.

When Ed's girl friend Lore Donner arrived in New York from San Francisco, sometime in early 1941, she had found a furnished room with a family whose name was Wassermann and who had an apartment next door to our apartment in the same building of course. It was a very tiny room, just with a little window. My brother (Ed) Emil, too, had now quit his job. He found a job with a stock trading company which paid him a much better salary than Mr. Field had. Lore too found a job to sustain herself.

Contributing to the family income were my parents and my old grandmother who were making hairnets at home. This was a miserable job. They had a large roll of a knitted fabric in front of them; they had to measure a certain number of inches, make a knot at both ends, and cut between the knots. This created one hairnet. They were paid by how many hairnets they could make a day. Of course, they worked from very early morning until late at night. My grandmother did her fair share by cooking. My brother and I helped our parents with the hairnets too. I would help during the day before work, and Ed helped when he got back home from work. Together we now earned sufficient money to cover the apartment rent of $40 a month and the food we needed to sustain ourselves. There were even a few dollars left over for emergency expenses.

I was lucky to have found my job with the Kosoffs. They were great and generous people. One day I told them what my parents did to make ends meet. They immediately told me to bring my father with me the next day, and they would give him a job too. This they did and paid him well. Dad learned very quickly how to make the spools which would fit into the shuttle to be used by the weavers to produce the cloth. Suddenly, and for the first time since November 9, 1938, together we all made sufficient money to start paying our debts back to Uncle Albert and Aunt Berta in Belgium and to Hermann and Edwin Elsbach in San Francisco.

In the spring of 1942, Emil and Lore got married. It was a small wedding. They were married in Rabbi Koppel's study, and the "reception" was in our apartment. The only people invited other than my grandmother, my parents and myself, were a few friends of Lore and Emil, and Hermann and Regine Kahn. Lore's parents and brother did not come from San Francisco because of their own financial difficulties. The young couple did not go on a honeymoon, but started their married life renting a studio apartment on the ground floor in the same apartment house where we were living. They bought the furniture they needed second hand and started life together.

# Memorial Pages

### Dedicated to our family and friends who were killed by the Nazis during the Holocaust Years 1940-1945. May their suffering and their names never be forgotten

## May they rest in peace

| | | |
|---|---|---|
| Machauf Ignatz | Ilse's Father | Liesing, Vienna |
| Machauf Kurt | Ilse's Brother | Liesing |
| Machauf Anna | Aunt | Liesing |
| Machauf Helene | Aunt | Liesing |
| Grohman Walter | Uncle | Liesing |
| Machauf Bernhard | Uncle | Liesing |
| Machauf Adele | Bernhard's Wife | Liesing |
| Machauf Moritz | Uncle | Liesing |
| Machauf Valli | Cousin | Liesing |
| Machauf Erika | Cousin | Liesing |
| | | |
| Beck Franciska | Ilse's Grandmother | Vienna |
| Beck Dori | Her Son | Vienna |
| Jonas Else | Ilse's Aunt | Hungary |
| Jonas Ignatz | Ilse's Uncle | Hungary |
| | | |
| Hoeflich Louise | Fred's Grandfather's Sister | Bedburg, Germany |
| Hoeflich Mathias | Louise's Husband | |
| Hoeflich Liselotte | Their Daughter | |
| Hoeflich Karola | Their Daughter | |
| Meyer Johanna | Fred's Grandfather's Sister | Essen, Germany |
| Meyer Leopold | Johanna's Husband | |
| Meyer Oscar | Their Son | |
| Meyer Miriam | Oscar's Wife | |
| Hirsh Anita | Their Daughter | |
| Hartog Jetchen | Their Daughter | |
| | | |
| Voss Hans | Fred's Cousin | Aachen |
| Voss Mathilde | Fred's Father's Cousin | Aachen |
| Voss Julius | Fred's Father's Cousin | Aachen |
| Voss Jeanette | Julius's Wife | Aachen |
| Voss Alfred | Fred's Uncle | Duesseldorf, Germany |
| | | |
| Kaufmann Alfred | Fred's Mother's Cousin | Aachen |
| Kaufmann Hugo | Fred's Mother's Cousin | Aachen |
| Kaufmann Elisabeth | Hugo's Wife | Aachen |
| Kaufmann Irmgard | Their Daughter | Aachen |
| Kaufmann Alfred | Fred's Mother's Cousin | Vaals, Holland |
| Kaufmann Otti | Alfred's Wife | Vaals, Holland |
| Kaufmann Erich | Their Son | Vaals, Holland |

| | | |
|---|---|---|
| Kaufmann Joseph | Fred's Mother's Cousin | Cologne, Germany |
| Kaufmann Henrietta | Joseph's Wife | Cologne |
| | | |
| Willner Tilly | Fred's Mother's Cousin | Krefeld, Germany |
| Willner Hugo | Tilly's Husband | Krefeld |
| Willner Ilse | Their Daughter | Krefeld |
| Kahn Edith | Their Daughter | Krefeld |
| Kahn Erich | Edith's Husband | Krefeld |
| | | |
| Levy Albert | Fred's Mother's Cousin | Wiesbaden, Germany |
| Levy Benno | His Brother | Wiesbaden |
| Levy Ruth | Benno's Wife | Wiesbaden |
| | | |
| Stiel Leo | Uncle Albert's Brother | Eschweiler, Germany |
| Stiel Friedel | His Daughter | Eschweiler |
| ~~Stiel Heinz~~ | ~~His Son~~ | ~~Eschweiler~~ |

*(found alive in Atlanta, Georgia, in 2013!)*

| | | |
|---|---|---|
| Weil Isidore | Fred's Grandmother's Cousin | Alsdorf, Germany |
| | | |
| Reinsberg Albert | Fred's Mother's Cousin | Duesseldorf |
| Reinsberg Martha | Albert's Wife | Duesseldorf |
| | | |
| StockJoseph | Fred's Cousin, Ruth's Father | Dueren, Germany |
| | | |
| Hartog Emma | Friend of Fred's Parents | Aachen |
| | | |
| Arensberg Kurt | Fred's School Friend | Aachen |
| Burghard Hans | Fred's School Friend | Aachen |
| Levy Guenter | Fred's School Friend | Aachen |
| Rubins Inge | Fred's School Friend | Aachen |
| Weil Hilde | Fred's School Friend | Aachen |
| | | |
| Czerner Eduard | Father of Ilse's Friend Julie | Liesing, Vienna |
| Czerner Gisella | Mother of Ilse's Friend Julie | Liesing, Vienna |
| | | |
| Rosendahl Hermann | Father of Fred's Friend Kurt | Aachen |

# Descendants of Natan Voss

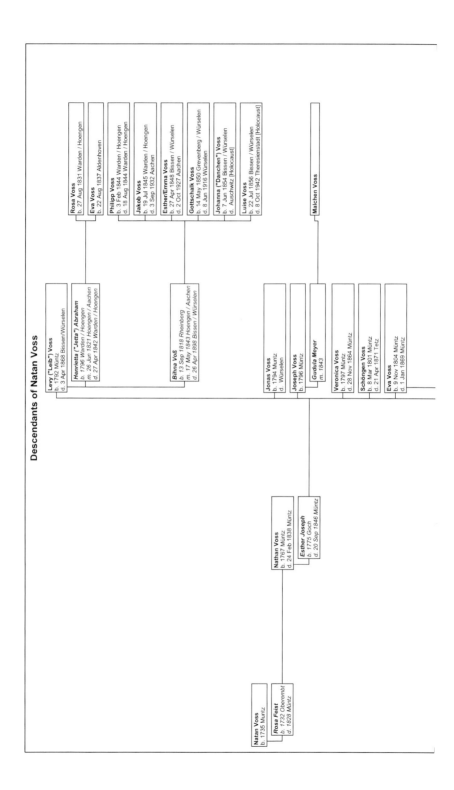

**Natan Voss**
b. 1735 Müntz

*Rosa Feist*
*b. 1732 Oberembt*
*d. 1828 Müntz*

**Nathan Voss**
b. 1767 Müntz
d. 24 Feb 1838 Müntz

*Esther Joseph*
*b. 1775 Goch*
*d. 20 Sep 1846 Müntz*

**Levy ("Leib") Voss**
b. 1792 Müntz
d. 3 Apr 1868 Bissen/Würselen

*Henrietta ("Jetta") Abraham*
*b. 1796 Warden / Hoengen*
*m. 26 Jun 1821 Hoengen / Aachen*
*d. 27 Apr 1842 Warden / Hoengen*

*Bihna Voß*
*b. 13 Sep 1818 Rheinberg*
*m. 17 May 1843 Hoengen / Aachen*
*d. 26 Apr 1898 Bissen / Würselen*

**Rosa Voss**
b. 27 Aug 1831 Warden / Hoengen

**Eva Voss**
b. 22 Aug 1837 Aldenhoven

**Philipp Voss**
b. 3 Feb 1844 Warden / Hoengen
d. 18 Aug 1844 Warden / Hoengen

**Jakob Voss**
b. 19 Jul 1845 Warden / Hoengen
d. 3 Sep 1932 Aachen

**Esther/Emma Voss**
b. 27 Apr 1848 Bissen / Würselen
d. 2 Oct 1927 Aachen

**Gottschalk Voss**
b. 14 May 1850 Grevenberg / Würselen
d. 8 Jun 1916 Würselen

**Johanna ("Danchen") Voss**
b. 7 Jun 1854 Bissen / Würselen
d. Auschwitz [Holocaust]

**Luise Voss**
b. 22 Jul 1856 Bissen / Würselen
d. 8 Oct 1942 Theresienstadt [Holocaust]

**Jonas Voss**
b. 1794 Müntz
d. Würselen

**Joseph Voss**
b. 1796 Müntz

*Gudula Meyer*
*m. 1843*

**Veronica Voss**
b. 1797 Müntz
d. 28 Nov 1864 Müntz

**Schöngen Voss**
b. 8 Mar 1801 Müntz
d. 21 Apr 1871 Tetz

**Eva Voss**
b. 9 Nov 1804 Müntz
d. 1 Jan 1869 Müntz

**Malchen Voss**

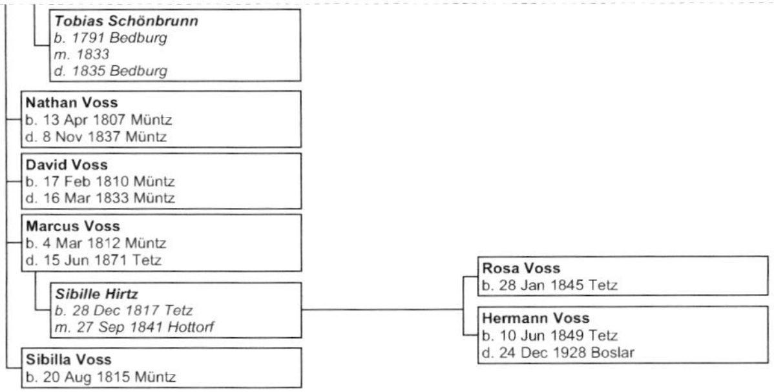

**Tobias Schönbrunn**
b. 1791 Bedburg
m. 1833
d. 1835 Bedburg

**Nathan Voss**
b. 13 Apr 1807 Müntz
d. 8 Nov 1837 Müntz

**David Voss**
b. 17 Feb 1810 Müntz
d. 16 Mar 1833 Müntz

**Marcus Voss**
b. 4 Mar 1812 Müntz
d. 15 Jun 1871 Tetz

**Sibille Hirtz**
b. 28 Dec 1817 Tetz
m. 27 Sep 1841 Hottorf

**Sibilla Voss**
b. 20 Aug 1815 Müntz

**Rosa Voss**
b. 28 Jan 1845 Tetz

**Hermann Voss**
b. 10 Jun 1849 Tetz
d. 24 Dec 1928 Boslar

# Descendants of Jakob Voss

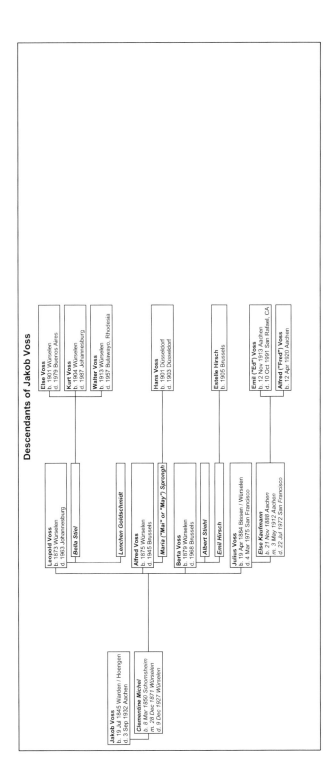

**Jakob Voss**
b. 19 Jul 1845 Warden / Hoengen
d. 3 Sep 1932 Aachen

*Clementine Michel*
*b. 8 Mar 1850 Schornsheim*
*m. 28 Dec 1871 Würselen*
*d. 9 Dec 1927 Würselen*

**Leopold Voss**
b. 1873 Würselen
d. 1963 Johannesburg

*Bella Stiel*

**Else Voss**
b. 1901 Würselen
d. 1979 Buenos Aires

**Kurt Voss**
b. 1904 Würselen
d. 1987 Johannesburg

**Walter Voss**
b. 1913 Würselen
d. 1957 Bulawayo, Rhodesia

*Lenchen Goldschmidt*

**Alfred Voss**
b. 1875 Würselen
d. 1945 Brussels

*Maria ("Mai" or "May") Sprongh*

**Hans Voss**
b. 1901 Düsseldorf
d. 1903 Düsseldorf

**Berta Voss**
b. 1879 Würselen
d. 1968 Brussels

*Albert Stiehl*

*Emil Hirsch*

**Estelle Hirsch**
b. 1905 Brussels

**Julius Voss**
b. 19 Apr 1884 Bissen / Würselen
d. 4 Mar 1975 San Francisco

*Else Kaufmann*
*b. 21 Nov 1888 Aachen*
*m. 3 May 1912 Aachen*
*d. 22 Jul 1972 San Francisco*

**Emil ("Ed") Voss**
b. 12 Nov 1913 Aachen
d. 10 Oct 1991 San Rafael, CA

**Alfred ("Fred") Voss**
b. 12 Apr 1920 Aachen

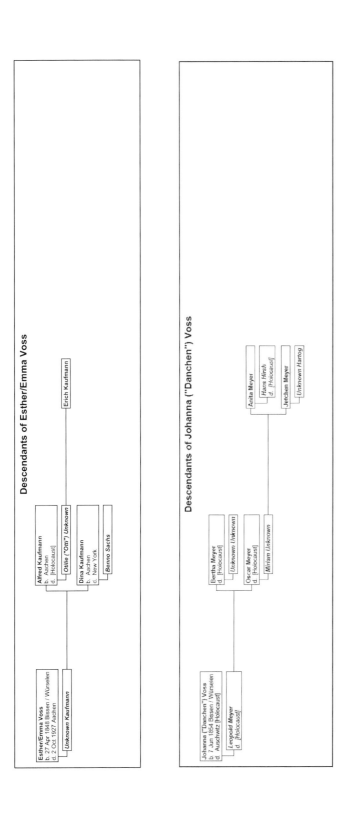

# Descendants of Esther/Emma Voss

**Esther/Emma Voss**
b. 27 Apr 1848 Bissen / Würselen
d. 2 Oct 1927 Aachen

*Unknown Kaufmann*

**Alfred Kaufmann**
b. Aachen
d. [Holocaust]

*Ottilie ("Otti") Unknown*

Erich Kaufmann

**Dina Kaufmann**
b. Aachen
d. New York

*Benno Sachs*

# Descendants of Johanna ("Danchen") Voss

**Johanna ("Danchen") Voss**
b. 7 Jun 1854 Bissen / Würselen
d. Auschwitz [Holocaust]

*Leopold Meyer*
d. [Holocaust]

**Bertha Meyer**
d. [Holocaust]

*Unknown Unknown*

**Oscar Meyer**
d. [Holocaust]

*Miriam Unknown*

Anita Meyer

*Hans Hirsh*
d. [Holocaust]

Jetchen Meyer

*Unknown Hartog*

# Descendants of Gottschalk Voss

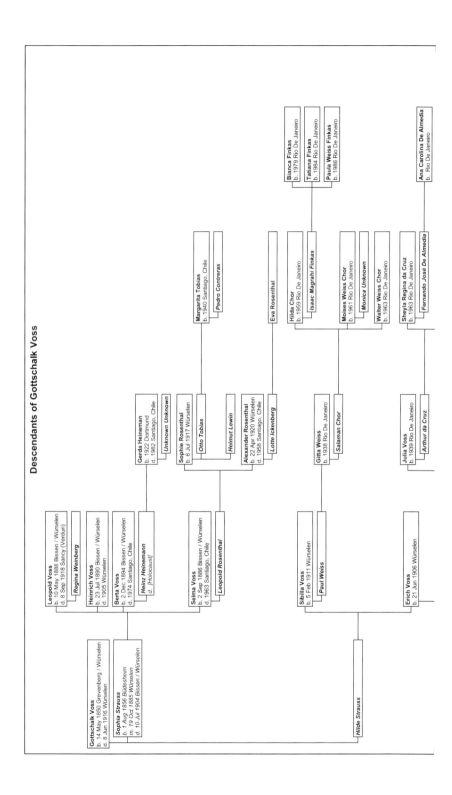

**Gottschalk Voss**
b. 14 May 1850 Grevenberg / Würselen
d. 8 Jun 1916 Würselen

*Sophia Strauss*
b. 1 Aug 1856 Büdesheim
m. 19 Oct 1885 Würselen
d. 10 Jul 1904 Bissen / Würselen

**Leopold Voss**
b. 10 May 1888 Bissen / Würselen
d. 8 Sep 1918 Sancy (Verdun)

*Regina Weinberg*

**Heinrich Voss**
b. 23 Jul 1890 Bissen / Würselen
d. 1905 Würselen

**Berta Voss**
b. 2 Dec 1894 Bissen / Würselen
d. 1974 Santiago, Chile

*Heinz Heinemann*
d . [Holocaust]

**Gerda Heineman**
b. 1922 Dortmund
d. 1962 Santiago, Chile

*Unknown Unknown*

**Selma Voss**
b. 2 Sep 1886 Bissen / Würselen
d. 1963 Santiago, Chile

*Leopold Rosenthal*

**Sophie Rosenthal**
b. 6 Jul 1917 Würselen

*Otto Tobias*

**Margarita Tobias**
b. 1940 Santiago, Chile

*Pedro Contreras*

*Helmut Lewin*

**Alexander Rosenthal**
b. 22 Apr 1920 Würselen
d. 1958 Santiago, Chile

*Lotte Ickenberg*

**Eva Rosenthal**

**Sibilla Voss**
b. 5 Feb 1911 Würselen

*Paul Weiss*

**Gitta Weiss**
b. 1938 Rio De Janeiro

*Salaman Chor*

**Hilda Chor**
b. 1959 Rio De Janeiro

*Isaac Magrabi Finkas*

**Bianca Finkas**
b. 1979 Rio De Janeiro

**Tatiana Finkas**
b. 1984 Rio De Janeiro

**Paula Weiss Finkas**
b. 1986 Rio De Janeiro

**Moises Weiss Chor**
b. 1961 Rio De Janeiro

*Monica Unknown*

**Walter Weiss Chor**
b. 1963 Rio De Janeiro

**Erich Voss**
b. 21 Jun 1906 Würselen

**Julia Voss**
b. 1939 Rio De Janeiro

*Arthur da Cruz*

**Sheyla Regina da Cruz**
b. 1963 Rio De Janeiro

*Fernando José De Almedia*

**Ana Carolina De Almedia**
b. Rio De Janeiro

*Hilde Strauss*

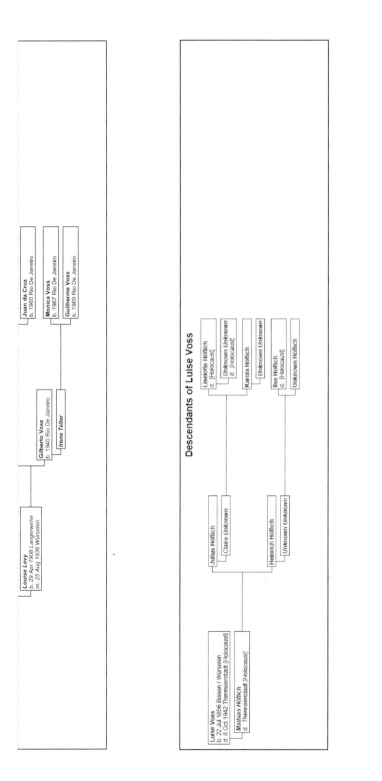

# Descendants of Luise Voss

**Louise Levy**
b. 29 Apr 1908 Langenwehe
m. 25 Aug 1936 Würselen

**Juan da Cruz**
b. 1965 Rio De Janeiro

**Monica Voss**
b. 1967 Rio De Janeiro

**Guilherme Voss**
b. 1969 Rio De Janeiro

**Gilberto Voss**
b. 1940 Rio De Janeiro

*Irene Teller*

Luise Voss
b. 22 Jul 1856 Bissen / Würselen
d. 8 Oct 1942 Theresienstadt [Holocaust]

*Mathias Höflich*
d. Theresienstadt [Holocaust]

Julius Höflich

*Clare Unknown*

Heinrich Höflich

*Unknown Unknown*

Liselotte Höflich
d. [Holocaust]

*Unknown Unknown*
d. [Holocaust]

Karola Höflich

*Unknown Unknown*

Ilse Höflich
d. [Holocaust]

Unknown Höflich

# Descendants of Leopold Voss

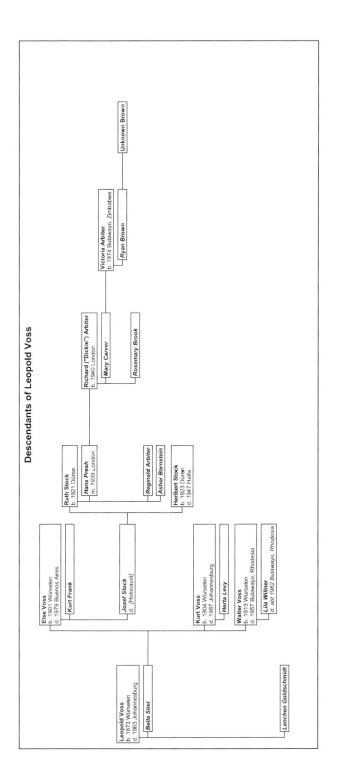

**Leopold Voss**
b. 1873 Würselen
d. 1963 Johannesburg

*Bella Stiel*

**Else Voss**
b. 1901 Würselen
d 1979 Buenos Aires

*Kurt Frank*

**Josef Stock**
d. [Holocaust]

**Kurt Voss**
b. 1904 Würselen
d. 1987 Johannesburg

*Herta Levy*

**Walter Voss**
b. 1913 Würselen
d. 1957 Bulawayo, Rhodesia

*Lilia Willner*
d. abt 1962 Bulawayo, Rhodesia

*Lenchen Goldschmidt*

**Ruth Stock**
b. 1921 Düren

*Hans Presh*
m. 1939 London

*Reginald Arbiter*

*Asher Bernstein*

**Heribert Stock**
b. 1923 Düren
d. 1947 Haifa

**Richard ("Dickie") Arbiter**
b. 1940 London

*Mary Carver*

*Rosemary Brook*

**Victoria Arbiter**
b. 1974 Bulawayo, Zimbabwe

*Ryan Brown*

**Unknown Brown**

# Descendants of Berta Voss

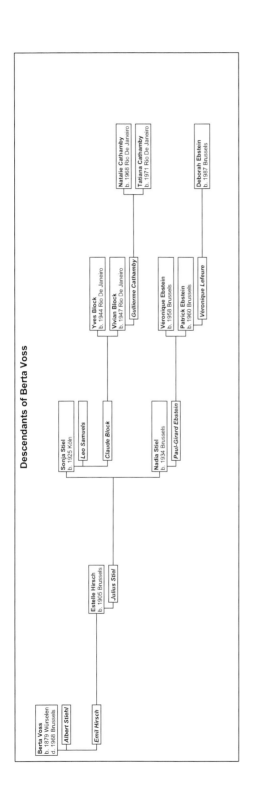

**Berta Voss**
b. 1879 Würselen
d. 1968 Brussels

*Albert Stiehl*

*Emil Hirsch*

**Estelle Hirsch**
b. 1905 Brussels

*Julius Stiel*

**Sonja Stiel**
b. 1925 Köln

*Leo Samuels*

*Claude Block*

**Nadia Stiel**
b. 1934 Brussels

*Paul-Girard Ebstein*

**Yves Block**
b. 1944 Rio De Janeiro

**Vivian Block**
b. 1947 Rio De Janeiro

*Guillerme Cathamby*

**Véronique Ebstein**
b. 1958 Brussels

**Patrick Ebstein**
b. 1960 Brussels

*Véronique Lefeure*

**Natalie Cathamby**
b. 1968 Rio De Janeiro

**Tatiana Cathamby**
b. 1971 Rio De Janeiro

**Deborah Ebstein**
b. 1987 Brussels

# Descendants of Julius Voss

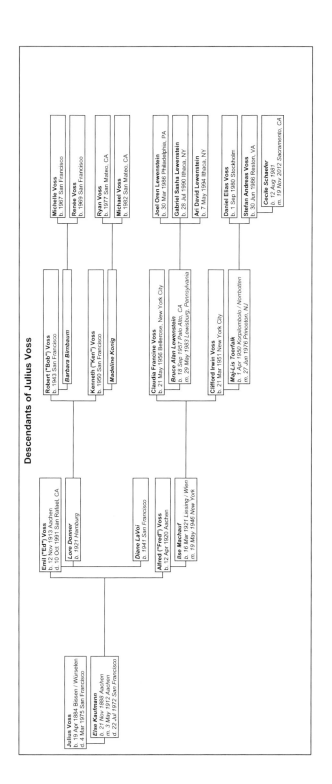

**Julius Voss**
b. 19 Apr 1884 Bissen / Würselen
d. 4 Mar 1975 San Francisco

*Elise Kaufmann*
*b. 21 Nov 1888 Aachen*
*m. 3 May 1912 Aachen*
*d. 22 Jul 1972 San Francisco*

**Emil ("Ed") Voss**
b. 12 Nov 1913 Aachen
d. 10 Oct 1991 San Rafael, CA

*Lore Donner*
*b. 1921 Hamburg*

**Robert ("Bob") Voss**
b. 1943 San Francisco

*Barbara Birnbaum*

**Michelle Voss**
b. 1967 San Francisco

**Renee Voss**
b. 1969 San Francisco

**Kenneth ("Ken") Voss**
b. 1950 San Francisco

*Madeline Konig*

**Ryan Voss**
b. 1977 San Mateo, CA

**Michael Voss**
b. 1982 San Mateo, CA

*Diane LaVoi*
*b. 1941 San Francisco*

**Alfred ("Fred") Voss**
b. 12 Apr 1920 Aachen

*Ilse Machauf*
*b. 16 Mar 1921 Liesing / Wien*
*m. 19 May 1946 New York*

**Claudia Francine Voss**
b. 21 May 1956 Bellerose, New York City

*Bruce Alan Lewenstein*
*b. 18 Sep 1957 Palo Alto, CA*
*m. 29 May 1983 Lewisburg, Pennsylvania*

**Joel Oren Lewenstein**
b. 30 Mar 1986 Philadelphia, PA

**Gabriel Sasha Lewenstein**
b. 28 Jul 1990 Ithaca, NY

**Ari David Lewenstein**
b. 7 May 1994 Ithaca, NY

**Clifford Irwin Voss**
b. 21 Mar 1951 New York City

*Maj-Lis Toerfalk*
*b. 1 Apr 1950 Korpilombolo / Norrbotten*
*m. 27 Jun 1976 Princeton, NJ*

**Daniel Elias Voss**
b. 1 Sep 1980 Stockholm

**Stefan Andreas Voss**
b. 30 Jun 1986 Reston, VA

*Cecile Schaefer*
*b. 12 Aug 1981*
*m. 19 Nov 2012 Sacramento, CA*

# America Declares War

Life was getting more secure and predictable for us when on December 7 in 1941, war again disrupted our lives. The Japanese Empire attacked our naval bases in Hawaii, and the United States declared war on both the Japanese Empire and their allies the German and Italians.

In March 1942, I tried to join thousands of young American men and women. I too volunteered to serve in the United States Army. There were two reasons for this. First of all I thought that this move would bring me back to England where Ilse was. Most troops from the Eastern United States were sent to Europe at the time. The other reason was that there was a mass hysteria to enlist in the Service. No young man wanted to be seen in civilian clothing. Socially, a young, healthy male felt guilty and ashamed if he did not sign up for military duty. There was an air of patriotism in America after Pearl Harbor like America had never seen, before and certainly not since. The pressure to join the army was everywhere. People who were sick tried to enlist by making false claims about their health.

Of course my parents were not too happy that I volunteered, but because of the general patriotism in the United States, they didn't oppose my enlisting. I am sure that they must have been very upset about it but never said so to me. I was sure that they really understood my feelings to enlist.

A few month after I had signed up, I received a letter from the army stating that my application was appreciated but put on hold because the current law did not allow non-American citizens to join the US army. The letter stated that my application had been forwarded to the local draft board because they expected that the law would be changed shortly. Of course, that was a blow to my ego.

In the meantime our family was making a number of changes. Emil and Lore had moved back to San Francisco where Emil got a well paid job in the accounting office of the Kaiser Shipyard. At the shipyard they were building "Victory ships" by the hundreds. These ships were used to transport American troops both to Europe and to the Pacific. I had found a new job paying a very nice salary at Buckminster Rug, a well-known hand carpet weaving company. Mr. Wassermann, our next door neighbor, had found a job for my Dad at Kohn and Goodman, a well-known factory for men's suits. My mother continued to make hairnets.

We had adjusted to our new life and life style in America. But suddenly my Omi got very sick. Doctor Levin, who was also from Germany and was our doctor, told us that she had an obstruction in her stomach and that there was not much that could be done. She was put on a very heavy medication, and on September 7, 1942 she passed away in her sleep at the age of 86 years. Of course we were saddened to have lost her, and I remember the day of her passing away forever.

The United States changed the laws and now allowed non-citizens to join the armed forces. I accepted this change with mixed feelings. I was lonely and wanted to be with Ilse. My home my life had changed. My brother had moved to California, and therefore I had second thoughts about leaving my parents alone in New York. I felt now, and my parents agreed with me, that if the military wanted me, the draft board would let me know in due time. My best friend at that time Julius Maier had enlisted as well for the army and passed his physical examination even though he had some medical problems which he did not reveal to the army doctors who examined him. Now we both awaited orders from our draft boards to report for active duty.

All over the United States "The Air Raid Warden Service" were formed. Anyone who was physically fit, male or female, between the ages of 18 and 50 was expected join to protect the homeland from potential enemy air raids. Blackout exercises were started; first aid courses were given, and the new Air Raid Warden Service was accredited as Police Auxiliaries. Those who worked at day time were asked to give of themselves at least three nights week, and those who worked at night time, served during the day time hours. A shift lasted only four hours per person. Of course, I joined as well at an office at 156 Street and Broadway. A police officer was in charge of each office, and both male and females were assigned to patrol duty. Here I met a lot of nice young people; among others were Curt Rosenfeld and his then girl friend Helga Rubel who got married in 1946. Ilse and I remained life long friends with Curt and Helga. Unfortunately, Helga passed away several years ago in Florida. Curt was drafted into the army only about two month before me.

Ilse and I had been corresponding on a daily basis as we had promised we would since that dreadful day in May 1940 when I left her in London. Ilse started numbering all her letters; I, of course, did not. Through the years right up until the present March 2004, we still have all those letters. Now and then we enjoy re-reading them. We realize that during the best years of our young lives we were separated, but that through this period, the hope of getting together was never abandoned.

Towards the end of 1943, I finally received the long expected notice from my local draft board stating that since I had volunteered to serve, I was now asked to come for a physical examination. On January 2, 1944, I went to Governor Island in New York City for my physical and was pronounced 1 A for military Service. My brother Ed had gone for his physical in San Francisco at the end of December 1943 but was rejected because of his poor eye sight. I received my official notice for induction and had to report for active duty on March 21, 1944. Once again I had to say good bye, this time to my parents and some good friends.

# I Am In the Army Now...
## and Discover Racism

On March 21, 1944, a blizzard hit New York City. It snowed for hours as we left by train shortly after six o'clock in the morning from Penn Station in New York City for Camp Upton in Brookhaven, Suffolk County on Long Island, NY. As soon as we arrived at Camp Upton, we recruits were all given snow shovels, and the army "fun" began. A Sergeant yelled at us, "You are in the army now; we can make your life miserable! If you want us to. Just don't try and find out." With those welcoming words, we started shoveling snow for at least three hours. After that job was done, we were tested for IQ, given more physical examinations, medical shots, issued equipment and uniforms, and so on. Finally, everyone was interviewed by an army Colonel who decided to which branch of the service the army would assign us. I was assigned to Combat Engineer training at Fort Belvoir in Alexandria, VA, about 18 miles south of Washington, DC.

As soon as we finished our basic training at Ft. Belvoir, which was at the end of May in 1944, groups of us were assigned to different camps for jungle warfare and additional and special training. In June 1944, the group to which we were assigned was the 1673 Engineer Utility Combat Unit.

At Ft. Belvoir, we had trained building bridges and blowing them up again. We trained installing telephone and electric wires and learned the regular utility requirements. While I was in the service, I never did any of those assignments for which I had trained.

We had no idea what assignment we would face once we were assigned to the 1673 Engineer Utility. Out of Ft. Belvoir the group consisted of about 18 men, but we soon learned that once the 1673 was fully staffed, our unit would be 45 men. These soldiers would come from other training centers. Mostly they were from other army camps in the southern part of the United States. At this point we had no idea as to where our new assignment was located.

Within only a day or two after we had been told about our new assignment, we were told to get ready on the next morning with all our gear and belongings to be transferred to our new post. Typically for the army, we were not told where the new post was located. Two army trucks took us to the Union railroad station in Washington, DC. There we were assigned on a train with a destination for Alexandria, Louisiana, via New

York and Chicago. It was a strange route for a journey to go about 1400 miles south of Washington.

From Washington we went first with the Pennsylvania Railroad to New York City. In New York we boarded a Pullman train to take us to Chicago, Illinois. Our seats were two seats together which at night time the porters would convert to two single beds, one upper and one lower bed. Each car had air conditioning, which was a real novelty. In those days the Pullman trains were really luxury. They had porters on them, who were all without any exception Black Americans. The trains had a dining car, where the waiters again were Black Americans. In the dining car they served from a standard Pullman menu, and for us that was great since it was better than the army chow. We could order whatever we wanted. I had never traveled on a luxury train before and had never been south of Washington, DC, so this was a great experience for me. First, I was a bit amazed that the crew on the Pullman trains were only Black Americans, which the "White" people  referred to either as "Colored" or "Negroes" or even the horrible "N" word. The word "African-Americans" was not known at that time in our history.  This only became a key word during the Civil Rights Movement only years after the war.

Once our train left the Grand Central station in New York City, we went directly to Chicago where we had to change railroad stations and trains, and after a long layover finally boarded a train for Alexandria, Louisiana. The train took us from Chicago first to Charleston, West Virginia. At this stop about another 15 or so men joined us. We still had no idea, and neither did they, the name of the camp we would be assigned to. That was a secret, only the army knew. In Asheville, Tennessee, another group joined us.  We were now a full platoon traveling to a place that we didn't know if it had a name.

When we got to Birmingham, Alabama, we had to leave the train and were picked up by army trucks for an overnight stay at some army camp close to Birmingham. Before we left Birmingham in the morning, two officers were assigned to us. One of them was Lt. Geoffrey, about whom I will write more later on. The officers told us that we would now leave for Camp Claiborne in Louisiana for further training. Why the additional training, they really didn't know themselves, so they told us.

This was a short train ride and was not on a Pullman train. We finally reached Alexandria, Louisiana. It was a terribly hot and humid day. Alexandria is about 170 miles northwest of New Orleans, but the climate is about the same as in New Orleans. It must have been about 80 degrees of burning heat and 80 percent humidity when we arrived at the end of May 1944.

Before we got there, the base was known for its large Air Force base. But it was now the home of the 82nd infantry division. To us it appeared to be a mud hole surrounded by swamps and mosquitoes, which were big and mean. The men stationed there already called them the "dive-bombers" and warned us that they are just as dangerous as our enemy.

We soon found out that we now would be trained for the Pacific Islands and that the weather and climate in Alexandria were very similar to any of the Pacific Islands. The main object of the training was to acquaint ourselves to the climate and learn all about jungle warfare. This was rather very bad news for us. At the mess halls a sergeant was assigned to make sure that after each meal, before we left the mess hall, we would swallow the salt pills in front of them. To prevent sunburns we had to be fully dressed at all times. Uniform shorts were not allowed to be worn on or off duty. We slept in tents whose entrance consisted of mosquitoes nets. So really we were not very happy troopers. Most of our exercise consisted of learning how to climb up on palm trees and install telephone and electric wires all at about the same time. We learned how to build fox holes and how to live on C and K rations for days and days, without regular army chows.

After being at Camp Claiborne for a week or two, we were able to get a two day weekend pass to visit New Orleans. By train it was about a three to four hour trip which went mostly through desolated areas. The homes along the railroad tracks were like the little shanty houses one would see on the Pacific Islands. The population along the roads were mostly all black and apparently from the looks of it very poor people. Whenever the train stopped at the many little villages, little boys and girls would try to sell us watermelons or other fruits. They were so thankful that we bought from them, which gave them a few cents to spend. We could see cotton growing and we could see people picking and bailing cotton.  It seemed to be back breaking work especially at those hot and humid days.

After a hot and sweaty miserable train trip, which was in very old railroad cars, we finally arrived in New Orleans. I don't remember at what time we got to New Orleans, but it was in the late afternoon. The USO had made hotel reservations for us, but we had to pay the hotel ourselves. The hotel was an old run down hotel in town. Of course, no air conditioning. All the rooms were small and smelly, two men to a room.  We were lucky we had a room with a window, most did not. But we were young and didn't care and it was a nicer place than our army camp. The first night we decided to spend in town, rather than at the hotel. The town was doing a great business with all the soldiers and lots and lots of sailors and lots of music and great restaurants. All the many bars in the French Quarters were loaded with military personnel. All American soldiers were happy to be in town.

The local population was another story, which shocked me personally and reminded me of my own life as a Jewish young man in Nazi Germany during 1933 when the Nazis came to power until I was able to escape in 1939. During that time the Jews in Germany were segregated by Nazi laws, from the rest of the German people. The Nazis had declared that the Jews were a different race by themselves and that they were not allowed to mix in any form, shape or manner with the rest of the German people and society. The Nazis claimed that the Jewish blood was different than that of the German people, which the Nazis claimed had pure "Aryan" blood. Black people, according to the Nazis, were also of a different blood than the Aryans, and people who were of mixed blood would not be considered as Aryans.

When I walked through the town of Alexandria, Louisiana and later on when I was in New Orleans, I saw park benches, public bathrooms and drinking fountains, clearly marked "FOR WHITES ONLY" or "FOR BLACKS ONLY." Restaurants would not serve black people, the same as the Nazi German restaurants that had signs saying "WE DON'T SERVE JEWS." To me, at least, it appeared that the racial prejudice was much more openly shown in Alexandria than it was in New Orleans. I really could not understand why this was allowed to happen in America, where I thought that all men and women were created equally free since the days of slavery had ended long ago. Yet the black people I saw were so much segregated from the white population. It was so sad for me to see. As I watched the way the black population accepted this segregation as a matter of fact, I realized that this was totally an unacceptable situation for me, but it was nothing new to these people. At that time of my life I had not too much knowledge of the Civil War and no knowledge of the widespread discrimination against black people. At a card store in town I purchased a few post cards which clearly showed how insulting and how insensitive the white people were about that horrible era in the southern United States. I still have those cards, but won't show them here. Google "racist postcards United States" if you want to see how badly Americans treated our fellow citizens.

On my next and last weekend pass to New Orleans, I signed up for a tour of the city. It was very obvious that the majority of the black people in New Orleans were employed to do manual labor in the entertainment and service industry. Some were musicians, others were porters or laborers. The tour took us to a number of plantations on the outskirts of New

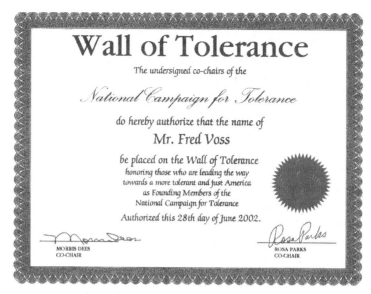

*My certificate from the National Campaign for Tolerance,*
*presented by Rosa Parks*

Orleans. I can still remember one of them very well. I believe it was named The San Francisco Plantation, which was built in the mid 1800s by slaves (but I am not sure of the name). The plantation mansions had very large rooms, and some even had the original furniture as they had in the mid-1850s, less than ninety years earlier. The properties were amazingly large.

Based on this experience in 1948 I joined and became active in CORE, the Congress of Racial Equality. In 2002 I was honored by the late Rosa Parks in person. I have a beautiful certificate which she presented to me.

After the training, our group was selected for overseas assignment; some of us were assigned to units serving in the Pacific and others for assignment in Europe. How the army picked us for serving in the Pacific or in Europe nobody was ever told. Somehow I was in the group assigned to Europe. We who were assigned for service in Europe felt relief. At least the climate in Europe would not be that oppressive, and most of all, it would not include jungle warfare. It definitely was the better of the two places to serve. I was especially delighted, hoping that we first would go to England for further training before deploying to the continent.

# Going Overseas with the U.S. Army

On June 27, 1944, we left New Orleans for Camp Miles-Standish in MA and arrived in Boston about two days later. From the railroad station we went immediately to Camp Miles-Standish to be given our assignment for overseas duty, receive all needed medical attention, receive the chaplain's final blessings, and be issued brand new equipment, uniforms and all other gear. About two days later, we were brought to a pier in the Boston harbor to board the "SS Manhattan" which had been refurbished to be an army troop ship. Our unit was assigned quarters at the empty indoor swimming pool of the ship.

On our second day on the ship out of sight of land, a call came suddenly through the ship's PA system. A clerk called out for attention, and called a long list of names. Among them was Pvt. Voss. At the end of the message he announced that all the names called must report to the ship's commanding officer without fail. Of course I was stunned, worried, and scared. I felt like when I was in school and would be called to the principal's office. To my relief, I saw one of my best buddies being called as well. His name was John Duffey. John was a few years older than I was; he was married and had a daughter. John, like me, was not an American citizen. John had come to the United States from Ireland as a child. He had never bothered to become an American citizen. Together we went to the Commanding Officer's Deck, and there we saw other men assembled already.

After a few moments came the surprise of our lives. The ship's Commanding Officer came out—our mouths dropped and didn't seem to close. It was Jack Dempsey in person! Jack Dempsey was at one time the world heavy weight champion boxer. I will never forget his words. He looked at us, smiled, and said "Yes, that is me, Jack Dempsey." Then he continued and said, "I have been notified that none of you men are American citizens. Under the present laws of the United States of America, you must be a United States citizen in order to bear arms in the defense of the United States. Therefore, raise your right hand, and let me administer the oath." I have no idea what he said, but I remember that he said, "Now all of you are American citizens." He then shook hands with each one of us and wished us God's blessings on our journey. That is how I became a US citizen. The photo on my citizenship paper shows me in my US Army uniform.

I can't remember if Jack Dempsey himself signed the original paper or the order that he swore us in. Many years later, Ilse and I were walking on Broadway in New Yorkaround 50th Street passing by a restaurant that Jack Dempsey owned. As we passed by his restaurant, I saw that he was busy talking with some people. I waited until he said good bye, introduced myself, and told him that he was my Commanding officer on our ship on its way to the ETO (European Theater of Operation) and that he had sworn me in to become an American citizen. He remembered that incident. We chatted a few moments, shook hands, and that was that.

The SS Manhattan crossed from Boston to England in July 1944 during the hurricane season, and the sea was very choppy to say the least. Since it was a wartime sailing, we traveled in a convoy of a number of other ships and were escorted by navy battleships all the way to Liverpool, England. The sailing took the better part of a week. By now it must have been late July 1944 or about six or seven weeks after D-Day. All of us were glad that we came after D-Day, and nobody was sorry that we missed that historical event.

The troopship arrived after dark at the Liverpool harbor. I remember that it was a real blackout. Not a single light was burning; not a single match was lit to smoke. We debarked from the ship in company formation, and then lined up at the pier, again in company formation with our duffel bags and gear. An English army band was playing songs like "Roll out the barrel - the Yanks are coming" and we would add to that, "Yeah and we won't be going home until it's over, over here."

Roll call was taken about every thirty minutes to make sure everyone was off the ship and was still present. Suddenly, without any warning, we heard the air raid sirens for the first time. We were under the control of jointly American and British Army officers. The American officers were just as new as we were and seemed to be taking orders from British officers. Within seconds, German fighter planes appeared out of nowhere and welcomed us with their machine guns, firing live ammunition. This lasted maybe two or three minutes or even less, but by the time it was all over and the "All Clear" was sounded, we had a few casualties, some wounded. We were totally unprepared for this welcome, not trained for it or even warned and had no idea what had happened until it was all over. Welcome to Europe to ETO, "European Theater of Operation."

Several hours later we boarded a train for London to receive our assignments. To write about my feelings and emotions on our train ride from Liverpool to London I just cannot do for the lack of the proper words to use. They are just not in my vocabulary, neither in English nor in German. Excited—maybe, I was dreaming of seeing Ilse on a furlough—re-living the day when I had left her in London for Liverpool and the States only a few years before—Scared, you bet I was scared.

What was ahead of me when we would get into France? Would I survive the military combat actions or become another one of Hitler's victims? Total uncertainty.

After hanging around the Liverpool train station, the troop train finally pulled out sometime during the night. Again, total blackout, not a light anyplace, no matches allowed. A light rain was falling; it was a moonless night. After our arrival experience, there was a somber and scared mood among us. We now had been under fire for the first time; we had not trained for it. We had not seen movies about it; we had not been told about it. It was an uneasy, scary new experience for us GIs.

The railroad cars we boarded were rather old ones. The seats were four-man across with small windows that had been painted black. The German Luftwaffe could not easily see such a moving troop train, but neither could we see anything. At that time the Germans were at the heights of the Battle of Britain flying and attacking with daily and nightly bombing raids. Once on the train, we were given our usual army cold K rations. Not much to eat, but a lot to complain about. K rations consisted of a very high energy chocolate bar, powdered milk, instant coffee, a can of spam, a few crackers, cookies, and 10 cigarettes. According to the army, this was a 1500 calorie diet. In the midst of this train trip, a few British soldiers came to each GI-filled car to welcome us to Britain and thank us for coming to help win the war. They had with them a large pitcher of beer and, of course, paper cups. "Welcome," they said, leaving the beer with us. We had no idea that in England beer was consumed warm— not chilled or even cold. In addition, the beer did not taste like the beer we knew in the States. So, nobody drank the British beer, and we spilled it all out.

At daylight our train pulled into London's Victoria station. We were unloaded from the train but kept waiting at Victoria station for a while. There we were served by our own American mess, a typical American mess hall breakfast—juices, cereal, bacon, eggs, hot coffee or tea, and so on. Every so often was another roll call. I guess they wanted to make sure that none of us had vanished, but this would have been impossible because we were in a heavily guarded area, guarded by both American and British MPs. We were warned not to leave what was referred to as the "compound." Of course, I was dying to make a telephone call to call Ilse, but there were no telephones in sight. In addition, none of us had any English money. When we had left the Boston harbor, we were not told what our destination was. The army had signs up everywhere, "Loose lips sink ships." Once the ship had left Boston and we could no longer communicate with anyone, then and only then were we told that we were sailing to England and from there to France. Never were we given specific towns in either country or told what was ahead of us. Would we go into more training or go into combat? We had no idea and neither did any of our officers. Always, everyone was told only at the very last minute what would happen in the next.

Then without any warning, a large convoy of British Army trucks which the British called "lorries," appeared from nowhere. We were told to get on these open trucks, about 25-30 men on each truck. I was one of the first men on the truck and was standing behind the driver's cab. We were told that we would be taken to a secure area in London to be assembled later on during the day to leave for the French coast and that the French area where we would land was "secured and safe" for us to go on shore. This of course was great news for all of us, except that very few of us believed it! The "lorries" pulled out around 8:00 AM and drove us through London on our way to the "secured area."

I will never forget entering the famous Oxford Street in London and approaching Great Portland Street. We stopped for maybe 10-15 seconds in traffic. As I looked out to my right, I couldn't believe my own eyes. Like in a dream—there standing, looking straight into my face, was the most beautiful girl, the girl of my dreams and my hopes, my future wife, my sweetheart, none other than Ilse herself on her way to work. We just looked at each other for two or three seconds, that was all. But we had seen each other again under the most impossible circumstances. Neither one of us had any prior idea or thought that this could happen. The lorries had stopped for a few seconds in a traffic tie up at the right time, at the right place, for the right people to see each other again  after four years. I remember my knees were shaking. I couldn't wait to get off that lorry. I could have screamed; it all had happened so quickly. Once when we were in France and could receive mail again, the very first letter I got from Ilse was one of joy at seeing me for just a split second and one of sadness that it was only a split second.

After a short ride, the convoy came to a halt in a section of London with which I was a bit familiar and which was very close to where Ilse and her mother lived. During the ride, we saw many of the bombed out parts of London. To prevent low flights and pinpoint bombing of London by the German Luftwaffe, the Air Raid Precautions (ARP) put up huge barrage balloons all over London and other towns in England. Each balloon looked like the German Zeppelin or the Goodyear blimp, was about 100 feet long, was silver colored and was moored to a wagon by a cable. These metal cables were strong enough to destroy any aircraft colliding with them. On the wagon was a winch that enabled the RAF

(Royal Air Force) Balloon Command to control the exact height of the balloon. The balloons achieved the main objective of discouraging dive bombing and machine gunning low-level attacks. Of course most of the American GIs had never seen anything like them before. I, however, had in fact seen them during my stay in London in the first months of the war from September 1939 to May 1940.

After our arrival experience at the Liverpool harbor, this view sobered us and made us think about what we could expect upon our arrival somewhere in France. Finally, the convoy stopped at a large movie house. As far as I can recall today, it was called "The Odeon Cinema." That place was huge! We were ushered in and seated, but no movies were shown.

Soon lunch was served; of course it was an American mess again with the usual GI lunch menu. After lunch we had group meetings; each platoon with the NCOs and officers was briefed about what was going to happen next.

We were told that under the cover of darkness, we would leave London by truck to go somewhere on the English shore to board landing crafts which would take us to the Normandy beach. Again we were assured that the place where we were about to go ashore in France was secured, and under the control of the US Army. But again most of us were not sure if what we were told were all the facts.

I really don't think that anyone of us believed that story, but it turned out to be true and accurate. We were told that we would travel by landing crafts rather than ships so that we could land a few feet from the shore and that we had to walk a few feet through the water to reach the beach. All this was actually true and happened. We had to leave our duffel bags behind in England and again were told that we would see them once we were assigned to a certain area in France. No further explanation were we then given. The afternoon was off, and we were told to take a rest. I don't remember that any one of us actually rested. We were all very nervous and scared; we chain smoked, talked, or played cards to make the time go by faster.

We had another gear inspection, rifles, bayonets, gas masks, combat boots, shovels, first aid kits, and live ammunition of one clip each, about 8-10 bullets per man. Our dress uniforms we had to leave behind with our duffel bags, so we all wore combat fatigues with leggings. We had no permission to leave that compound. It was guarded by both US and British MPs for our own security, so we were told.

The movie theater must have been large enough to hold about 300 men because it took about 10 trucks with 25-30 men each to take us there. I was burning to call Ilse, but again, there were no phones in sight.

Besides the money problem was still the same; we had no coins to make a call. But I was determined to get in touch with Ilse. Finally, I found a piece of paper, and my buddy John Duffey had an envelope. I wrote a letter to Ilse telling her that I had seen her that morning, waiting on the street corner as our convoy passed her on Oxford Street and that we were being sent somewhere in France. Then I found a British soldier; he was what we called "a real nice chap." I started up a conversation with him, and he was very friendly. I told him my problem, that I wanted to get in touch with Ilse, that I had written her a love letter but had no stamp. He said that this was no problem, that he would mail it for me. I gave him one US dollar bill for the stamp which he accepted. But he never mailed the letter, or at least Ilse never received it

# Leaving for France

The convoy left London as soon as it got dark and arrived somewhere on the English shore during the night. There the landing crafts were waiting for our arrival. Roll call was once again, and each platoon boarded one of the landing crafts. No sooner had we boarded these vehicles then they pulled away from shore with tremendous speed. We were in the open British Channel. The ocean was anything but friendly to us, and the waves were high. We all wore life preservers and were scared to death. Everyone was deadly quiet; everyone was thinking back over his life and what was ahead. Anyone who would have said that they were not scared would have been a liar. None of the officers even smiled or tried to talk to us in encouraging words as they often did. For the first time we saw that even they were scared and quiet and were human after all.

Shortly before day break we reached the shores of Normandy beach. We could see some sunken landing crafts at the shore, possibly sunk by enemy fire on

D-day, on June 6, 1944, many weeks before we got there. The coast was still littered with a lot of barbed wire. About 20 feet off shore the landing crafts came to a halt. Only later did we find out that we had actually landed on what the army code named was "Omaha Beach" which by now was under the control of the First Army under General Bradley.

Fortunately, the tide was low. We could see a long stretch of skeleton-like obstructions erected by the Nazis in a vain attempt to prevent our troops from landing there on D-day. The front of our landing craft came down and extended maybe another 10 feet or so into the water. We were told by the skipper of the landing craft that we would have to wade through 3-4 foot deep water to get to the beach, and so all rifles had be carried overhead so that they would not get wet. Never mind that all of us got soaking wet almost to our chest! It was a cold miserable day and certainly not the right temperature for us to dry quickly. But at least it was true, that the area was safe under American control. As soon as we got off the landing crafts, we were directed by American MPs to walk up a little steep hill and await further orders. We now saw for the first time a group of German soldiers, all prisoners of war, being marched by the American MPs to board the same landing crafts from which we had just disembarked to take them back to England as prisoners of war.

I would be lying if I wouldn't admit that I envied them for going back to England even as prisoners of war.

As we walked up that little hill we could clearly see the German fortifications, heavy concrete block houses overlooking the Normandy beach where we had just arrived. We passed a few captured German tanks and finally were met by some American MPs who assigned our Lt. Geoffrey to an area to set up tents until we would get further assignment. Our lieutenant was given a map and a compass so that he could find the specific area. With only cold K rations to eat, we set up camp for the night. This was our first night in France. It wasn't too long before we could hear in the far distance German planes or rockets flying towards England. All I could think of was Ilse and her mother, fearing that one of those bombs or rockets might hit wherever they might be at that moment. That fear had especially been on my mind since we drove through London and saw all the horrible destruction caused by the Blitz, the German Luftwaffe attacks on England.

Shortly before daylight, around five o'clock in the morning, some MP officers came and asked our Lieutenant who the idiot was who had put up tents on a clearly marked mine field. The "idiot" was our own Lt. Geoffrey. Long before this incident, we GIs had called him "Lt. Goofy," "A ninety day wonder" (ninety day wonder was a term we used for 2nd Lts. who had taken officer's crash training courses to become officers within 90 days). Now, very carefully we broke up our bivouac area and were led by some MPs away from this spot. It was a miracle that none of us got hurt or killed. Of course, Lt. Geoffrey had now lost all our respect, and he soon found out when a few hours after this incident he was released as our commanding officer and replaced by First Lt. Murray.

Lt. Murray was a very friendly man and officer. Like us, he had just arrived in France. In civilian life he was an attorney somewhere in Ohio. He was given orders to march us approximately ten miles east to a little French village called Montebourg. It was an interesting march, along bombed-out roads, passing an occasional abandoned farm house and seeing a lot of destroyed armor, both American and German. Food, of course, consisted only of our K rations. We were warned not to get off the "paved roads" because the areas to the left and right of the roads had not yet been cleared of mines. Eventually, very tired, hungry, and exhausted, we reached Montebourg. As we came close to the town, we saw a bombed out-church and next to it a grave yard where we clearly could see lots of new graves. They appeared to be mostly German graves because above the graves were crosses, and on top of each cross was a German army helmet. Again, a sobering site to see. Some officers from some American Ordinance Unit were awaiting our arrival. We were led to a real army mess for our first hot meal in days. Also a hot water shower had been rigged up. That Ordinance Unit was fully equipped! We got new, clean army fatigues and new, clean underwear, felt real good to be clean again. We were a bit rested and ready for our first assignment in France which came a few hours later. Our outfit now called the 1673 Combat Engineer Utility Detachment was temporarily assigned to an Ordinance unit. We had trained to build and destroy bridges, and every man knew exactly what to do on such assignments, but here we had no idea what was expected of us. Soon we found out.

An officer from the Ordinance unit told Lt. Murray that some Colonel had ordered that we were to participate in "cleaning up" the area. Of course, we had no idea what that meant. Lt. Murray picked half the platoon and had us report for duty to some sergeant from Ordinance whom we had never seen before. We were about to encounter the end results of combat and war, what we had never trained or heard about in basic training. A detail of men was assigned to an area outside of Montebourg where the casualties of the recent fighting had not been all "cleaned up." This area had seen heavy combat about three weeks earlier but since then had been secured by our infantry. As the guys from infantry moved on, some of the dead, not many, were left behind. It became our assignment to search for these bodies, find their "dogtags" for identification, and search their pockets for personal belongings which were stuffed into little bags to be returned to the next of kin. Then an ordinance unit would come with bulldozers and prepare the graves. We nailed one of the dogtags to a white cross, recorded the proper location of the fallen soldier, attached the other dogtag to the report, and moved on to the next area. Some days we didn't find any victims, and on other days we found a few.

Today, almost 60 years later as I write this story, I can still feel the agony that each and every one of us had. There were times when none of us could eat, drink, or even felt like smoking or talking. Mentally none of us was prepared for our assignment, but that did not mean anything to the army. Today, I can still feel the sadness that we had for each of our fallen comrades, none of whom we knew. It was only by the grace of God that we were not in that area some weeks earlier. This assignment affected me somewhat mentally. I just could not eat or sleep and kept on thinking about my own mortality. After about a week or so on this detail, our army chaplain came and talked to us. As it turned out, this chaplain was a Rabbi, Captain Widderer, and like me had lived in the Washington

Heights section in Manhattan. He asked about our personal welfare, and I was open and honest with him telling him how distressed I felt. He asked me if I was, according to the Jewish religion, a "Cohen," a high priest, who was forbidden by religion to handle and touch the dead. I was not but looked him questioningly in the eyes, as if to say, what shall I do?

Like Jack Dempsey before him who had made me an instant American citizen, Chaplain Widderer made me an honorary, instant "Cohen." Without my knowledge and without saying a word to me, he went to the sergeant in charge and explained to him that for religious reasons I should be transferred to a different assignment.

It didn't take this sergeant too long. The next day I was assigned to another unit with the same Ordinance company whose assignment was—to clear the mine fields. I was never really trained for this either except for several days of basic training. This reassignment taught me a big lesson. I remembered for the rest of my army days in the service—never complain. Do what you are told, and keep your mouth shut!

My buddies quickly taught me how to go about it. The word here was, be very careful. One mistake and you will not have a chance for a second one. With only a few minor accidents we all survived that assignment. It wasn't as bad as I had feared it would be, and it certainly was better than my previous assignment. I stayed with this until about mid-August 1944 moving ahead daily, clearing the mines when they were spotted.

Somewhere in a field while clearing up the mines, I came across what was once either a German or an American silk parachute. It looked dirty, it had been out in the rain, and it was torn. A part of a harness was still attached. I had an idea. I took my bayonet and cut all the good material off. This, I thought, will make a bridal gown for my love! I asked Lt. Murray if I could keep it and send it to my future bride. He gave me his OK. Years later on May 19th 1946, I saw the most radiant, and most beautiful bride I had ever seen wearing a beautiful, silk wedding gown made out of parachute silk, standing under the Chupa, the wedding canopy, while we were promising each other to be united forever, until death would us part.

Sometime during mid-August we had advanced to about 150 kilometers west of Paris. We knew at the time that our front line troops were closing in on Paris. Suddenly our mine clearing assignment came to an end. We could see that our officers were excited and nervous to say the least. We were pulled back by maybe 20 kilometers or so, where a temporary command post had been established.

A new captain whom we had never seen before was put in charge of us. Captain Edward Kearns came from someplace in Indiana, had been with the US Fifth Army under General Clark in Italy where he was wounded and was now assigned as commanding officer of our unit. He called all of us together to let us know that we would be on a temporary assignment to the 2 Battalion of the 12th Infantry regiment, the 28th Division which was also known as the Keystone Division. Captain Kearns spoke to each one of us in the platoon, and when my turn came, he asked me where I was born. Of course, he immediately noticed my German accent. I told him the circumstances under which I had left Germany and was now in the US Army. His next question, the answer to which changed my life in the army drastically was, "Besides German, do you speak some French?" When I answered in the positive, he said, "You are the man I am looking for." Of course at the time I had no idea what he meant and whether it was good or bad news.

Lts. Murray and Geoffrey were still left in charge of us, and Captain Kearns was now the Company Commander. Our 1637 attachment was now going to be being trained in removing booby trap devices. There were rumors galore that the Germans were about to leave Paris shortly and had put booby traps on anything and everything. Earlier, as we had removed the remains of both US and German soldiers, we had come upon planted booby traps on some of their remains. There was a specially trained unit from ordinance with us who removed the booby traps before we could move the remains. As it turned out, once we got into Paris, the German exit from Paris was so sudden that they had no time to booby trap anything.

# The Liberation of Paris

The Germans left Paris on the 25th of August 1944. At that point we were about 50 kilometers west of Paris. As soon as the city was taken and the local fighting had cleared up, we were brought into Paris by truck to the former German Army headquarters which was in the American Express building in the center of Paris. We were told that one of the demolition men threw a hand grenade at the main entrance door, and that the door blew open. The building was totally empty; there was not a single piece of paper about. There were no booby traps anyplace. This building became the temporary US Army headquarters, and we remained in this building. Now for my unit the war was over, except that we didn't know it at that time.

First of all, our job was to move in office furniture and together with other engineer units, quickly we hooked up electricity, water and telephone lines. We spent our first few nights in Paris in this building and then moved to a very large department store which the Germans had cleared out and used for their troops as a staging area of some sort. This place was in the Montmartre section which then and still is today the "red light district" of Paris.

Because of the mission which we had accomplished of clearing mines, Capt Kearns promoted each one of us. I was promoted from a Private First Class to a Corporal. Now I was an NCO, a non-commissioned officer.

Several days later we were reassigned once again. This time we became part of the Headquarters Company, Seine Section, Com Z. We left the department store and were temporarily billeted in a lovely hotel on Boulevard Housemann in the center of Paris. Four men were assigned to a room which had no beds. We slept on army cots. For our meals we were assigned to eat at the Casual Mess at 34 - 6 Blvd. Bonne Nouvelle. Paris was under the command of General Rogers.

Our new assignment was now to allocate building material to the Paris population. During the Nazi occupation of Paris, all building materials were shipped to Germany which had left the Parisians without that commodity. Hundreds and hundreds of homes were in dire need of repair, missing glass windows, broken pipes; you name it. Since we were the liberators of Paris and not the occupiers, it was headquarters' assignment to help the population. The Parisians were instructed to fill out forms requesting building materials to fix up their homes.

*In front of the St. Maur POW carpenter shop, left to right: Sgt. Reilly, me, Cpl. Lougherman, 1945*

Because I was able to converse somewhat with the people in French, Capt. Kearns assigned me now to the job of going to those homes and seeing what was needed. Based on my findings, building material was found by others in our unit and delivered to these homes. In order to do this assignment, I was even authorized to use a jeep from our motor pool. Since no soldier was ever allowed to go alone into a French home, my buddy John Duffey was assigned with me for this task. Of course we always carried side arms, never knowing if a trap was set up for us or not. Despite this, it was a great assignment. We met many lovely people who were truly and honestly happy to see American soldiers trying to take care of their problems and treating them as friends.

During this assignment, I discovered that the largest temple in Paris was in excellent condition, and the Germans had done nothing to it. I decided one Saturday while I was off-duty to go to services and see what it was all about. I had expected many other GIs at the services, but none were there. When the service was over, a young couple came over to me and invited me to their home for lunch, which I gratefully accepted. Food was still very scarce for the French people, but they quickly prepared a Shabbat lunch. I was introduced to the 18-year-old sister of the hostess. They were French Jews who had lived in hiding during

*At work in the St. Maur POW camp, 1945*

the entire German occupation. Their family was not that lucky, and all were deported to Poland never to be heard from again. As I remember, the girl's name was Rachel; her last name I have long forgotten. Following this lunch, I was invited almost every Shabbat when I was off duty. It didn't take me long to figure out that they hoped that I would be interested in Rachel and take her home to the States with me. Consequently, I was not interested and declined further invitations.

Captain Kearns was now assigned to an entirely new adventure. US Army headquarters had decided to open a German prisoner of war camp in a suburb of Paris called St. Maur. There was a large lumber yard and a saw mill in St. Maur which were turned over to the American army by the French authorities for the purpose of constructing army furniture, desks, chairs and other items, rather than taking them away from the French people. Captain Kearns was given 10 men of his choice to set up this prisoner of war camp. One GI in our unit was in the construction business in civilian life and also had his own carpenter shop. He was Sergeant Lawrence (Larry) Reilly, at the time the oldest of all of us, at 39 years, whom Kearns now put in charge of the entire operation. However, he also needed a German-English interpreter to deal with the arrival and job assignments of the German prisoners. There would be about 150 German army prisoners assigned to us. Because I spoke German fluently, I was assigned and promoted from Corporal to a Buck Sergeant.

Several days after Sgt. Reilly had set up the prisoner of war camp and before we were permitted to receive prisoners, the international Red Cross came to inspect the camp. They inspected the camp housing, kitchen, sanitary and first aid set up. I remember that they also called our company together and read us aloud the international law on prisoners of war, what we were

*In front of the POW camp in St. Maur, France, April 1945. Sgt. Reilly is second from left; I am third from right.*

allowed to do and what we were not allowed to do. We were never allowed to have loaded or unloaded weapons with us in the presence of the prisoners. Other rules directed that when speaking or dealing with a prisoner, we were to be standing or sitting at least six feet away from the prisoner, and that no one would be allowed to take any close up pictures of any prisoners. About a week later the trucks arrived with about 150 German army and air force prisoners of war. I must admit, that I was not too friendly at their reception but was glad to see them as our prisoners rather than our captors. They certainly did not at all look like the supermen of the super Aryan race as Hitler wanted them to look, which made me feel good.

Among the prisoners was one German Army doctor, one male nurse, and one German army chaplain. Since the doctor and the chaplain were both officers, they requested separate quarters as required under the international law. We also found a couple of men among them who said that they were cooks. We took their word for it, and they were assigned to the kitchen. I started my job by finding a clerk who spoke English very well. He had been an English teacher at a German school. He immediately wanted to know where I learned my perfect accent-free German. I just looked at him and told him that I was doing the interviewing and not he. That set up the ground rules very quickly. Then I found a German Sergeant who spoke only a little school English. His name was Ernst Gabriel. He was my age and surprisingly was a nice guy. Under normal circumstances we could have become good friends, but these were not normal circumstances. He was my prisoner. He became our spokesman dealing directly with the prisoners. We put him in charge of all prisoners, even of the two officers. Shortly after that the German army chaplain came to me and objected that he would not take orders from a sergeant. I checked with Captain Kearns and was told to tell him that as an officer he is only entitled to separate quarters and that he will not decide from whom he takes orders. I relayed that message and that was the end of his complaints.

I had to interview each and every prisoner, and we filled out forms with their personal data. After that the German army doctor had to give each prisoner a physical examination and record results on the same forms. It then became the job of the clerk to translate everything into English. I had to review the English translation and sign off on it. One interesting question on the forms was, "When did you join the Nazi party?" Not one of the prisoners answered that question, and when I asked them, they would only tell me that they never had belonged to the Nazi party.

Time passed, and early February of 1945, I asked Lt. Murray for a furlough, his permission to visit Ilse in London, and for permission to get married to Ilse during my furlough. Permission was granted for the furlough but refused for the marriage. I was granted a one week furlough starting on February 27 and left a week or so later for England. I really wanted to be in England for Ilse's 24th birthday on March 16, 1945, but that didn't work out. I had only told Ilse in my letters that I had asked for a furlough but was not sure if it would be granted. Since the army mail was very slow between Paris and London, she received this letter only one day before I arrived in London.

# Furlough in London

On February 27, 1945, I left Paris for a little town on the French coast called Etertage. It was a long train ride on a military train taking wounded American GIs back to England for (R&R) rest and recuperation. The next morning we left on an French ferry boat from Etertage to Dover, and by early afternoon of February 28, I arrived at Victoria station in London, took a taxi to 91 Elgin Crescent, London W II where Ilse and her mother lived. When I rang the door bell and Ilse's mother opened the door, the poor woman almost fainted when she saw me. Later on I found out that she had almost fainted not because she saw me but because I looked so skinny and haggard. I must admit that by that time, all of us who served overseas in the army had lost a lot of weight, and the stress was showing as well. I believe that I had lost 20 pounds or even more at that time from my normal weight. I wanted to call Ilse at work, but my future mother-in-law convinced me that I should surprise Ilse by picking her up as she came from work at the subway (tube) station that evening. I could not wait for the time to go by, and finally her mother and I went to the Holland Park subway station to meet her. Ilse's mother had a "secret plan" to see how I would react. As we waited for people to come off the subway, she spotted a very heavy set woman in the distance.

*Ilse's mother during my London furlough, March 1945*

*Ilse in my Army uniform, 1945*

Very quietly she said to me, "Here she comes." I looked at the woman and turned to Ilse's mother and said, "That is not Ilse!"

A minute or so later, there came Ilse, as beautiful and as unchanged as I had seen her in my dreams and had held her in my memory. We held each other a long time. Ilse's tears were running down her cheek,s and I could not speak. We had found each other again. We went to her apartment where she, her mother and a very jealous cat by the name of Lumpi lived. The cat did not like me at all. That first evening together we talked all night until the sun came up in the morning. Ilse took the week off from work.

*Ilse and me on Oxford Street, London, on furlough, February 27, 1945*

(For a followup photo, see page 248)

Within a few minutes of being together again, we both felt that we had only been apart for five minutes and not that five years had passed. We didn't even realize that we were separated for that long. We told each other details of our lives during the past five years and then went on to discuss our wedding plans, an event which we hoped would happen very soon. There was no doubt in either one of our minds that we belonged together forever.

The one-week furlough went by too quickly. We mostly took long walks and planned our future. The V II rockets were still hitting London daily, and here and there an air raid siren sounded. Being stationed in Paris at that time, I was familiar with the constant sound of the air raid sirens but not to the hissing sound of V II rockets. But we really did not care what was going on in the world all around us. We were so happy that we were together again, neither the air raids, the bombing of London nor the burst of the VII rockets could spoil our happiness. Once again I had to leave London without my beloved, but this time I felt sure that it just could not be that much longer until we would be together again. It was only a matter of a few months but certainly not years. We now were both in Europe, and only the English channel separated us, not the big Atlantic Ocean.

We had such a sweet, great time together, so much joy and so much love, so many smiles and so much laughter. A young couple in love, in love we were, and in love we still are on the eve of our 58th wedding anniversary in May of 2004.

# From France to Germany and Back Home

𝕸*arch 1945*

After spending a glorious week with Ilse in London, I returned to St. Maur. Needless to say how sad I was to be without Ilse once again. I could hardly wait for the war to end, return home to New York, and finally start our lives. Now I could see "the light at the end of the tunnel" and had something to look forward to for the first time since I left London in 1940.

Upon returning to St. Maur from London in early March of 1945, I was told that prisoners of war camps would receive an additional 100 German prisoners, among them a number of officers. At the time the German army was surrendering "en masse," and the US army was running short on barracks to house them. Hastily from the prison population, our Sgt. Larry Reilley got a group of carpenters together and built additional barracks for enlisted men and separate quarters for the German officers within the prison compound. When the new group arrived, I had to interview them. Some of the officers refused to be interviewed. I had to "persuade" them to be interviewed. Like the first group, these people, except the officers, were used in the lumber yard as well, cutting trees to be used for construction lumber.

*My good friend, Captain Ed J. Kearns and his forever happy smile, somewhere in France, 1945*

One day, one of the newly arrived German prisoners, considerably older then the others, around 40 years old, asked me if I would permit him to talk to me. I had no idea what he wanted. He told me that his name was Walter Rausch, that he was from Leipzig, Germany. He told me that he was a painter, was listed in the "Who is Who" in the German books of painters, and that his paintings in Germany were sold for high prices. He asked me if there was a possibility for him to paint rather than work in the lumber yard and forever ruin his hands. Somehow or the other he was very convincing, and I believed him. I remembered that a while back I, too, did not like my assignment of picking up the remains of the dead. I relayed Rausch's story to Lt. Murray who immediately was in favor of having him paint for us but told me to get the final approval from Capt. Kearns. In no time at all, it was decided, although we all knew that it was illegal, both as far as the rules and regulations of the international Red Cross were concerned as well as the American army policy regarding prisoners of war. Kearns told me that we should go ahead and accept his offer. He justified his decision that nowhere in the American policy or in the rules of the Red Cross were any stipulations forbidding prisoners of war to be used as painters. What

*German prisoner of war Walter Rausch painting the Matterhorn for me*

kind of painting was not specified. As far as Capt. Kearns was concerned that was it. (Of course that was before the Geneva Convention in 1949 established iron clad rules regarding prisoners of war.)

Rausch was a very nice chap and was very convincing to the point that I "almost" felt sorry for him. We faced the problem of how to obtain all the artist materials, oil paint, canvas and so on. Reilley came up with the idea of cutting the canvas off the broken army cots of which we had a few. Rausch felt that they were excellent for his paintings. After several days Lt. Murray told me that he had seen on the left bank of the river Seine in Paris a number of art supply stores. But how would we get the proper paint and all the other stuff Rausch needed? That was the big question. Capt. Kearns came up with a quick solution. We would dress Rausch in an American army uniform. Duffey and I would escort him by jeep to the artist section on the left bank, and he could pick what he needed. However, the problem was, should the MPs stop us to check our ID which they often did, it would not have been funny at all. One German prisoner dressed in an American uniform without an ID, another American in a GI uniform with proper credentials but with a heavy German accent (me), and poor Duffey with his pronounced Irish accent would be holding the "bag," so to speak. The other problem was, how would we deal with a possible escape of Rausch while he was in a US army uniform? None of us really gave this a lot of thought, except

Reilley who could see nothing but disaster. After all, we had loaded side arms, and Rausch knew that only too well. He had seen us on the pistol target range a few days before. A jeep was requisitioned from the motor pool. Capt. Kearns authorized the vehicle to be used for official business into Paris about 12 miles south of St. Maur. A conspiracy if there ever was one. If caught, it would have been a disaster for all of us including Lt. Murray and Captain Kearns. But Kearns was the "old daredevil," and so we went with his blessings.

We left St. Maur, drove into town, and found the artists supply store. Rausch was like a child in a toy store. He ordered all he could think of that he would need. We made our purchases without incident. That was what was known in military jargon as "a joint military operation."

Larry Reilley built a little studio for Rausch at our GI quarters so that Rausch could paint and not be disturbed. In addition our quarters were very safe because when the Red Cross came for an inspection, they never inspected our quarters. The Red Cross couldn't have cared less about our quarters. Rausch was fully at work painting within several days. Sometimes he worked on two paintings at the same time. The first paintings of course were for Capt. Kearns and Lt. Murray; they each had about two or three paintings done. Then there was only Larry, John Duffey and me left. We all got our fair share. He painted a portrait of Ilse from a photograph, and I was sitting for him to paint me. We still have these paintings. Ilse never liked hers, and so the portraits were never hung up. They are hidden in one of the many closets in our present apartment in Ithaca. Then he painted two landscapes for me which were lovely but nothing that was outstanding. Finally he painted the master-piece, the Matterhorn. All three paintings were hanging in our homes in Bellerose and later on in Lewisburg, PA until in August 2002 when we prepared to move to Ithaca, NY. At that time an auctioneer asked us if we wanted to sell some antiques. He saw the two landscapes and offered us $ 700 for the two. Since Ilse and I never really liked them, we took him up on it. When he saw the Matterhorn, he offered us $1000 for it, and we said no, we would keep that one. We still have it, and as long as we live, we will not sell it. That is the story of the painter and paintings.

Either before Rausch was put to work painting for us, or shortly there-after, another little story had developed. Captain Kearns called me into his office, told me that he had to tell me a very strict "Military Secret" and that only he and I were to know about it. The "secret" went like this. Captain Kearns was a devoted Roman Catholic who had become friendly with a Catholic Army Chaplain in Paris who was an ordained priest. This chaplain who had the rank of a Major had forgotten his vows, and consequently had met a "lady of the night" in Paris from whom he caught "syphilis." What to do now? This was a very embarrassing situation for all concerned. Any GI, never mind an officer, who contracted syphilis would automatically be busted to the lowest rank. A GI would be reduced to the rank of a private and an officer to the rank of a second Lieutenant. The only available "cure" was a treatment every three hours, day and night, with a new wonder drug called penicillin which was then administered by injection only.

Kearns already had his plans worked out. He knew one of the army medical officers, a Protestant chap at the military hospital in Paris. From this doctor, whom Kearns had taken into his confidence, he obtained sufficient penicillin to treat this priest. Now comes my "military secret." I was to get the German army medical doctor (an officer) at the prisoner of war camp who also was a Catholic and tell him to give this chaplain a shot of penicillin for the next seven days, every three hours, day and night at Capt. Kearns's quarters where he and the chaplain would be billeted. That meant the doctor was to be transported to Kearns's quarters and stay there for the duration of the treatment period. I was to tell this German doctor all about it, and threaten him that if he ever should talk about it, he would be shot (period end). Fortunately for me, the German doctor spoke enough English to converse with the chaplain and Kearns, so I was not needed.

Again, the question of security came up, and Kearns assured me that he would personally make sure that this guy could and would not escape. How he did that, I never found out. But after the "treatment" was over, he came back to the camp. He looked especially well fed and appeared to be very happy. That is the end of that story and the "military secret."

We were still in St. Maur on May 8, 1945, at the time when the war ended in Europe. Germany had surrendered, and Hitler was dead. The little town of St. Maur went crazy for joy and of course, the GIs as well. The French population came with flowers and champagne to celebrate with us. Most French families had hidden and stored champagne just for this day, and now, all over town, the bottles were popping. The French girls kissed every GI they saw, and of course we reciprocated gladly and kissed every French girl we saw. What a night that was! At midnight there were big fireworks. After almost six years of total blackout, the lights came on again all over France. People celebrated for days; I never saw so much wine and champagne consumed. It was a moment that can never be forgotten. Hitler dead—the nightmare was over.

Another little side story about Captain Edward Kearns. His family in Indiana owned a number of liquor stores, and every month Kearns would receive a little crate with his favorite brand of scotch. Usually, this lasted him for a about two weeks. Shortly before V-E Day, one evening I came back from Paris late. My orders were that before turning in for the night, I first had to check the prisoners' quarters and sign off that everyone was accounted for. That evening, around 9:00 or 10:00 PM, I went back to the camp, spoke to the French army guards at the gate and was advised that all was quiet and under control. As I walked into the prison quarters, Ernst Gabriel, the German Sgt. whom we had put in charge of the prisoners came to me with a fully loaded weapon, a US army .45 in his hands, the same weapon which we had. At first, I was stunned and scared to death and could not believe what I saw. He was holding the .45 in a safe military position, pointing to the ground. He told me that in case I was looking for Cpt. Kearns, he was lying in one of the German prisoner's bunks, totally drunk, and that he, Gabriel, had disarmed him by taking the loaded .45 away from him before he could use it, or some prisoners could get their hands on it. Needless to say, I was shocked. On our two way communication system, I called Reilley. He came right over, and we decided to get two fellows from the guards. The four of us carried Kearns out and took him to his quarters. We put him on his bed and left. Early the next morning, he came to Larry and me, and told us that his .45 was missing; it was gone. At first we didn't say anything and let him stew. He was very nervous and started cussing, telling us that he had no idea what had happened to his weapon. Finally, after a while, Larry pulled the .45 out of a drawer and told him to use this for a while. Kearns looked at the serial number and of course it was his. He kept on repeating that he had no idea what had happened. The story he finally told us was that he remembered to go by the French guards outside the compound to check, had a sudden headache, and that was all that he could remember. We just smiled.

During the Italian campaign, Kearns had been hurt by enemy fire, and always claimed that a shot or two or three or even four of scotch would reduce his discomfort. He was so lucky that we were his buddies. He could have been court martialed and gone to jail for that. I must say, he never forgot our kindness. He was some character; he was a very good and very compassionate man and officer. His biggest problem was that he was an alcoholic which eventually killed him. He liked his liquor better than anything else and would get very upset if any one of us would not join him in a few drinks. With the exception of Lt. Geoffrey, I don't think he ever had a problem with any other officer or a GI. But then again, Lt. Geoffrey never could do anything right. He tried, but he was a real "screwball" as Kearns always called him, even to his face.

Shortly thereafter, a new chapter began for our unit. The war with Japan was still going on, and now the army started what was called the re-deployment of the forces. Troops on non-essential assignments were first sent back to the States and from there to Japan. At the prisoner of war camps, while the administration still remained with the American troops, the guarding of the prisoners was turned over to the French troops of General De Gaulle. What this involved was that all my buddies with whom I had trained and come with from the States were returned to the States for re-deployment to Japan. This involved my buddy, John Duffey (whom Ilse met in New York when he was on leave for his re-deployment for Japan), as well as Sgt. Reilley and Lts. Murray and Geoffrey. The only ones who were not re-deployed were Capt. Kearns and I. I was sad and would have loved to stay with my platoon and go to Japan with them, but because I was a German native and spoke German fluently, the army had other plans for me. Captain Kearns was assigned a new command and I was assigned to him which of course he had arranged. I still believe that he knew what was coming, but I was not privileged to know about it—yet—"military secret." There were all kind of rumors flying around that Kearns and I would go to Vienna or to Prague, and then there was the rumor that I would be assigned as an interpreter at the Nuerenberg War Crimes trial.

Just the other day, Ilse showed me her diary which she kept from the time that she left Austria until we got married. There was an entry written at the time when the war in Europe came to an end. She wrote in 1945, "Now that the war is coming to an end, and now that all my immigration papers for America have been approved by the American Consulate, I am scared, that I will be in America and my Darling will be in Europe. I just can't take it anymore." Of course when she wrote these lines, she had no idea how accurate and close to the facts of life she was. While our unit was preparing to return to the States without me, Ilse was about to sail with her mother to New York, and I remained with the US Army in Europe for my next assignment.

The next assignment was in Versailles outside of Paris. Kearns promoted me to the rank of Staff Sergeant. Our new assignment was an already established 300-man Waffen SS camp in Versailles. Capt. Kearns now became the Commanding officer of the camp, and I became the Sergeant in charge. The American officers and men who had been assigned to this camp before us including the MP guards had been assigned to relieve the combat troops in Germany, and we were to relieve them. The guards were under the command of an MP Major. We were the new command and the camp administration. There was really hardly any work for us at that camp. These prisoners were not from the regular German army; they all had the Swastika tattooed under their left arm close to the arm pit. They were Hitler's elites. They were not the concentration camp guards; they were the fighting units, the ones who would prevent the regular German army from retreating or defecting. If they would have been together with the regular German army prisoners in the same camp, they would have been constantly at each other's throats. That is why they were now in separate camps. They all were previously interviewed, and we had all their records.

The US Army did not recognize the Waffen SS as a unit of the German army. Their officers and enlisted men all volunteered to belong to the

*The Boss: Lt. Col. James Ramage,*
*Frankfurt, Germany*

Waffen SS. They shared the same prison housing; their various ranks were not recognized by us. They were not assigned to any type of work. Their prison uniforms were old worn out US Army summer khaki colored shirts and pants. POW was painted front and back in large letters. They were inspected by the International Red Cross on a monthly basis even though the United States army considered them as non-combatant.

The previous camp administration had worked out a schedule for them which was mostly just physical exercises which they enjoyed. But the fact that they had nothing to do, had nothing to read, and generally waited from one army chow to the next, made them very miserable to deal with. There were three or four German chaplains with them as prisoners, and Kearns had now set up a special office for these chaplains so that the prisoners could go and consult with them. Since none of the chaplains spoke any English, they would come to me with their problems which were then presented to Major Kearns and two other officers who were in the command. Their problems were addressed in accordance with the international law as provided by the international Red Cross of which all of us had copies. Our officers and we had to follow those rules. It was not a very pleasant assignment. I personally considered each and every one of them as killers and Gestapo agents.

Kearns knew that, and he enjoyed that I felt that way about them. With the exception of their chaplains to whom I had to speak, I never spoke one word to any of the killers.

Sometime in June or July of 1945, an old army buddy of Captain Kearns came to inspect the camp. His name was General Larkin, a highly decorated one star General, about 50 years old. After his inspection of the camp, he called all military personnel together, the administration, and all officers. He told us that he was appointed by General Eisenhower to be the commanding officer of the city of Frankfurt on Main in Germany, and that a part of our unit would be attached to the Military Government for the city of Frankfurt under his command. We would be relieved within a few days and moved to Frankfurt. As he was about to leave, he said that he had not yet had a chance to review all of our service records, but was there by any chance any German speaking soldiers among us. Before I could even raise my hand, Kearns volunteered me to become his interpreter. Major Kearns had known Larkin from their days during the Italian campaign when Kearns was a Captain and Larkin a full Colonel serving under General Clark's fifth army. The two became good friends. They were both in their fifties and much older than the rest of us who were only in our early twenties.

# Leaving for Germany

About a week or so after this meeting, Major Kearns, a few others, and I were told that we would leave for Frankfurt the next morning. It was an interesting journey, which took us all day. We had a few jeeps available. I drove one of them with Major Kearns and the two other officers assigned to Larkin. They were new arrivals in Europe and so far were unassigned. Larkin had them quickly assigned to our newly formed outfit. One was Lt. Jim Smith about my age, and other one was Lt. Murray Sobelman from Brooklyn, NY. Our trip took us from Paris through Strassburg up the Rhine river to Frankfurt on Main. We now had become a part of "SHAEF"—Supreme Headquarters Allied Expeditionary Forces. The main office was located at the I. G. Farben compound in Frankfurt, the same place where General Eisenhower's headquaters were located. General Larkin had promoted Kearns to Major, and now I was promoted by Major Kearns from Staff Sergeant to Tech Sergeant which meant that I now had what we called two rockers under my Sergeant stripes. It also meant that I got an increase in pay as a Tech Sergeant, and I had many more privileges.

We were assigned to new quarters. The enlisted men who were all non-commissioned officers were billeted in a school building which became our office as well as our living quarters. Two men were assigned to a room. The officers were billeted in private furnished homes which the army had confiscated. The first few days we were unassigned and were told to get oriented with the city of Frankfurt. Slowly our duties were assigned. I was assigned to a new office which had been requisitioned by the army in a large German insurance building. The German insurance company was called the "Alliance Versicherung." It now became the headquarters for the military government of Frankfurt. Here were the newly established offices for General Larkin and Major Kearns and for two other officers, all previously known to Larkin and Kearns. They were Lt. Col. Jim Ramage from Atlanta, GA (whose wife was a sister of Nancy Reagan, later on the First Lady of the United States), and Major Clarence Olson. Olson was single but very friendly with a US army Registered Nurse. Ramage who was married and had two children He always acted like he was single; he just loved the girls. Other offices were occupied by the newly established police in Frankfurt, another by the fire department, a press office, and so on. Our office was the liaison office between the American officers and the newly established German authorities.

My partner was Sergeant Fred Koeth. Fred was about two years older than I. His parents were from Germany. Fred was born and raised in Chicago, and he spoke German as fluently as I did. He came from an replacement unit. Fred had seen a lot of combat and had been in Luxembourg during the famous Battle of the Bulge at Christmas in 1944. Most of his unit was also re-deployed to Japan, and like me, because he spoke German fluently, he was held back and assigned to SHEAF. Fred and I became close friends quickly. He did not have a girl friend and was flirting and dating several German speaking WACS who were assigned to our unit as well.

As soon as we got set up in Frankfurt, I got my first letter from Ilse. As she had feared, she was now in New York, and I was in Europe. She wrote about her sailing from England to New York and about her arrival in New York. It was an army troop transport, and she wrote about the great time she had with the American soldiers coming home from overseas. Her last fling, as she put it. They were the first civilians to leave England for the United States after the war had ended in Europe on May 8, 1945.

My parents were at the pier to welcome her and her mother. Both Ilse and her Mom had moved in with my parents. My parents wrote glowing letters, as if I didn't know already, what a beautiful girl Ilse is, how sweet and lovely. They now had the daughter they always wanted. They were very happy that the first step of our reunion in New York was fulfilled and hoped that I would follow soon. Ilse had already met my old friend Julius Maier who for medical reasons had been discharged almost six months before.

In the meantime Major Kearns and I had become real good friends. Since he was the oldest of all of us, including the officers, he was called Pop by everyone who knew him well. Now Kearns told me to call him Pop as well, if and when we were not on official duty. Jim Ramage who was a Lt. Colonel also took a liking to me and told me to call him Jim. Soon Lt. Colonel Clarence Olson told me to call him by his first name. These was a wonderful group of men. I am still proud of them and very happy that I served with them rather than under them. We were a group of very responsible men who respected each other for what we were and not for who we were. Enlisted men or officers, we were all real friends who in the evenings would sit around at Pop Kearns's quarters and have a beer or other drinks together, mostly talking shop, about the day's events, and bitching about army life in general, like soldiers always do. Also, Fred Koeth was always invited, but he rarely appeared. He preferred the company of one female or other, as I said always a

WAC. Kearns, who owned a liquor store in Indiana, had served some years before the war in the Indiana National Guard and had left as a first Lieutenant. During the war his unit was activated, and he was called back into active duty as an officer in the army Corps of Engineers. Like the rest of us, he was not too happy about it.

General Larkin had moved into the offices of the former German President of the Alliance Insurance. Kearns, Olson, and Ramage had adjoining offices. Fred Koeth and I were given an office in the center of all the others, so that they could get a hold of us when they needed us as interpreters. Since this was the headquarters of the military admin-istration of Frankfurt, each of the officers was assigned his area of responsibility, reporting to General Larkin. Ramage was in charge of the German police, city busses and the fire department. Olson was in charge of reopening the banks in Frankfurt, and Kearns was in charge of all engineering which included the safety of all the bombed out build-ings and the bridges over the Main river to make sure that they did not create a safety problem. Two new officers Sobelman and Smith were also assigned to Kearns's staff. Their assignment was to get the local utilities operating again. When we moved into Frankfurt the water and gas works were still not operating. The retreating German troops had blown them up. Sobelman and Smith were two young guys and did not play their role as officers who would rather be closer to Fred Koeth and me than to the senior officers. I became friendly with them as well. In addition we were given two more German speaking GIs. One had only a school knowledge of German which was not too bad, and the other fellow was of Swiss heritage He had a problem between his Swiss German and the German-German. I was the only one who was born and raised in Germany, knew the German "culture" only too well, and was able to cope with the various dialects which even Fred Koeth couldn't do, especially the dialect in the Frankfurt area. Our jobs were to go with the members of the US Army Corps of Engineers who inspected these damaged places and gave us their recommendations about what had to be done. These recommendations were given to Kearns, Sobelman, and Smith for their study and disposition. If the building was to be torn down, we had to get German contractors for that purpose and follow up with reports to Kearns on a daily basis. For me, the war had long ended. Except that I was not at home, I had a rather good time.

Around the early part of June 1945, General Larkin called me to his office. He told me that he very much regretted that he had to assign me on temporary duty to a Displaced Persons Camp in Offenbach which was about 25 miles from Frankfurt. I would keep my living quarters where

I was now. I'll never forget. I looked at Larkin, and I said, "General, what is a Displaced Persons Camp?" His answer was, "Sergeant, that beats the shit out of me." I am writing this especially so that the reader should know that until that day in June of 1945, none of us had any clue about what had happened at the Nazi Concentration Camps.

I was to report to a Lt. Curt Kroner the next day who would be in charge of this camp. Curt Kroner's parents were from East Germany. He was a real nice compassionate fellow who spoke German well and had a good knowledge of Yiddish. When I reported to him, he already had a staff of foreign language speaking GIs. I soon found out that most of the men came from an American Intelligence unit, and now they were assigned

*Photo of me taken in May/June 1945 at the Offenbach Displaced Persons Camp*

on temporary duty as well. I believe that every European language was represented here. Kroner told us about the Concentration Camps, what had happened, and how the survivors were now being distributed all over Germany into camps until proper dispositions could me made. He warned us that these people had to be treated as if they were Americans; we were not allowed to have any weapons. Our job was to help them to get back to health and reunite them with their families. He warned us about their physical and mental appearances, that they were in bad health, malnourished, and mistreated by the Nazis.

The Camp was used before we occupied it as an SS training center and had a hospital unit attached. Kroner had already put the barracks in shape. They were newly painted, all new beds, super clean, and so on. They looked just like our barracks in the States did. An American Medical Unit was already stationed at the adjacent hospital, and a full and well stocked Army Mess Hall was set up to feed about 300-400 people. German civilians were assigned to do all the hard labor.

Our job was to interview each person, take all their personal information. We asked them for names of those that they knew who died at the camps, and where they had lived before the Nazis occupied their countries. That would have been a great job if there had been computers those days. All the reports went to the International Red Cross. When the survivors of the Holocaust finally came to the camps, we asked them to write the names of their missing loved ones on paper, and we posted these sheets for everyone to read, hoping that one or the other might know something. Sometimes these notes were interchanged with other Displaced Persons Camps. Sometimes we were able to reunite some survivors with other members of their families.

The Holocaust survivors who came into our camps were just skin and bones. They had nothing with them but the rags they wore. Some were still in their blue and white concentration camp "uniforms." They did not trust us and were scared of us. We had large signs up indicating where each language was spoken. Most of them were Jewish and were from Poland; some were from Germany, Hungary, Austria, France and so on. In addition we all wore home made armbands indicating our native languages. Since I knew Larkin personally, Kroner asked me to contact General Larkin to get a Jewish chaplain assigned to this camp as soon as possible. That was done, which helped a lot. A very unfortunate incident happened the very first night. The hospital staff, US Army doctors and nurses, were to come the next day only, so we had no medics available. The first transport of about 100 people got in late in the afternoon. Our Mess Hall was all set up to receive them. The fellows at the Mess had prepared a nice meal for them. These poor people had not had a warm meal, never mind a full meal in years. They had been living on soup and bread for years. They fell over the food, and we were so happy to see them eat. That night a few of them got very, very sick. We called for Medics to come in a hurry, which they did. They gave us hell because we fed these people the way we did. Their systems were no longer used to such meals. We were all saddened when one of these people died. We didn't know any better and no one had warned us. Of course Lt. Kroner got the blame for it and was almost court martialed.

FAST FORWARD: Many years later, around 1948 or 1949, Ilse and I were at the Pinehill Country Club in Pinehill, NY, on vacation. We were sitting at the swimming pool, and as I looked around, I could not believe my eyes. There were two girls in their early twenties sitting by the pool. I was sure that I had seen them before, but was not sure where. All of a sudden I remembered them sitting at my desk in Offenbach doing my interview and filling out their forms. They had survived one of the killing centers. Ilse thought that I might be wrong, but I could not resist going over to them. I asked them if they by any chance had ever been at the Offenbach Displaced persons camp. They looked at me, looked again, and meekly said yes. Of course they did not remember me. A number of years had gone by, and they looked no longer like skeletons.

We talked a lot. They had found a home in New York City and were leaving the next day.

In the meantime Ilse's letters came in on a daily basis. She sounded much happier; she had met Ruth and Julius Maier who were not married yet. Ilse and Ruth had both found jobs dressmaking, working for a Mrs. Martin who had a high priced clientele at Central Park West in New York City. Julius was working at an upholstery shop learning the trade. Later on Julius had his own upholstery shop in Mt. Vernon, NY, and Ruth was working with him. Through Ruth and Julius, Ilse soon met other people, but her daily letters indicated how lonely she felt. I missed her terribly as well. It reminded us of an old German song which translated into English went like this: "Once upon a time, there were the children of two kings, but they couldn't get together, the waters separating them were much too deep." After about a month or so, our assignment was taken over by UNRA, the United Nations Relieve Agency. We in the military were only too glad to be relieved of this assignment. Some problems had occurred where some of the Concentration Camp survivors had ventured against all military rules and regulations into the town of Offenbach and confronted and beat up some Germans. However, the army had to stop this by no longer allowing people to go into town. Now we had some real nasty problems since the survivors resented the army restrictions and called us "Nazis.

Just at that point UNRA (The United Nations Relief Authority) took over, and we walked away from it. I was reassigned to my previous duty with SHAEF headquarters at the Alliance building. I must admit that it made me very happy. But soon rumors started flying again that both Fred Koeth and I would be reassigned to the interpreter pool for the upcoming Nuremberg war crime trials. Neither one of us was re-assigned.

During the following month, I made a few trips to Brussels to visit Uncle Albert and Aunt Berta. Aunt Berta was my father's sister who had helped us to escape from Nazi Germany with the forged Cuban visas. I also visited Uncle Isi and Aunt Irma. Aunt Irma was my mother's sister. They had both survived a Nazi Concentration Camp in Gurs which is in the south of France. Uncle Albert and Aunt Berta had survived by hiding in France. I also found my old boyhood friend Kurt Rosendahl who had survived three years of the Buchenwald Concentration Camp and three years in Auschwitz. He was still in very poor condition when I saw him, very thin and very pale. I was able to get him some of my used army clothing and a pair of shoes, items which he didn't have since he had returned, and items which were both very expensive in Belgium and difficult to get.

*This is a photo taken of me in front of our former house, about February 1945*

Another trip was to Aachen and to Wuerselen, especially to visit the cemeteries in both places. On an earlier assignment to Aachen, I was able to send a lot of photos home to my parents showing them the destruction of Aachen and especially of the Kaufmann homestead, the place where my mother, my brother and I were born. All the old familiar places in Aachen had been totally destroyed by the Allied air forces for which we were not sorry. The city of Aachen was severely damaged; about 80 percent of all houses had been bombed, and a lot of them were no longer safe for people to return to them. On my visit to Aachen I was mostly interested to find certain people who had made our lives miserable, for example, my former music teacher who made my life into a nightmare whenever we had our music class. Unfortunately I couldn't find him or anyone else I was looking for. Most of the civilians in Aachen had fled as the American army approached to capture the city. There were some old people still there, and I found an old lady who used to live across from us and had a grocery store, Mrs. Leroy. After Kristall Nacht she had secretly slipped food to us nightly, food we could no longer buy. I was happy to reciprocate her kindness by getting her some food packages through her son and daughter-in-law who lived in New York. Her children in New York had the packages sent to me, and I was able to get them to their mother in Aachen. The Leroys were not Jewish, they were some of the righteous Christians who helped Jews to survive.

Ilse and I kept on writing letters to each other daily. We were getting more and more desperate as time went by. There just was no light at the end of the tunnel. Because I was with military government, my status was frozen, and it appeared that my discharge from the armed services would never come. After all I was serving at the pleasure of the President of the Unites States. Rumors were flying once again that our headquarters would be moved either to Vienna or Prague. But they turned out to be just more rumors. Every day, almost every hour, rumors were spread; none of them were ever accurate.

Frankfurt, Germany September 1945:

Today Col. Clarence Olson asked me to come to his office when I have a free moment. He started his conversation by saying, "Can you keep your mouth shut?" I had no idea what was up and of course said "Yes, of course." He then told me, that so far nobody else knew that he was about to marry the love of his life, a lovely Army nurse, whom I knew well. He said that I was his "confidant." He asked me to arrange the wedding. I had not seen that in my army job description although I had been called about other non descriptive assignments. At first I could not believe what he was saying. He needed somebody who spoke both German and French. He wanted me to locate a German jeweler for the wedding rings. Find a jeweler and then the three of us would go there and make sure they fit. However, this was much easier said than done. During the Hitler years, the Nazis had banned any jeweler to have any gold objects. I tried and tried, but it was not possible to find golden wedding rings in all of Frankfurt and vicinity. I had an idea. I told him to get me a jeep and travel papers, and I would go to Brussels to see my uncle and aunt. I was sure that they had all kinds of connections that would help. He agreed. The next day he came again; he had two rings. Both were his and his bride's college rings. He gave them to me to take them along for size. I drove from Frankfurt to Brussels over Aachen. I found out quickly from the first jeweler in Brussels whom Uncle Albert knew, that there, too, the Germans had confiscated all the gold. However, he knew of a jeweler in Antwerp who might help us for a price. Uncle Albert and I drove to Antwerp, and we soon found the jeweler. Sure enough, he had the gold rings I needed. I have no idea how much they were, but they were expensive. He only wanted to be paid cash in US dollars. I contacted Olson who said that was fine, and that I should come back to Frankfurt. He would give me the money, then I should drive back to Antwerp and have the rings properly sized. I had a few US dollars in my pocket and gave them to the jeweler as a deposit. Within a week I was back in Antwerp and paid for the wedding rings. He fitted them to size, and back to Frankfurt I went. In military jargon, "Mission accomplished."

I thought that this would be the end of the story. Olson had another request which he wanted me to take care of. A friend of Olson's who was stationed in England had been contacted by Olson for live lob-

*General Larkin, Commanding Officer, City of Frankfurt, Germany, 1945, and Madeleine Carroll (movie star)*

sters for the wedding meal. The problem was that his friend in England who was a pilot would put the lobsters in packed containers filled with water and ship them with other cargo on a scheduled flight to Frankfurt. The pilot of that plane was told to turn the package over to me. I went to the airfield outside of Frankfurt. The plane came in; the pilot came out and handed the "cargo" over to me.

This still was not the end for me. A few days before the wedding I was asked to find flowers for a bridal bouquet which the groom had forgotten all about. His bride made up a list of flowers which she wanted, and now I was the recipient of that list. I soon found out that in all of Frankfurt no fresh flowers were available, only plenty of artificial flowers. After some more checking around, I found a gardener who grew chrysanthemums in his garden. I talked him into making them into a bridal bouquet, the American style, and to my surprise he did.

I was the only enlisted non-commissioned officer who was invited to the wedding. Good old General Larkin was the best man and gave the bride away. A very famous American movie star Madeleine Carroll was the bride's best girl friend from her college days and was the matron of honor. She was with the American Red Cross serving somewhere in Europe but came to the wedding. Earlier during the war she had lost her sister during the German bombing of London. She was a very charming and pretty woman. She had asked me to tell her the unbelievable story about how I got the wedding rings and all the other

*The wedding picture of Lt. Col. Olsen and Mrs. Olsen, Frankfurt, Germany, 1945*

things together for the wedding. She had heard about it from the Olsons, but she just didn't believe the story and begged me to tell her myself.

The story of my army life would not be complete without writing about an experience which occurred around the Jewish High Holidays (Rosh Hashanah) in the fall of 1945.

During Kristall Night, November 9, 1938, the Nazis burned down about 99.9% of all synagogues in Germany, Austria, and all other occupied territories. Of the many synagogues in Frankfurt, only one of them, also totally burned out inside, was still standing. It was the "Freiherr vom Stein Street synagogue in the heart of Frankfurt."

A Jewish army chaplain had contacted Major Kearns at SHAEF Headquarters to inquire how this synagogue could be refurbished to make it available for the Jewish military members to observe the High Holidays. Kearns had lost no time in passing the message onto me. I met with the chaplain. We toured the burned out temple. The question was how safe the construction was to be used.

Within a few days Major Kearns and some army engineering personnel established that it was safe to be used. Kearns told me that he knew that there was sufficient paint in one of the German warehouses which we could confiscate to be used for this project. We contacted Military Police headquarters in Frankfurt for manual labor help. They were holding a number of Waffen SS members at a nearby location and made about 15 of them available under MP guard, of course, to be used to clean up and paint the synagogue. The paint we located was a blue color, and there was plenty available to give the inside of the temple two coats of paint. The prisoners also constructed sufficient wooden benches for about 150-200 GIs to be used. The Erev Rosh Hashanah Service (The Jewish New Year) was for many of us very emotional, especially for me, since it was the first time since November 1938 that there was a Jewish religious service held in a synagogue in Germany and in the city of Frankfurt.

When Ilse and I visited our good friend Curt Rosenfeld in Tamarac, Florida in February of 2004, we talked about our army lives for the first time ever. As it turned out, Curt was stationed in Aschaffenburg not far from Frankfurt at the same time I was stationed in Frankfurt. During the night of Erev Rosh Hashanah in 1945, he was at the "Freiherr vom Stein Synagogue." Although we knew each other very well and were friends, neither one knew where the other was stationed at the time, and with close to 200-300 men present, we did not see each other. Another interesting side story. Shortly before Rosh Hashanah 1945, I don't remember under what circumstances, I met an old Rabbi and his wife who had just returned from the Thersienstadt Concentration Camp. It was Rabbi Neuhaus, the last Rabbi of the Freiherr vom Stein Synagogue. I visited with him several times thereafter. Talking with Curt, he too had met him and had visited with him a number of times. Yet, the two of us never knew about it until 59 years later.

The synagogue is still standing in 2004 and is Frankfurt's largest synagogue. The name has been changed from "Freiherr vom Stein" to "the Westend Synagogue." If in time any of the readers should visit Frankfurt, go and visit the synagogue which is located at the Freiherr vom Stein Strasse. During my recent research with the Jewish Museum in Frankfurt, I was surprised to find out that my above story is recorded at the museum as a part of the history of the synagogue.

Sometime in January of 1946, I got a letter from Ilse that my mother was seriously ill and had cancer. I got a follow up letter from my Dad that my mother needed either X ray or similar treatment. At the same time, my Dad and Ilse got in touch with the American Red Cross to obtain an emergency furlough for me to come home and see my mother. However, I was not aware of this until I was called by General Larkin to come to his office. He told me that he had just received a notice from the American Red Cross regarding my mother's condition. Since I had served my time in the army, and had an excellent military record, he told me that he was sending me home within the next few days with the recommendation for my honorable discharge from the service. Of course I was stunned. I went to Pop Kearns, who already knew about it. Kearns told me that Larkin wanted to tell me personally about my Mom. Within a day or two I found myself packing all my gear and was ready to leave for Antwerp in Belgium to get on a troop ship bound for the States. I called Ilse from Antwerp; she assured me that my mother would survive and that my Dad was doing well. I then told her that I was on my way home, and in her English accent, she said, "I can't believe it."

On January 30, 1946, the day before I was leaving Frankfurt, Germany, Lt. Col. Olson called the entire unit for an award ceremony. I had no idea that I was the recipient of the award. He read the following letter aloud. (The original is in my army book.)

SUBJECT: Letter of Appreciation.
TO : T/Sgt Fred Voss 42127828
At this time, when you are terminating your service with this headquarters, preparatory to leaving the United States Army, I wish to extend my personal appreciation for the fine service you have rendered. During the seventeen months that you have been a member of this command and Seine Section in Paris, you have

exhibited loyalty, good sound judgment, and executive ability, to a marked degree. The service that you have contributed to the United States Army and to our country has not only aided to the proper function of our headquarters but has been a factor in establishing the respect for our American way of life with the German Prisoners of War and with the German Civilian population, with whom you have worked. I wish to thank you for the material results that could not have been accomplished without you and which were far above the call of duty, and beyond a mere routine conception of duty, your loyalty is one that brings credit upon our military forces where ever we are, and upon you as an individual. I wish you all the success that I know is coming to you in civilian life, and I hope that I will be able to see you again when we are both back in our normal way of living, that of a civilian.

(signed) CLARENCE O. OLSON
LT. COL., INF.
EXECUTIVE OFFICER
SUPREME HEADQUARTERS
ALLIED EXPEDITIONARY FORCES

A few days later I was on a troop transport bound for New York. The ship docked in New Jersey at an army pier. I was the first one off the ship. I ran as fast as I could to a pay telephone and called home. My mother answered which made me very happy. Ilse was at work, and I told my mother where I was. However, from the pier in New Jersey we had to go by train to Fort Dix which was also in New Jersey to be processed for discharge. That night I called Ilse again from Ft. Dix.

The six year long nightmare had come to an end. The army discharging process took a while. Medical checkups, paper work, and all the other red tape. After all this was done, I had to see the discharging officer who gave me a long sales pitch that I should re-enlist and offered to me, if I would re-enlist, a second Lieutenant promotion. I turned him down very easily and now had my discharge papers in my hands. On March 3, 1946, on a Sunday afternoon, I took a train from Ft. Dix to New York and from there the subway from the Pennsylvania Station home to 580 West 161 Street Apt 47. Ilse and my parents were anxiously waiting for me. I was home—it was all over—Ilse and I were in each other's arms, promising never to leave each other again, as long as we lived.

About three months after my discharge from the army, I received the following letter from Kearns (the original is in my Army book):

Indianapolis Ind
14 May 1946
Friend Fred;

Sure glad to receive your letter of 21 April and would have answered it sooner, were it not for the fact that the Medics have had me all trussed up so that I could not write. Imagine me, letting them get away with that, well I did because I could not get them to do anything else despite all my cussing and hell raising with them.

No doubt, that you will recall, that I had a bad left shoulder from back when I was hit, in the days of the Italy campaign. Well, we were coming back on the boat I was sitting on the boat deck, on a bench, and sitting next to me were two chaps that weighed a couple of hundred pounds a piece. The weather had been fairly smooth and I was somewhat relaxed, when all of a sudden we hit a big wave and the ship took a 30 degree list, and of course I had to be on the low side and the others piled onto me.

I quickly grabbed the stanchion hook with my left arm and the others having nothing to grab, piled into me, and I took the combined weight on my injured left arm. I did not pay much attention to it, even when my arm got a bit stiff. However, when I got to camp Atterburry the examining Medic told me to raise my arms like a butterfly, and when I was unable to do so, they threw me in the hospital over my objection. The hospital medics trussed me up like a wild steer to be branded. So, as of this moment, I am still in the army, but hope to be out in about two weeks. From now on I will be spending my days at the hospital and my evenings at home. Fred, I sure wished that you were here to help me overcome these darn Medics, as you have so often helped me in the past. Olson and the new Mrs. Olson came back on the same boat with me. We drove from Frankfurt to Le Harve in France, via Paris. Stopped for a few hours in Paris. Our old spot at 24 Le Grand Armee is now a very elaborate PX and our saw mill and camp in St. Maur certainly has gone to hell. I had to wait around for several hours before a Lt. Gelman finally showed up. I guess he had found out that I was there and he tried to stay away from me. Turner, our former French police officer at the camp, is supposedly in charge with Lt. Gelman. The POWs were sitting around smoking and doing nothing when I came in, but man did they jump up when they recognized me, and were now running around madly with nothing to do. Very evident from their action, that they were now in the habit of doing nothing all day long. The smooth working empire that you created out there certainly went to hell when you left Paris. By the way, I recently run into Lt. Geoffrey, down at Camp Atterbury the other day. He found out I was in the hospital and came over to visit me. You will recall he was that screwball Lieutenant, who was with Lt. Murray. He is now assigned to an MP outfit that is being trained for duty in Germany. God help them, unless he has changed a lot. Sorry, I did not get the chance to call your hand on that promise of a good Kosher dinner, but the facts are that we landed at Ft. Kilmer and I was stuck to take troops to Atterbury, so did not even have a chance to make a phone call home. Well as soon as I get out of this man's Army, I will have to make a trip to New York and will sure call on you to deliver that dinner with possibly a midnight snack in addition. How are your folks much improved I hope, now that you are at home to look after them. And what about that good looking girl, the one you always talked about, were you able to talk her into marrying you. If not, you better get busy my friend you better get started and get a set of twins, because from the looks of things another war is in the making, and you know if I get called back, I will insist on you going along to look after me. So, you had better get married in a hurry and get started building up points, so you will be one of the first ones out the next time around.

Believe, I recall in your letter you said that you had talked to Fred Koeth, Larry Reilley and John Duffey. Next time you write send me their addresses please. How does it feel to be a civilian again? Bet it is or was hard to get out of the habit of raising hell with those around you, as you did with the Krauts civilians and the Heines POW. Before I close I had better mention the fact, that Lt. Safforn, was so sure that you were coming back to Frankfurt, that he insisted on setting up your desk, in the new office building. Better close for now, best of luck and once gain thank you, for your invaluable assistance in those trying days of France and Germany.

With my best regards
Major, ED. J. Kearns (POP)
Army Corps of Engineers.

When by Christmas 1948 the United States got involved in Korea, I received a Christmas Card from Kearns which I have also in my army book, and I would like to quote a part of it here, as a memory to him.

"Freddy" It now looks as though we will be back in uniform soon. If I am called back into the Service, which I do expect shortly, I hope, it is my good fortune to have with me Sgt. Fred Voss, the best soldier, that ever wore the army uniform in the ETO.
(signed) Pop Kearns.

One day in 1951, I received a very sad letter from the Kearns family that my dearest friend, Major Ed. J. Kearns had passed away of a liver ailment at the age of 53. I was really saddened, and the cause of his death, as far as I was concerned, was suicide by alcohol. I still think of him. When life was dangerous and tough at times, he always tried to protect his men from harm. He was a friend, a father image, and I still miss him.

Lawrence Reilley passed away in 1962 at a New York City hospital of cancer. I visited him there several times at the hospital before his death. Jim Ramage passed away in 1973 in Atlanta, Georgia. I had spoken with him on telephone a few times since I had left the army, and yearly I received a long letter around Christmas time telling me all the news. When his brother-in-law Ronald Reagan was inaugurated as President of the United States, he tried to get tickets for Ilse and me to be at one of the inauguration balls, but at the end he could not get the tickets for us.

John Duffey got back to New York in June of 1945 to be re-deployed to leave for Japan. The war with Japan came to an end, and he was discharged from the army. While I was still in Europe with the army, he went to visit Ilse in New York and told her about our friendship. For reasons I really don't remember, somehow we lost contact with each other.

With the Olsons I was in touch for a while, but when the war with Korea broke out, he was still on active duty here in the States. His unit left for Korea, and that was the last that I heard from him or his wife.

From Lt. Murray and Lt. Geoffrey, I never heard from either one and was not in touch with them.

From General Larkin I never heard again. I was told that he had returned home sometime in April of 1946 and retired from the army.

## Army of the United States

### Honorable Discharge

*This is to certify that*

FRED VOSS      42 127 828      TECHNICAL SERGEANT

HEADQUARTERS COMMAND THEATER SERVICE FORCES EUROPEAN THEATER OF OPERATIONS

### Army of the United States

*is hereby Honorably Discharged from the military service of the United States of America.*

*This certificate is awarded as a testimonial of Honest and Faithful Service to this country.*

*Given at*      SEPARATION CENTER
                   FORT DIX NEW JERSEY

*Date*      3 MARCH 1946

WILLIE Y DUNCAN
MAJOR F.A.

# Our Story

*From Aachen, Germany, and from Liesing-Vienna, Austria*
*to Ithaca, New York*
*Via London, England; Bellerose, New York; Lewisburg, PA*

*This was the house in Liesing where Ilse was born and raised*

*This was the house in Aachen*
*where I was born and raised*

*This was the house in London*
*where Ilse and I met in 1939*

*This was our first house in Bellerose, NY, from 1951 to 1967, where Clifford and Claudia were raised*

*This was our second house, in Lewisburg, PA, from 1967 to 2002*

*This is now our apartment in Ithaca, NY, since August 2002*

# Together at Last

Sunday, March 3, 1946 was a day that I will never forget. Ilse and I were together again—no more war, no more letter writing, no more immigration papers, no more visas, no more ocean separating us. We stayed up all that night, just looking at each other and holding one another's hand. We didn't want to let go for fear that it was all a dream.

We had so much to talk about. We both could not believe what we had endured since May 2, 1940. It had been almost six years and 2000 letters later. It seemed that the years had suddenly gone by so fast that we could not believe it. That very night we decided to get married in two months on Sunday, May 19, 1946, on the Jewish holiday of Lag B'Omer, and the same Jewish date on which my parents were married which was on May 5, 1912.

On Monday, March 4, 1946, the day after I came home from the army, Ilse took the day off from work and we stayed at home. We kept on holding each other's hands; we talked about resuming a normal life. We were so much in love. We couldn't believe that the nightmare was over. I had bought a New York newspaper to see what jobs were offered. I was amazed about the number of jobs which were open in the textile industry. On the following day, Tuesday morning, March 5, Ilse returned to her job with Mrs. Martin who had an atelier for expensive ladies' dresses on Central Park West in New York City. Ilse and Ruth Maier both worked there.

I was still in my army uniform when on the same day I went and applied for a job at a weaving mill in the city. The owner of the mill hired me on the spot, and I started working the next day on Wednesday, March 6, 1946, only three days after my army discharge. Since I had no civilian clothing, I bought some and went to work.

Looking back, I realize that the transition from army life to a civilian life was not so easy. I was no longer used to taking orders from civilians and had a tough time getting along with the owner of the mill. The straw that broke the camel's back was when he told me a few weeks after I had started to work, that I should get a broom and sweep the floor because he was expecting visitors. I looked at him and told him to give me his right hand. I put the broom in his hand and told him to sweep the place himself! He was kind of stunned and kept looking at me as I walked out of his place and out of his life.

To understand what I was facing at the time, one must realize that when we were discharged from years in the service, we had no coun-

*Our wedding day, May 19, 1946. My mother, Ilse's mother, bride and groom, my Dad*

seling and had to change our life within hours from years of military life to the life of a civilian. At our discharge the army had not mentally prepared us for what we might have to face in the real world and in many cases at home. At discharge time, there was a short ceremony; some lieutenant addressed us and said, "Thank you for all you did for our country. Now go home stay well and good bye." American civilians had no idea and certainly no understanding that we had spent our military life at arm's length from danger and far away from our homes and our loved ones.

I had a tough time readjusting from my army life to civilian life. When looking for a job I met with narrow-minded people in management. Most, if not all, of the people I came in contact with had not been in the army, and it seemed to me that they were sorry that the soldiers had come back alive and into society and the work force.

In April of 1946 I found an other job, also with a small weaving mill. The owner of the company was a Mr. Pessener who also had a knitting mill in New York City. The weaving mill was called Modern Woven Fabrics. It was located on the sixth floor of an old factory building at 204 Green Street in Manhattan which was part of Greenwich Village. The manager was a man about my father's age, Frank Wirtz, a nice man and most of all an understanding human being. He and his wife who had no children, lived in New Hyde Park on Long Island. Frank hired me with a starting salary of $65 a week which made me well paid in 1946. At that time he employed only four people, but the company was rapidly growing both with customers and employees.

At the time he hired me, I told him that Ilse and I were getting married on May 19 and that I hoped that he would understand that I would like to take a week off for our honeymoon to which he agreed. He asked me to return to work with the company after we were back home again which of course  I did.

Like my brother Ed and Lore, we also were married by Rabbi Koppel in the study of his apartment on Ft. Washington Avenue. We had hired a limousine which took us from our apartment to Rabbi Koppel's apartment. As we entered the Limousine some people yelled "YOU'LL BE SORRY." During the ceremony Rabbi Koppel played on his record player "Here comes the bride." Ilse looked so beautiful in her silk parachute white wedding gown which I had brought for her from the battlefield of France. A reception for the family and friends consisting of about 15 people was held at a little restaurant at 158th Street and corner Broadway in Manhattan, a few blocks from where we lived. We were all in a somber mood because we had no information about the fate of Ilse's father and brother who were still missing after having been deported by the Nazis to Poland in 1941.

My good friend Julius Maier was to be my best man. However, he and Ruth showed up about three quarters of an hour late. I quickly asked Herbert Hirsch another old friend of mine from Aachen to be my best man. Rabbi Koppel delivered a sermon at the reception that we have never forgotten. It was based on the old German song "Es war einmal ein treuer Hussar" which translated into English went like this: "Once there was a faithful soldier, who loved his girl an entire year, an entire year and still much more. Their love never ended for ever more." After the reception hosted by Ilse's mother, we got ready to leave for our honeymoon. We had reservations at the Strand Hotel located on the Boardwalk of Atlantic City in New Jersey.

We took a bus to Atlantic City, and on that ride there were no seats for us to sit together. We had to split up, and my new bride sat down next to a soldier and had a good time. I wound up in the rear of the bus next to some drunk. We finally arrived in Atlantic City around 10:00 PM and checked in at our hotel. Our reservation called for one room with an ocean view. The clerk insisted that we had requested two separate rooms. Well, that wasn't so, and we convinced him that we only needed one room to which he finally agreed. He took us to our room from which we couldn't see the ocean, and we told him so. He told us that all we had to do was to look around the corner, and we would see the ocean. The Strand Hotel was a first class hotel in Atlantic City. We went for a late snack, and I got sick smoking a big cigar. By the time that we called it a day, it was very late at night. On the next day we took a sightseeing boat around Atlantic City. It was a very hot and sunny day, and both of us got a painful sunburn. On Friday we returned home to prepare ourselves to go back to work on Monday, as well as to set up our living quarters at my parents' apartment.

When we got married it was impossible to find an apartment for us to rent. During the war there was no housing construction, and when the war was over there were not enough apartments for the returning soldiers to live with their wives. Consequently, most families doubled up for the time being until they could find homes of their own.

Living at my parents' apartment, I went back to work at Modern Woven Fabrics and got involved in all aspects of the mill from receiving to production to shipping. I really loved the job very much and received a wage increase from time to time. By 1955 we had about 12 employees working on two shifts, and sometimes even more employees working on three shifts. My working hours got longer and longer and by then included Saturdays as well. When I sat down with Frank and told him that I felt that I was more at the plant than at home, he got upset with me. In the fall of 1956 after ten years with Modern Woven Fabrics, I finally had enough and had a fallout with Frank Wirtz. He was more and more away from the mill, went on long vacation trips to Florida and fishing trips on weekends, and I was having more and more problems, responsibilities, and work without getting any help while he was away.

Since I was considered as management personnel by the owner of the company, Mr. Pessener, I worked six days a week without any overtime pay. The mill was exclusively used for the play shoe division of US Rubber who actually were the main stock holders and owned the mill. But the pressure was getting too much for me to live and work under, so I decided to leave the company for my own sanity. My father was very much upset with me and told me so, that I left that job with my obligations as a married man and father. At that time I was 36 years old.

When I returned from the army, I had a tough time getting along at home as well, especially with my father who was still the "German" disciplinarian whom I had left when I entered the American military service. However, when I returned from the military I was a Tech Sergeant which was only one rank below a Master Sergeant and as such had a lot of power and most of all a lot of respect from soldiers and officers of all ranks. I was used to giving orders and rarely had orders given to me. If so, they were in the form of discussions between my officers and myself. There never was any yelling or screaming as was the custom in my father's younger days in Germany.

When my brother and I were children and would misbehave, our Dad would yell, scream, and spank us which was typically the discipline of the German men of that generation. He was very strict with both my brother and me. We experienced this same "tough upbringing" from our male teachers at school. I am sorry to admit that this German model for being a man was part of my culture and upbringing. Unfortunately, it was every boy's role model as well. This authoritarian approach of the Germans was passed on from one generation to the next generation. Of course it was reflected in how I brought up my own son Cliff. I am forever sorry for how wrong this was. For my excuse, if there can be one, is I must admit that I was plain ignorant. It took me years to realize this. I do apologize to Cliff.

Later on in life, I realized that this Prussian-German generation under which I was raised and the generation before me and their parents' generation with their strict disciplinarian attitude, also produced the Himmlers, Mengeles and Eichmanns of the concentration camps during the Nazi era.

Ilse, on the other hand, was brought up in an Austrian culture which was much more civilized and relaxed than the German culture and opposed my tough "German" authoritarian way of raising Cliff for which I am forever thankful to her.

When I was in the army, I had become used to a different life. Most of all a different and better culture. I dealt with highly educated men like Larkin, Kearns, Olsen and Ramage. People like them I had never met in my life. Truthfully, they had great respect for me, not for who I was, but for how I conducted myself. In addition, I had now been integrated into the American way of life and the American culture which was so different from the one under which I was brought up. I was together with Americans, day in and day out, and tried hard to adopt their culture and thinking. No longer was I the little refugee boy who had left the German way of life when I joined the US Army.

When I came home from the army I really thought very highly of myself, but my Dad thought that I was a nobody who had to learn a lot yet, which of course I refused to accept and proved it later on in my life. It was hard for me since I loved my Dad very much. He was my role model for better and for worse, working very hard, taking care of his family, and being very honest. He loved my Mom dearly, loved my brother and me very much as well but in his own way. He was always there for us when we needed him; he always protected us. He had been raised by a strict father himself who believed that children should always be seen but never be heard. This is where Ilse's and my upbringings and maybe even our cultures were totally different. Certainly her Dad was totally different from my Dad, and Ilse was not used to this disciplinarian environment at home. The Austrian people were relaxed and easy going as compared to the aggressiveness of the German people, especially males.

There could have easily been more severe problems between my Dad and me in this period, but fortunately Ilse's cooler head as always prevailed, and I kept quiet. After all the two families lived together in the same apartment, and the three women shared one kitchen. This alone had created some minor problems, but they were little ones which the three women managed to overcome.

Early in 1948, while still living with my parents, Ilse and I bought our first car. It was a used 1941 Chrysler, a lovely car. The model was called "Highlander," and the interior was in the famous Scottish plaids. The top was a light beige and the body in a maroon color. We used it only during the summer. In the winter we put the car in storage. We often took my parents and Ilse's mother on weekend trips into the country. We would pack lunch and stopped for a picnic at some lakes within 50 miles north of Manhattan. Everyone loved it and enjoyed a day away from the city. Until we bought the car and took my parents and Ilse's mother on outings, they had never seen the New York City surroundings. This was their first time since they came to this country.

Although Ilse and I had married in 1946, we still lived in my parents' apartment until the winter of 1948. Of course we split all the expenses with my parents. At that time my mother's sister Aunt Irma arrived from Brussels to join my parents. My parents took her in to live with us in the already cramped apartment. This of course created some problems; by now four women were sharing a small kitchen! This became a little bit too much for Ilse and me. It also led to some additional friction between my parents and me. My parents felt very loyal to Aunt Irma and were so sorry that her husband, my Uncle Isi, had died right after the war from being denied medical help for bladder cancer while he was interned in a Nazi concentration camp. Aunt Irma's daughter Edith had escaped Germany and was married in Israel where their children were born. They too were preparing to move to the United States joining Aunt Irma.

Ilse and I started looking for our own little apartment. At the time apartments were still impossible to find. Apartments were at a high premium, and when one was available, it was rented within minutes. We were listed with a number of rental agencies, and daily after work we went there and looked at their bulletin board to see which apartments became available. But one had to pay a lot of money, not for the rent, but to the people who moved out. Everyone tried to make as much money as they could on the returning soldiers. In the summer of 1949, through our good friends Curt and Helga Rosenfeld, we were able to rent an apartment. We had to decide to rent or not to rent within two hours as other people were also interested in the same apartment. The apartment was located at 608 West 135th Street in Manhattan. We had to pay $1000 for an old beat up table and four chairs. The apartment was on the fourth floor, walk-up, no elevator; the monthly rent for the two bedroom apartment was $45 a month. We could hardly afford the $1000 for the furniture which was a lot of money especially for us. But we very much wanted our own apartment and needed the two bedrooms because Ilse's mother was going to move with us. We would not leave her behind.

My parents had decided at just about the time to travel by train to San Francisco to visit my brother and his family. Commercial flights were rather new, expensive, and only very few people traveled by air. When they returned we told them that we would move out. My father got very upset with me for having decided to rent our apartment while they were away without consulting with him first. The guilt complex was put on Ilse and me, that we were not grateful to my parents for all the time that we lived with them.

At about the time when our apartment was ready for occupancy, my Dad told me that Aunt Irma's daughter Edith, her husband Alfred Melzer, their son David and daughter Sonja were to leave Israel and would move to New York, as well. Dad told me that he and my mother had decided to move to San Francisco to be near my brother. Since we had decided to move out, he had invited Aunt Irma and her family to stay in the same apartment, and he also sold them the furniture for only a few dollars.

Now my mother and father had suddenly decided that they were moving to San Francisco for two reasons. The first one was that my brother who had his own accounting office in San Francisco had offered my Dad a good job in his office which would be easier for him than what he was doing until now for which I could not blame him. The second reason was that my then sister-in-law, Lore, in San Francisco was expecting her second baby, Kenneth, in November of 1950. My mother claimed that my brother wanted her to be there when the baby was born. I can never forget my mother's words to Ilse and me, "When my son calls me I go." However, Ilse was already six months pregnant with Cliff, our first child, whom we expected to arrive in March. My mother knew that we expected our first baby, and her remark hurt both Ilse and me.

Some years earlier Ilse had found a very well-paying job in the ladies garment industry on Broadway in New York City. She was hired by a very famous and well known dress designer whose name was Emily Wilkens. Ilse created the sample dresses which Ms.

*Clifford, 8 years old*

Wilkens sketched and designed. She had to join the International Garment workers union in order to work there. There, Ilse became very friendly with Gerti Halberstadt, Ingrid Naylor, and some other girls. Ilse and Gerti are still friends to this day. Ilse loved her job and worked there until shortly before Clifford was born on March 21, 1951.

Clifford was named after Ilse's brother Curt because in German the letter C is pronounced K. Therefore the C was used in Clifford, and his Hebrew name is Yitzchak Ben Avrohom. Yitzchak after my paternal grandfather's Hebrew name and Avrohom after me. About a year after Cliff was born, Ilse went back to her old job at Emily Wilkens in New York. Ilse's mother, Omi Olga, took over the cooking, baking, and Cliff.

Cliff was our firstborn, and what a beautiful baby. Ilse and I had been at Dr. Bamberger the afternoon before his birth and were told that his birth was not imminent. We were surprised when on the same evening around midnight, Ilse had labor pains. I drove her to the Mt. Zion Hospital in mid town Manhattan. I stayed with her at the hospital until Cliff was born at 3:30 PM. He was the handsomest baby boy we had ever seen. I kept on calling my mother-in-law every couple of hours to keep her posted. For Ilse, it was a tough birth, but all went well. His Brit was on Easter Sunday, and on Monday morning we took him home to our walk-up apartment at 135th Street. There Cliff spent the first seven months of his life until we moved into our own home in October 1951.

So, Ilse became a Mommy; I became a Daddy, and Ilse's mother became now Omi Olga. Omi Olga was overjoyed that we had a little boy! Cliff reminded her so much of her own son, Curt, whom she had so tragically lost at the age of twelve years when he was killed in Auschwitz by the Nazis.

In the fall of 1950, Ilse and I decided that we would not bring up the baby in the neighborhood where we lived, especially not in a walk-up building, and so we looked for our own home. Finally, we found a house which we could barely afford to buy. It was a Cape Cod at 83 - 30 241 Street in Bellerose, Long Island, NY. The house had two bedrooms, an expansion attic, a full basement, a front lawn and a nice size back yard. The house was on a 40 x 100 ft. ground. The price was $12,999. Down payment was $1500 and a VA guaranteed loan was at 4%. Only a model home was available at the location we chose. Ilse was already six months pregnant, and after the down payment, all we had left between the two of us was a total of $10. This was the second time in our lives that we had only $10 to our names. We would have never asked either my parents nor Ilse's mother for any financial help because neither had any money to give or loan us. In the meantime, because of our financial position, not making too much money, I sometimes worked on two jobs at a time, one day job and one night job.

With the help of our neighbors I did a lot of construction work myself. When we bought the house there was no drive way. I built one along the side of the house so that we could park the car there. With the help and neighbors' supervision we built out the attic by constructing two bedrooms, one for Cliff and the other one for Ilse's mother, Omi Olga. Some years later we had the basement built out with a bathroom and a full kitchen, so that Cliff and another baby waiting to be born would have a nice playroom in the basement.

Cliff was our pride and joy, the sweetest and cutest little fellow we had ever seen and watched growing up; his head was full of blond curls. People used to stop and admire his blond curls. His playmates were a little girl next door, Annette, neighbors Debbie and Susan Risch, a little boy Tommy Gross and Norman Camen. At his Bar Mitzvah in 1964 we made a party at a lovely restaurant to which all our relatives and friends were invited. My parents came all the way by train from San Francisco. At the time my Dad was 80 years old, and my Mom was 76 years.

Cliff was always a hustler, selling Christmas cards at the age of 12. He sold enough that the company for which he sold them gave him a record player as a present. When he was 15 years old he worked as a caddie on the golf course, and he sold ice cream for Good Humor using a tricycle as a form of transportation. He always tried to make some pocket money; he knew that our financial situation was very tight, and he never asked for anything. He went to PS 18 in Bellerose and skipped from third grade to fifth grade and did junior high school in two years, instead of three years. From there he went to an excellent high school in Brooklyn, the Brooklyn Technical high school from where he graduated at the age of 16 years in 1967. He was always a very bright boy and a smart young man. He was a good boy, but once in a while he would feel his own oats, especially after he had entered Bucknell University and had his own ideas with which we would not always agree, and this would upset him as well as us.

He spent four years at Bucknell University in Lewisburg, PA from which he graduated at the age of twenty. While Cliff was at Bucknell, he worked during his vacation time at a number of places. The first job was at Perkins Pancake House as a short order cook. He worked the night shift at Chef Boyardee in Milton and at the maintenance department at H. Warsaw also in Milton, PA.

Next he studied geology and geophysics for two years at Boston College. In Boston he worked at an apartment house as the caretaker. He always worked and always made money. From there he went to Princeton University, NJ, where he earned his PhD in civil engineering developing a computer model of underground fluid flow. In 1976 he married Maj-Lis Torfalk who was born and raised in Korpilombolo, Sweden. On September 1, 1980, their first son, our first grandson Daniel, was born. Six years later on June 30, 1986, their second son Stefan was born.

In 1981 he joined the U.S. Geological Survey as a researcher. In May 2004 he is still with the Survey. He and his family live in Reston, Va.

Maj-Lis enriched her education by earning in 1986 a B.A. in Geography at the George Mason University, Fairfax, Virginia. In 1990 she earned her M.A. in Economics at Virginia Polytechnic Institute, Falls Church, VA. and is currently doing research in progress towards earning her Ph.D. (Public Health) at Umea University, Umea, Sweden. *[In 2006, Maj-Lis and some of her colleagues created a new non-governmental international development organization, the NorthSouth Group for Poverty Reduction.]*

After I had decided to leave my job at Modern Woven Fabrics in 1956 I found another job with a large weaving mill with about 100 employees in Brooklyn, NY. The company's name was Roy Weaving. The owner was a Manny Seiderman. Seiderman was a cheap, miserable, and nasty person. I was paid rather well because I was well experienced in the weaving operation. Around 1954, the US immigration had opened its doors to the survivors of the Nazi concentration camps. Seiderman obtained his help for the plant from HIAS (Hebrew Immigrant Aid Society). Seiderman's business and personal friends were associated with the

HIAS organization. At the time, a large number of textile workers mostly from Poland were coming to the United States and HIAS was referring them to Roy Weaving. Seiderman hired these people. Most of them spoke only Yiddish and no English at all. He treated them a bit better than slaves which bothered me very much. While I was in Frankfurt, Germany, with the US army I had seen what these people suffered in the concentration camps during the war. First of all he had hired them on a six month probation period during which time they were paid below the then federal minimum wage law. This was allowed at that time for new workers for the first six months. After the six months he would let these people go and hire a new group. There were a few of us who became upset about how he treated these people. Very few could help themselves, and most of all they didn't know the American laws or the culture. When they complained to HIAS, they didn't get any help from them and were told by HIAS to be glad that they had a job. One day a few of us, whose names I hardly remember except for Siggy Wolle, met for lunch and decided to stop the abuse of these unfortunate people. I was picked as the spokesperson for the group and gladly accepted it. Previously, at some occasion, I had met a man who was an organizer for the Textile Workers Union (TWU). I contacted him, and our little group met with him. It was decided that we would start by calling a strike against Roy Weaving for mistreating their workers.

Before that day came, we had spoken to a few of the workers whom we trusted, and who joined us. By the time Monday came we had the majority of the employees on our side. On Monday morning about an hour before the mill opened, we had all these people lined up carrying ON STRIKE signs and preventing the rest from entering the plant. We had accomplished about a 95% of a walkout. Seiderman called the police and tried to stop us from blocking the door to the mill. We already had the union lawyer with us. The lawyer asked the police to see the court order empowering them from ordering us to make access to the entry way. The police had no such court power and left. We knew that Seiderman was too cheap to get a lawyer for a court order against us and counted on that.

We were on strike for a week or ten days; there were no negotiations, and finally Seiderman told the TWU that he wanted to meet with them. I was one of the six delegates and with the union lawyer we met Seiderman the following day. He was not represented by his lawyer, as usual he was too cheap for that too. As the meeting started, he tried to throw his weight around by telling the union lawyer that there were some people whom he didn't want to be on the committee. I was one of them. The lawyer told him that this was up to the membership to pick their committee and not up to him. He was asked if he wanted a membership vote on this issue or if he wanted to start talking to us. He asked to think this over, and our union lawyer gave him until the next morning to think. We met again the following morning. This time he had a lawyer with him. Our demand was a very simple one. No more probation time for new employees. All employees were to

*Claudia, 3 years old*

be paid federal minimum wages for the first 30 days, thereafter increases of three percent per month for the next five months, plus the union health benefits and a vacation package. Seiderman and his lawyer walked out. The next day he totally capitulated to our demands. The strike was over; we went back to work. Shortly after that I left Roy Weaving. "Mission accomplished."

From this incident I learned a lot about how unions work. These experiences came in handy several times many years later when I was dealing with the Teamsters Union when they tried to organize H. Warshow and Sons in Milton. The lessons I had learned prevented the Teamsters Union from winning several elections for which Henry Warshow was very grateful.

I left Roy Weaving in January of 1958, about two years after I had started there. Long before leaving Roy Weaving I had made contact with the owner of a knitting mill, Duke Knitters, also in New York City. The owner was a Syrian, Bob Trabalsi, a great and fantastic person with whom I became a good friend. His Dad really owned the mill, but Bob, his son, was the one who was in full charge. I had no idea about knitting and took the job mostly with the idea that I was still young enough to learn and to expand my textile knowledge in the knitting end of the textile industry, which turned out just as I had planned.

On May 21, 1956, Claudia was born at the Long Island Jewish Hospital. On May 20, Ilse, her mother, Cliff and I had gone out for dinner to a seafood restaurant on Long Island. Ilse and I had lobster for dinner, my mother-in- law had some other kind of sea food. On that same night shortly after midnight Ilse let me know that it was time for her to go to the hospital to have the baby. We woke up my mother-in-law and let her know that we were leaving for the hospital. In the morning when we told Cliff, who by now was already five years old, that he had a little sister, his comment was, "I thought that this would happen after the lobster Mummy ate." The family was now complete, a boy for me and a girl for you—as the old song goes. We were one happy family.

*Claudia, 6 years old; Clifford, 11 years old*

Of course Claudia was also so cute, except she had no hair, bald like a plate. I saw her before she was cleaned up. I still remember her little pinkie was standing up, the rest of her fingers were a fist, and the nurse told me that she is a lady already, drinking a cup of tea. Whatever that was all about, I don't know. Everything was just beautiful; we had two lovely and healthy children and our own home. What else could we want? We were so happy; both Ilse's and my dreams had now become realities. No babies were ever more wanted than Clifford and Claudia. Claudia Francine was named after my paternal grandmother whose name was Clementine, and Ilse's maternal grandmother whose name was Franciska. Her Hebrew name is Alisha bas Zipora, Alisha after my maternal grandmother's mother; Zipora is Ilse's Hebrew name.

About a year or so after Claudia was born Ilse found a part time job at The Mays' department store in Bellerose, and Omi Olga helped out again. However, by the time Claudia was about three years old, Ilse stopped working. Claudia was always a sweet girl, never gave us one moment of problems and worked hard in school. Like her brother Cliff, she always was very smart and very bright and did well in school and later on in college.

Her childhood friends were Joann Nagler, called JoJo, Jeffry Kirshner, who wrote to her in Kindergarten that she is a "Knockout," and little Marisa Montecalvo. Like her brother before her, she also went to PS 18 in Bellerose but only up to the 5th grade because we moved to Lewisburg, Pennsylvania in 1967. There she went to elementary school for the sixth grade, as well as her junior high school and high school years. In Lewisburg she had many friends, Kathy Wilson, Nancy Rheam, Rick Rose, a boy Zimmy, and many others.

While in the Lewisburg school system, Claudia worked during the summer at a variety of restaurants as a waitress, The Fence, The Country Cupboard, Kentucky Fried Chicken, at H. Warshow and Sons in Milton and many other places. Claudia, like her brother, always knew that our financial position was not the greatest. Her love was to participate in school plays. Of course her high school achievement was that she became the valedictorian of her graduating class, and we were so proud of her. While she had won a scholarship for the University in Rochester, NY, she preferred to go to Wesleyan University in Middletown, Connecticut for her undergraduate studies majoring in government. She spent one year abroad studying at the Hebrew University in Jerusalem in 1976-1977. Following her graduation from Wesleyan in 1978, she studied at the University of Chicago for two years, earning a master's in international relations.

While in Chicago she met Bruce Lewenstein from Palo Alto, CA, and they both left after their graduation for Washington, DC, where both of them had found jobs. Bruce decided to leave for the University of Pennsylvania to earn his PhD. They decided to get married in 1983. They had a lovely wedding on a rainy Memorial Day weekend. Their ceremony which should have been in our back yard in Lewisburg was moved to a reception hall at Bucknell University.

Claudia worked in the field for six years before taking time off to have a child. During that time, she decided to return to graduate school and earned her MSW from Syracuse University in 1992.

On March 30, 1986, their first son Joel was born followed by Gabriel who was born on July 28, 1990. He was followed by Ari who was born on May 7, 1994. We were now the proud grandparents of five wonderful and caring grandsons whom we love very much.

As of May 2004 Claudia is still with Family and Children's Service in Ithaca, NY, practicing as a child and family therapist.

While Passover shopping in Harrisburg in April 1968, Ilse's mother had an unfortunate serious accident. She fell over one of the concrete car stops on a parking lot and fractured her hip. At the time we had no idea how serious this was. She went back home with us, and once home we called a doctor who came to the house and told us the bad news that she had broken her hip. A few days thereafter she was operated on; a new plastic hip replaced the broken one. This surgery led to many serious complications. She fell again some time later and broke her other hip. This made the complication even worse. She had an awful lot of discomfort and pain. The doctors decided to replace the first plastic hip with another one, and this third surgery really ruined her, physically and mentally. I don't know when, but I would guess that it was around 1974 that she was finally admitted in a Williamsport, PA nursing home. Two years later she transferred to another nursing home in Northumberland, PA where she passed away in 1980 at the age of 91 years.

Ilse's mother was a great lady, I loved her very much. In her younger days I consulted with her many times; she always had good ideas and was always there for us when we needed her. She was a mother to me, rather than a mother-in-law. I still miss her ever so much.

In May of 1969, we had planned Claudia's Bat Mitzvah. It would have been a nice affair. We invited our closest friends from New York, new friends from Lewisburg, and all of Claudia's friends for a party at a local motel. My parents had flown in from San Francisco; this was the first time in their lives that they flew. My brother Ed put them on a non stop plane from San Francisco to Pittsburgh, and I flew out to Pittsburgh to meet their incoming plane. Together we flew to Williamsport and drove home to Lewisburg. They had arrived in Lewisburg on a Sunday afternoon. On Thursday afternoon, two days before the Bat Mitzvah, my mother stepped outside and fell. She had broken her hip. An ambulance was called, and my mother was taken to the local hospital. We canceled the party for all the grown ups but made a little party for all of Claudia's friends at home.

Of course the religious part of the Bat Mitzvah went on without a schedule change. After surgery, my mother came back to be with us to recuperate for the next six weeks.

Now both my mother-in-law and my mother walked around the house with the help of walkers. A very sad sight to watch. About six or seven weeks later my parents insisted on going back home to San Francisco. I took them to the Harrisburg airport from where they got a direct flight to Chicago, and from Chicago they flew home to San Francisco. My mother was in a wheelchair to get on and off the planes. Like my mother-in-law, she really never fully recuperated from this accident.

In July of 1972, my mother passed away in San Francisco at the age of 84. She had suffered from asthma ever since I can remember. At times she had very severe attacks. My parents had consulted many doctors; she had tried every diet and had injections galore, but nothing helped. Several years before she passed away, the asthma had turned into emphysema, and that was the cause of her death. The sad part of it is that we did not understand or know those days that direct smoking or second hand smoking could lead to her death. Today, we know that asthma is an allergy and smoking was what caused her asthma. My father always was a heavy cigar smoker; my brother and I were cigarette smokers, and my poor mother was exposed to our smoke all her life. I remember that at home, when the family got together, all the men were smoking cigars; the rooms smelled, and the cloud of smoke was very dense. My mother had a tough life. She really was never a happy woman. She was always worried about my father, her mother, and her children. For her everyone came first in her life, and she was never concerned about herself, always only about the family. She was always pessimistic and rarely optimistic. For her the glass was always half empty. People tell me that I inherited her negative view.

# H. Warshow and Sons

In 1959 I was still working at Duke Knitters in New York City when Clara Reinsberg, my mother's cousin, introduced me to a man named Ernie Horn who was related by marriage to the Reinsbergs' son Kurt. Ernie Horn was born in Fulda, Germany. He had left Germany under Hitler, going first to Sweden, and then in 1938 to the United States. He was hired by H. Warshow & Sons shortly after he came to the US. Ernie Horn had an engineering degree in textiles from a well known university in Germany. By coincidence Ernie's father owned a large weaving mill in Fulda, and my father had been a customer and knew his father well. By now Ernie Horn was the director of operations at H. Warshow and Sons located at 45 West 36th Street in New York City. At the time, H. Warshow's largest customer was Jantzen and Jantzen, a famous women's wear company. While in Sweden, Ernie Horn had developed a technical procedure for elastic woven and knitted fabrics which could be used to make two-way-stretch fabric

*Ernie Horn, my mentor and good friend*

for the manufacturing of ladies' girdles. For many years Warshow was the only world-wide manufacturer of elastic woven fabrics used in the manufacturing of ladies' girdles. Later the same method was used for manufacturing bathing suits.

Ernie Horn invited me to meet him for lunch; we had a long discussion about the textile industry and my knowledge of the many products. He left me by promising to think about hiring me but warned me that the owners of the company, the president Mr. Joseph Warshow and his brother-in-law Mr. Jack Feldman, would interview me and that they would decide my fate. I recognized that this might be the break I would need in my life. I went to Bob Trabalsi and told him. He said that he would help me as much as he could, and also I could give his name as a reference. Years earlier at Modern Woven Fabrics I had met Harry Cooper, a salesman for the yarn division of US Rubber. During the interview Ernie Horn had dropped the name of Harry Cooper. I called Harry Cooper and told him about my Warshow interview with Ernie

Horn. Cooper told me that Horn had spoken to him previously, asking him if he knew somebody who would fit the job requirements. He said that he would now call Horn and tell him about me. The catch was, as Cooper told me, that Warshow would never hire anybody for a management position unless he was a college graduate. He advised me to tell them that I had graduated from CCNY (City College New York) and assured me that they would not ask for a college transcript; he knew the company only too well. About a week later Ernie Horn called me again and told me that he had set up a meeting with Mr. Warshow and with Mr. Feldman. I went to this meeting—shaking—I wanted that job so badly. I was escorted by the receptionist into a large conference room. Mr. Warshow's private secretary came in, introduced herself and asked a lot of questions, mostly regarding my past involvement in the textile industry as well as my educational background. Now I was really nervous. I was sure that she could hear my heart pounding. I told her that I had left Germany not getting my high school diploma, but had passed the high school equivalency test by taking the test upon my entry into the military which was the truth and is so noted on my army discharge paper. Now, she asked me for my higher education and the degree. As rehearsed with Cooper, I told her that I had attended evening courses at CCNY and had a degree in mathematics. That was the one and only time that this question ever came up for the next 26 years at Warshow.

She walked out of the office, and had me wait for about thirty minutes or so, which seemed to me like thirty hours. Then she came in with Mr. Warshow and Mr. Feldman, as well as with Ernie Horn, who introduced me to the others. I was hoping that my shaking was not noticeable to the naked eye. Both Warshow and Feldman asked me lots and lots of technical questions about the mechanics used for weaving and knitting. Now I really felt great that I had left Roy Weaving and went into the knitting end of the textile industry. They were all technical questions for which I had the answers. After interviewing me for an hour or so, they told me that they would think it over. I was not asked any questions as to what salary I expected, nor what I was planning to do in the future. I left them with a negative feeling about getting that job.

As I wrote earlier, since I often was working on two jobs at a time, I wanted that position with Warshow desperately. Almost two weeks went by, and I was sure that I would not hear from them again, when suddenly Ernie Horn called me to have lunch with him, adding that afterwards he would show me around the office before I had another meeting with Warshow and Feldman. I met Ernie, and he told me that he believed that I had made an excellent impression on those two gentlemen and that they might hire me. He himself was not really sure of their decision, or so he said, which I never believed. We went to Ernie's office where I was introduced to Ernie Horn's right hand man, Bernard Greenberg. When I walked into the office Bernard was making a calculation with his slide rule. I had never seen a slide rule before, never mind used one. Now I really had second and third thoughts about the job: Could I do it? After all "I had a degree in mathematics" and had no knowledge how to use a slide rule. I was sure that my charade was over. I was taken into Mr. Feldman's private office. Feldman was the CEO of H. Warshow and had an engineering degree in chimney construction; he was also Joe Warshow's brother-

*Budd Greenberg*

in-law. Both gentlemen came together into the office, and Mr. Feldman told me that they had decided to hire me to be Ernie Horn's assistant. My jaw dropped. They offered me a starting salary of $9000 a year which at that time was a lot of money. I quickly calculated that this would be close to $175 a week, plus a profit sharing plan, plus full medical coverage, two weeks paid vacation, Jewish holidays off, and my salary would be reviewed in six months. I had not dreamed of making that kind of money at that time.

Because of the July vacation period, I was to start on Monday, August 1, 1959. As it turned out, this was another lucky break. Ilse and I had planned to leave the first week of July for a week's vacation at the Rose Garden Hotel in the Catskill Mountains of New York. Prior to this vacation I purchased a slide rule and found some college students at the hotel who taught me how to use it. When I reported for work at Warshow, I went there equipped with my "very own slide rule." Since I was uncertain that I could handle this job, I had made arrangements with Bob Trabalsi that after my day ended at Warshow at 5:00 PM, I would go to his place and work the second shift until midnight. Bob had agreed to that and was only too happy to help me. So, the first morning I purchased only two subway tokens, one to go to Warshow and one to go home. I arrived at Warshow at 9:00 a.m. Ernie Horn was there to greet

me and took me into his office. On the prior interview I had met Budd
Greenberg, and now the three of us would share the same office. Ernie
told me that he was sure that I would know what to do (I was glad that
he thought so) but wanted me to spend a few weeks with Budd training
me. Mr. Feldman had suggested to Ernie that I experience this training
period. Budd had already been working there for five years and was
only too glad to throw all his work over to me, and at great length he
taught me what he called the crazy Warshow system. His words, which
I have never forgotten were, "There are three ways of doing something
here, the right way, like we learned in school, the wrong way, as if we
didn't know any better, and the Warshow way, which is the crazy way
of doing things." We became close and good friends quickly and are still
friends 45 years later. The first day I was there, Budd, Shelly Bernstein,
and Henry Warshow, the son of Mr. Joseph Warshow, took me out for
lunch. I was impressed. This had never happened to me before. Budd
Greenberg had served during the war with the famous 8th Air Force as a
gunner on a Flying Fortress. Shelly Bernstein had been an air force pilot
during the Korean war. I felt better already because I had now found two
former GIs, and the three of us exchanged our various experiences in the
military as well as our stories about how tough it was to find the right
jobs after we left the service.

I admired Ernie Horn for his great knowledge in the textile industry.
He became my role model. He didn't like my cigarette smoking and
presented me with my first pipe and taught me how to smoke it. Ernie
was a great collector of road maps; he would get upset with me when
I folded them the wrong way. Ernie was a good friend with whom I
consulted many times during our time together. I missed Ernie when
he retired from Warshow. He gave me the break in my life which I will
never forget. He gave me the opportunity to get my job with H. Warshow
and Sons. May he rest in peace.

Within the first few months at Warshow I had made tremendous progress. My knowledge about the textile industry was based on practical
hands-on experiences and not on a book-college education, like Budd
had. Budd had graduated from a first-class textile college at Lowell, MA.
By now both Ernie Horn and Budd consulted with me about problems
which had occurred at the mill which was in Montoursville, PA. Lucky
for me, I often had the right answer on how to resolve some critical problems. More luck than I knew! One day Mr. Feldman came to me saying
he had a production problem at the plant and wanted to take me there to
see if I could shed some light on the problem. On a Sunday afternoon I
met him and his wife, and we drove to Montoursville, PA to meet Gerry

Berube. Berube was the assistant plant manager. However, in charge of the plant was Henry Warshaw's cousin, Donald Layton. Layton was a big man with a voice like he was using a bullhorn. You could hear him miles away. I had no idea what the problem was until I went into the plant with Mr. Feldman and Don Layton. It was the simplest problem that "anyone" with a mill background could have solved it in a few moments. I resolved the problem very quickly as I had experienced it many times before. I couldn't understand why the people at the plant couldn't resolve such a simple problem themselves. I always thought that this was the "acid test" to see if I was full of bull...or really knew my stuff. I never believed that they didn't know what was wrong as Berube was a well-experienced hands-on mill technician. Now, as far as everyone was concerned, I was fully qualified for the job. That night Mr. Feldman and Mr. Layton took me out for dinner. When we came back to the New York office, my salary was increased even though the six month trial period had not ended. I was so excited that I called Ilse right away.

At Christmas time I got another raise and two weeks pay as a Christmas bonus. I could hardly believe it. Either I knew so much, or they didn't know anything. Until today I still don't know which was which.

Over the following years I came more and more to the attention of Donald Layton who by now was promoted as the CEO in charge of all plants. At the time we had a rubber covering plant in Talladega, Alabama, in Tappahannock, VA, a weaving plant, in Milton, PA, the dye house, and in Montoursville, PA, another weaving plant. The corporate office was New York City. The annual company sale was close to four million dollars at the time and employed close to 800 people.

In 1963, Don Layton called me into his New York office and made a proposition which he claimed that I could not refuse. He wanted me to move to Pennsylvania to be involved in the physical operation of the Milton dye house. Cliff had just entered Brooklyn Tech, and I told Donald Layton that I would not move until Cliff graduated from Brooklyn Tech in 1967. In the meantime I traveled a lot to the mills both in Pennsylvania as well as to Virginia to help to resolve technical problems.

In March of 1966, as a birthday present Ilse's mother, Omi Olga, bought Cliff a dog for which he had begged for a long time. He was a real beautiful one year old wire haired terrier, Mr. Chips. He was Cliff's dog. Cliff trained him, and boy and dog bonded early on. In 1968, a year after we had moved to Lewisburg, Mr. Chips got sick and was diagnosed as a diabetic. We had to give him insulin shots every morning, and his food was controlled. With the excellent care we gave him, he survived and had a relative normal life to the age of 15 years until he died in

1980. He was a sweet but also a stubborn little dog. We loved him very much.

A few months after we had Mr. Chips, we decided to tour the United States by rail. Mr. Chips, as we called him, stayed with our neighbors Larry and Jo Risch and their daughters, Susan and Debbie. We went by train from New York, across the country to the Grand Canyon in Arizona, from there to Disney Land in Anaheim, California, and then we flew on to San Francisco to see my parents and brother and his family. On the way home we traveled by train through Colorado. We stopped at the Air Force academy out-

*Ilse's girlfriend Julie and her husband Harold Cohen*

side of Denver for a tour and then finally back to Bellerose. Omi Olga spent that time with Ilse's childhood girlfriend Julie Cohen who now lived in Boston and was married to Harold Cohen.

A notable incident happened on this trip during our stay in California. We had made reservations at the Holiday Inn in Anaheim, California, for our stay and a planned a visit with Fred Kaufmann a third cousin of mine on my mother's side of the family. When we got to the motel we quickly found out that we were the only "white folks" there. The rest of the guests were all African-Americans. The NAACP had their yearly convention there, and Dr. Martin Luther was the keynote speaker that evening. In the morning, while we waited for my cousin to pick us up from the hotel, a sound truck pulled up. On this sound truck stood a number of brown shirted men, wearing swastika armbands identifying them as members of the American Nazi Party whose leader at the time was a Lincoln Rockwell.

No sooner had the sound truck pulled up when their "screaming started." The Nazis addressed the African-Americans by telling them that the Jews and only the Jews were their problem and spouted off anti-Semitic propaganda. I watched them for a few minutes and then I had enough. I will never know what came over me but I felt 10 feet tall and 500 pounds heavy. I started screaming at the Nazis and intended to jump on the sound truck and tear these Nazis apart. However, Ilse and Cliff tried to hold me back, but I kept on yelling at the Nazis. Fortunately for me, some members of the African-American group grabbed me and held me so that I couldn't move. They tried to calm me down, while Ilse and Claudia were hysterical. This incident might have triggered a flashback, reminding me what the Nazis had done to us in Germany.

Back home again from this trip, I was having lunch with one of my many bosses Don Layton one day when he reminded me about our conversation of four years earlier. At that time I had refused to move from Bellerose, NY, until Cliff graduated from Brooklyn Tech. Now, he made me an offer which I felt that I really could not refuse. The offer included an immediate increase of ten percent of my current salary and the job of setting up a new yarn dyeing division to be known as "Milton Yarn." I was to be in full charge. I told Don that I had no idea about yarn dyeing, and his answer was, "So, what you do is hire the people who do know, and then you run the show." That, I found out, was the Warshow concept. Hire the right people. I guessed that this was why they hired me. In addition, he wanted me to be the Corporate Purchasing Agent, a position which Ernie Horn held at the time, and he was about to retire within a few years. I would also be responsible for the Milton division meeting its projected budget. I had no idea of what was involved, and most of all I had no intention of moving. I kept on delaying and delaying until there was no longer a way out. The more I delayed, the more interesting he made the offer, adding that I should buy a new car, paid for all moving and legal expenses, including what he called the "kitchen sink." After a long discussion with Ilse, and most of all Ilse's mother with whom I always discussed any decisions involving the family, the three of us decided that I was still young enough and should accept the offer. Cliff had decided to go to Bucknell University in Lewisburg PA. Now all pieces fell into place. I accepted the offer. We put our Bellerose house up for sale. We had paid $12,999 in 1950 and asked for $30,000 in 1967. (The re-sale value of this house in 2004 would have been close to $225,000.)

In Bellerose I spent a lot of time working to improve our home. I had the help of some of my handy neighbors, Emil Zazzy, Tony Renner, Larry Risch, John Sussino and others. They helped me to build a driveway along the house, so that we could park our car there and not in the street. With their help, I built out the attic. Whenever I needed help, these fellows were always there to lend a hand. I am forever thankful to them because without their help, I could not have afforded all the improvements made to our house in Bellerose.

*These are some of our many friends from our days in Bellerose, NY, 1967*

We all had served in the army during World War II. We understood each other, had a lot in common, and had the same financial problems. They were a great group of men. They all were men of "the greatest generation," and our common bond as veterans was very strong. I owe them as much for their help in peacetime as I would have owed them in wartime, had we served together in the same unit.—And so I had to leave them and move on to Lewisburg, PA.

I started my new position in Milton on March 1, 1967. I rented an apartment in nearby Sunbury which I didn't like at all. Then, I rented a furnished room in Milton. The agreement with Warshow was that I would drive home on Fridays at noon time and return again to be at the plant on Mondays at 9 AM. I was now the "Manager of Milton Yarn and Corporate Purchasing Agent for all raw material."

Some time in April Ilse called me in Milton to let me know that our house was sold, and we would have to move out by July 15, 1967. I had already started looking for a home in Lewisburg, PA, but could not come up with what we really wanted. One day, however, Jack Farell, who was the dyehouse plant manager, called me to let me know that the night before a "For Sale" sign was put on a house around the corner from him. He thought that this would be the right house for us. At lunch time Jack

*These are some of our many friends from our days in Lewisburg, PA, 2002*

drove me by the house. It was a big ranch home sitting on .50 acres in Lewisburg. I liked it at once. I called Ilse and made arrangements with Ed Mensch the realtor to show Ilse the house while I was working. Ilse came to Lewisburg, and Mr. Mensch showed her the house as well as another house. But Ilse loved the house which Jack had called me about. The very same evening we met with Mensch again, and now both Ilse and I went to see the house with Mr. Mensch. The house belonged to Dr. John Arborgast, Jr. We made an offer of $32,000. Later on that same night Mr. Mensch called us at the motel to let us know that Dr. Arborgast had accepted our offer which included our occupancy as of July 15, 1967. We were happy that we had found a new home in beautiful Lewisburg, PA.

# Moving to Lewisburg, PA

The job at Warshow's Milton plant was very difficult for me to handle because I did not have the experience for it. I followed Don Layton's advice, and I hired the right people. One man was Ralph Garner and the other was Lyman Fields. Both were from Charlotte, NC and had been experienced in the yarn dyeing as well as with a new Uster yarn testing system which I had set up. Things began to go pretty smoothly. I was getting in full control of what was expected of me. Garner and Fields both quit their jobs a year later, as they didn't like living "up north" in Milton. But by then I had sufficient knowledge to run the show without them.

We were now settled quietly in our Lewisburg home when one day once again, history and politics showed their ugly faces. These were turbulent politically charged times in our history. President Kennedy, his brother Robert, and Dr. Martin Luther King had been assassinated in the previous few years. The American Nazi party had come out in the open using their anti-Semitic hate propaganda.

I can't remember exactly when, but sometime in late 1968, Warshow had entered a new venture in the textile industry. The Montoursville weaving plant was closed, and in its place it became a weaving mill for narrow woven fabrics. Since I had 10 years of experience in that field with Modern Woven Fabrics, Don Layton got me involved with the operation. I was transferred from the Milton Yarn operation to the converting department of which Shelly Bernstein was in charge. My job was now the production scheduling, material purchasing and the inspection of the narrow fabrics finished goods. This job was an easy one for me and since Shelly was my friend and my supervisor, I had no real responsibilities and enjoyed this work with Shelly. This assignment was too short and didn't last long.

In the spring of 1969 the American Nazi Party's leader, Lincoln Rockwell, announced that he would be speaking in front of the Lewisburg Post Office. A local Jewish business man Harold Stiefel who owned the Campus Theater, a local movie house, organized a committee of Jewish residents which included Bob Heyman, Robert Lyons, Mike Freemont, Attorney Leonard Apfelbaum as well as myself to face this challenge. We met and decided that we would not permit Rockwell to speak. We first contacted the local police Chief Mr. Hufnagle who told us in no uncertain terms that according to the first amendment of the constitution, Rockwell had every right to speak. Then we contacted the ADL (Anti-Defamation League) and had a follow-up meeting with an ADL representative. The ADL representative made it clear to the Lewisburg police chief that should Rockwell be permitted to speak, we would also have the legal right under the first amendment to have a protest rally against him across from the post office. The police chief told us that he would review this request with the county legal authorities before granting a permit for such a counter protest. But he never came back with an answer. ADL called him several times but he was always unavailable. There was nothing we could do about it except obtain a court order to prevent Rockwell from speaking. On the day that Rockwell was to speak, Leonard Apfelbaum, an attorney, was trying to get a court order. Telephone threats against Rockwell were called into a local newspaper and radio station. Two hours before Rockwell's scheduled time, the American Nazi Party issued a statement that Mr. Rockwell was not speaking as scheduled. A few weeks after this incident, Rockwell was shot to death by one of his own men in a fight for leadership of the American Nazi Party.

In 1970 a serious business problem hit Warshow. Mr. Joseph Warshow, who was the president had passed away and his nephew Donald Layton had taken over as CEO of Warshow. Henry Warshow's brother Alan became the President of H. Warshow. In 1983 Alan Warshow retired and Henry became president.

Mostly due to the large textile imports and a major recession here in the States, business at Warshow came almost to a standstill. The Milton dye house operation was reduced from a seven day a week operation to only three days a week. I came up with the idea of soliciting some knitting mills in the New York City area to obtain their business both for yarn and piece goods dyeing. I knew most of them from my earlier New York days in the textile industry. I talked to Don Layton about my idea, and his comment was, "Nothing ventured, nothing gained—go for it." The following week I was in New York City knocking at the doors of the people I knew including my friend David Zinger who was then the plant manager of a large knitting mill that did not have their own dye plant. Within a few weeks, I was able to get more commissioned work for our dye house than we could handle. Now Layton and Henry Warshow thought that I really did a good job. Once business had turned around in 1971, and Warshow was busy with its own customers again, the commission dyeing came to an end. We needed all the equipment for our own business by then.

Shortly thereafter a new problem arose. Henry Warshow and his cousin Don Layton had a serious fall out. An emergency meeting of the board of directors was called, and Donald Layton was fired as the CEO of Warshow. Henry Warshow took over that position himself. Henry hired Norman Schneider to be the Senior Vice President in charge of the northern operation. I had met Norman through Bob Klausner long before that and knew him well. Norman and I are still friends. Norman is an excellent textile engineer, has an outstanding knowledge of textile machinery and the dye house operation, and has an excellent reputation in the industry.

In 1975 Henry appointed me as an assistant Vice President to help Norman. Some years later Henry Warshow made me what he called "the Czar," responsible for the purchasing of raw material for both the Milton and Virginia plants, production scheduling, and for the Milton receiving and shipping department. Since Norman was the Senior VP, I reported to him.

In the fall of 1972, a new American Nazi leader had emerged by the name of Frank Collins. This time we had a serious situation on our hands. Collins had promised to have a major rally on Sunday, June 26 in Skokie, Ill., a Chicago suburb. Skokie was home to close to five hundred Jewish Holocaust survivors. All the Jewish organizations had protested to the local authorities to stop Collins from organizing this event. But again the first amendment permitted him to come to have a rally and to speak. The Jewish War Veterans to whom I belonged had mobilized every Jewish war veteran post to come to Skokie not only to protest but to be prepared, if need be, for a confrontation with the American Nazis. In Lewisburg we organized with members of the Williamsport Jewish Veterans to get a bus load of men and to be ready to leave for Chicago. I signed up to go, and so did my good friends in New York City, Julius Maier and Curt Rosenfeld with their local JWV chapters. The day before we were to leave, the governor of Illinois stopped Collins from coming to Skokie. He was permitted to speak at a park in Chicago, but Collins rejected this alternative.

By the mid 1970's our family had gone through its natural growth and changes. Cliff had graduated from Bucknell University and was studying at Princeton University in NJ, and Claudia was in the Lewisburg high school. In July of 1972 my mother had passed away. Three years after my mother passed away, my Dad passed away in San Francisco. Dad passed away in his sleep. Dad was 91 years old. Dad had lived a good long life and during most of it he was in good health. Around 1947 he had a mild heart attack which only kept him at home from work for a few weeks. He had a bad case of sleep apnea which might or might not have been the cause of his death. Dad's family health history is interesting. His father died at the age of 87 due to complications of prostate surgery. His mother passed away at the age of 78 due to a massive heart attack. His brother Leopold and his sister Berta all lived into their 90's. His brother Alfred died as a result of the Holocaust; he probably would have lived to be in the 90's.

Dad always was an optimist, while Mom was always the pessimist in the family. For Dad, the glass was always half full. He had worked hard all his life, always concerned with helping and supporting his family. He always refused to accept any help himself, right up to his death. He had survived World War I and imprisonment in 1938-1939 at the Nazi Buchenwald Concentration Camp. In his later years he had mellowed very much and was a warm, kind, and sweet man. He, like my mother, was totally selfless and so much concerned about the welfare of my mother, my brother and me. Up to the minute of his death, he was sharp, independent and always concerned for the poor. At the time of his death, we found mailings from ten charity groups that he had financially supported, although he could hardly afford it.

In 1976, Claudia decided to spend her junior year in Israel studying at the Hebrew University in Jerusalem. While Ilse and I had been Zionists all our lives, we had never traveled to Israel. So we decided to take that opportunity and visit Claudia there. We had a great time with Claudia, met her Kibbutz parents, Shemek and Shoshanah Nitzan, as well as their daughter Orna. Claudia took us sight seeing to the places she knew. We went on daily tours with the Egged bus lines, and we toured a great part of Israel. We went all the way south to the Negev and north to the border with Syria in the Goal Heights and then on to Haifa and Tel Aviv. We spent some time with Ilse's cousin Johnny Bauer and his family at Kfar Shmariahu. While in Haifa we met with two women who have Ilse's maiden name of Machauf. Ilse and I are always searching phone books for her family lost in the Holocaust. Their parents also came from Vienna like Ilse's family did but we could not establish a relationship. We became good friends with Liora and Jonatha Machauf. Liora is the chair of the English Department at the Technion University in Haifa. We have met both of them several times and are still in touch with them in 2004.

Everything was going just great for us, when suddenly in April of 1979, Ilse didn't feel well one day and went to our physician, Dr. Steckel. He was convinced that she had a heart attack and hospitalized her. After a number of tests, and consultation with some top heart specialists, it was decided that she did not have a heart attack, but a heart murmur. A medication was prescribed which would prevent future complications. But certainly these were trying days for us until we got the "all clear" which was three weeks after she was hospitalized.

In the summer of 1979, Ilse, Claudia, and I took a trip to Stockholm, Sweden to visit Cliff and Maj-Lis. Cliff and Maj-Lis were working in Stockholm at the time, and we were missing them both. On our way to Stockholm, we had stopped over in Amsterdam and took in some sightseeing of the town. In Stockholm we stayed at Wenner Gren Center where Cliff and Maj-Lis lived. They had found a furnished apartment for the two of us, and Claudia stayed with Cliff and Maj-Lis. It was a lovely trip which we all enjoyed. From Stockholm the five of us went with the Silja Line a combination of a cruise-ferry ship through archipelagos into Helsinki, Finland. In Sweden Cliff and Maj-Lis went with us to the glass factories, and together we toured Uppsala, next to the glass factories in southern Sweden. Cliff and Maj-Lis had taken us around Sweden in a little Saab. Soon after returning home again we adopted a new puppy. We named her after that car because that car was cute and so was "Saabie."

Saabie was a mixed breed dog, part wire-haired terrier. She was a sweet dog who was the healthiest of our dogs. She lived for 14 years in good health and then suddenly got sick. At first the vet diagnosed a lung problem, but changed that a few days later to a failing heart condition from which she did not recover. On the vet's recommendation, we had to put her to sleep. We felt so bad; it was terrible to lose such a sweet, loyal companion. We could not stand to be without a dog, and so in 1994 we got a new dog, a lovely little white Bichon Frise whose name was Cherie, French for "darling." She was truly our darling, and we loved her dearly. Unfortunately we had Cherie put to sleep on February 17, 2005. She had cancer and could not be saved. She was only ten and a half years old.

On March 11, 1980, after suffering for years from the after effects of breaking her hip in April 1968 and later on again in the spring of 1970, Ilse's mother, Omi Olga passed away at the age of 91. Upon hearing the sad news, Claudia came home from Chicago where she was a graduate student at the university, and Cliff came home from Stockholm, Sweden, where he was working. The funeral was at the Cedar Park Cemetery in Oradell, NJ, where my family is buried—my grandmother, my Aunt Irma, as well as my cousin Edith. The day of the funeral was a wintry one. Only Ilse's cousins Eva and Bob Suchman, our friends Ruth and

Julius Maier, Rabbi Silverman, Ilse, Clifford, Claudia and I attended the funeral. After the funeral we drove home and encountered a severe blizzard on the way. It forced us to get off the road and stay overnight at a motel.

In April of 1980, Henry Warshow had a fallout with his new New York "side kick," a guy with the name of Paul, I don't recall his last name, who was in charge of all production in all plants. Henry called Ilse and me to his office in New York City and offered me that position. He wanted to move Ilse and me back to New York at his expense to be promoted to Vice President in charge of all production. I declined his offer. I told him that by now I was 60 years old and was thinking about retiring in two more years. Accepting such a responsible position would not be in the best interest of the company.

Actually neither Ilse nor I wanted to move back to New York City. I knew that this position was a no winner and would involve too much politics. Henry was not the easiest person to get along with. To get the most out of everyone he played one manager or one Vice President against another. I refused to become his partner in that game. However, I did promise Henry that I would stay on with the company for at least two or three more years. Surprisingly, Henry asked me what he could do for me. Since I was only entitled to four weeks paid vacation, I told him that I would like to have three additional weeks vacation to go to Israel and Europe, and in the winter would take the other four weeks to go to Hawaii. Henry agreed without even blinking an eye. I went back to Milton feeling satisfied, and all was going rather well. Henry was always generous both with money and in giving me time off but only when it served his purpose. Henry was a fair boss at times, but he could also be a tyrant when things went wrong. Then he would go plain nuts with hysterics, yelling, screaming, throwing things around, pounding on tables, and so on. I didn't want to work close to him on a day by day basis.

Two years later, shortly before my 62nd birthday in April of 1982, I decided to leave Warshow while I still had my sanity. The pressure was getting too much. I followed company protocol and handed in my resignation for my retirement to Norman Schneider who was a senior VP and my superior in Pennsylvania. Norman tried to talk me out of it. He could not, and he had no other choice but to forward my final resignation on to Henry. A few days later I got a call from Henry to come to the New York office again and to bring Ilse along. We met in his office, and Henry dramatically tore up my letter of resignation in front of Ilse and said that this was the end of the conversation. However, as devious as he was, turning one against the other, he told me in what he called "the greatest confidence" that he was no longer happy with Norman Schneider. (Norman knew this already and had mentioned it to me.) He then called Marvin Shepherd into the office and introduced him to me. He told me that Shepherd would take over Norman's position in Milton. Norman he said would be assigned to an other position in Milton. Shepherd had a Ph.D. and was a VP at Dupont. In front of Shepherd he said, "Fred, I want you to watch Marvin. Don't let him jump off a cliff; if he does, stop him, and call me." Then he proceeded to tell Marvin, that I had his, Henry's, fullest confidence and that I had promised to stay on with the company for some time to come. I couldn't believe what he said! I had not promised him anything like it. But I knew right then that this would be the end of my association with Warshow and that Marvin would try and get rid of me as soon as he could. Nothing was said to Norman until a week later when Henry called a manager's meeting in Milton. An hour before the meeting he had a private meeting with Norman and told him that he was being replaced by Marvin Shepherd and that his new title would be "Vice President for special assignment."

Marvin appeared on the scene on or about May 15, 1982, and immediately took over Norman's office. He made Norman move into an empty little office. Since Norman and I had adjacent offices, Marvin let me stay in my office for a while with the understanding that I would stay on with the company until he was settled. I soon found out, to no surprise, that Marvin had zero actual hands-on experience. He came to me daily with all kind of questions. I was not about to educate him since he had a lousy and sneaky personality. He was very arrogant, "a know it all," who would try to take credit for everything that anyone else was doing, but refused to take the blame for any of his mistakes. Soon he moved me out of my office and assigned me to another empty place to work in.

In mid-September 1985 Henry called me and wanted my "honest comments about Marvin Shepherd." I was honest, and I told him not only what I thought about him, but also what most people who had come in contact with him thought of him. Of course I knew Henry well enough and knew that he would pass my comments on to Marvin. I really couldn't have cared less about that, and so it was. About a week later, Marvin called me into his office and told me that he would like to have a memo from me outlining what I had achieved for the company within the past six months. I just looked at him and said, "That would be my pleasure." I had my secretary take a memo addressed to Marvin Shepherd, with a copy to Henry Warshow. Here is a copy of my memo, which I still have. —

Milton, PA. October 1, 1985
To: Marvin Shepherd
From: Fred Voss
As per your request to account, to you, for my contribution to the company for the past six months, it is my greatest pleasure to make the following statement. It was a pleasure to work for H. Warshow and Sons since August 1, 1959 until the day that you came to join this company. I have no intention to account to you for anything. However, I would like to advise you, that herewith is my resignation of my position with H. Warshow, effective as of Dec. 31, 1985. I will so advise Henry Warshow personally.
Sincerely yours,
Fred Voss

A few hours later I met him inside the plant, arrogant as ever. He told me that my resignation was accepted. And that was that. A few days later Henry called me and wanted to know what was going on. What could he do for me? I told him that it was all over and in the best interest of everyone concerned that I leave. Henry invited Ilse and me to come to New York for a social visit and to see him. He and his wife took us out for dinner at a very expensive restaurant and gave us tickets, front row, to a new Broadway musical.

Henry Warshow invited Ilse and me out for breakfast the following morning, and he asked me in front of Ilse if I would stay on if he were to let Marvin go. I couldn't believe his question and knew it was a loaded one. Of course, he knew that this was a moot question and that my answer would be negative. He told me not to be hasty with my answer and to think about it for another week. Three days later I called him and told him that I had decided in the best interests of the company to leave at the end of the year.

When I left H. Warshow, the corporate total sales had reached close to forty million dollars a year and employed about 800 employees.

Shortly before I left Warshow, I found out that Shepherd wanted to give me a surprise party. I wrote him a note, telling him that of course he could do as he pleased, but that I was not coming. That was the end of the party and the end of my 26 years at H. Warshow and Sons. More about Marvin Shepherd later on.

Despite his efforts, Henry Warshow had not been able to talk me into staying any longer. During my years at Warshow not everything was always "Gold or Silver, Black or White." I had many ups and many downs to cope with. My responsibilities were just too great to handle alone, and I did not have the luxury of hiring my own assistant. I had felt similar pressure at Modern Woven Fabrics in 1956. The stress caused me to be on high blood pressure pills, smoke two packs of cigarettes a day, smoke a pipe, and use tranquilizers. I had a note pad next to my night table, so when I would wake up during the night I could make myself notes for the next working day.

I was always extremely nervous and suffered back pain. These were diagnosed as being a stress reactions to the pressure at my job. Henry would call me at home at any time in the evening, sometimes as late as 11 PM or on Saturdays and Sundays to talk about problems at the plant. He always had lot of questions. Months after I left Warshow, my back pains disappeared, as well as all the other symptoms.

# Liberty Travel

One of my areas of responsibilities at Warshow had been the corporate travel arrangements for the Milton division. Based on personal travel experiences using Liberty Travel, I had decided to make Liberty Travel Warshow's exclusive travel agency.

One day in October 1985, after I had advised Henry Warshow about leaving the company, Ilse and I were shopping at the Susquehanna Valley Mall in Selinsgrove, PA. I visited the local Liberty Travel office. I told Donna Diggens, the manager of the agency, that I was leaving Warshow at the end of the year. Donna asked me what I would do after that, a question that Claudia, Cliff, and many friends had asked me as well. I told her that I had not given it any thought. Donna looked at me, smiling as she always did, and said, "Fred, with all your bull....., you would make an excellent travel agent. I will personally train you and hire you. We really need a guy like you." I told her that I would have to think this one over. A week later she called me and said that she and her manager would like to have lunch with me. We had lunch at Ted's in Shamokin Dam, and I left having accepted the challenge of their offer.

Even before I started working at Liberty Travel, the district sales manager told me that Ilse and I should take a week's vacation in Cancun, Mexico. Everything was pre-arranged and paid for by Liberty Travel. They wanted me to become a part of their sales team.

Two months before I left Warshow in December of 1985, I started an on-the-job training with Donna Diggens. I would go to the Liberty Travel office on Tuesday and Thursday evenings after work and stay until the office closed at 9 PM. Saturdays I worked at Liberty Travel from 10 AM to about 4 PM and worked an occasional Sunday as well. At that time the Liberty Travel office had no computers. Besides Donna, there were only two girls in the office, one an agent and the other one a secretary.

When I left Warshow at the end of 1985, Donna had offered me a full time job, but I had declined to accept. I did not want to work again from 9 AM to whatever time, plus weekends. I opted for a part-time salesperson. I had given Liberty Travel a mailing list of the people whom I knew and who were associated with the Lewisburg and Milton industries. Liberty Travel sent letters to them to let them know that after 26 years with Warshow, I had joined Liberty Travel as a market representative. I went to visit them all, and before long I had built up a nice sized private and commercial clientele. When the office switched over to computers a few years later, I purchased my own computer too, and through American Airlines was able to hook it up to the main office computer. Now, I could do the same work from home as I was doing from the office. That worked out just great.

Liberty Travel offered me many wonderful travel benefits. In 1983, Cliff invited Ilse and me to join him, Maj-Lis, and Dani in Hawaii. We went there for the first time and fell in love with Hawaii and its people. We even seriously considered buying a condo in Honolulu, but Ilse vetoed my idea. From then on, however, Ilse and I did spend most of February in Honolulu. This later on led me to organize escorted tours to Hawaii which became a successful and lucrative part of the Liberty Travel business. This then gave me the idea for organized escorted tours to Alaska which became even more successful. Ilse and I went to the Hawaiian Islands close to 12 or 15 times over the years, and five times toured with groups to Alaska.

In May of 1993, while escorting a group to Hawaii I suddenly got ill and felt really bad. But since I had a group of forty people, the trip had to go on. I could hardly walk; I had pain all over and felt generally just miserable. I had no time to see a physician while I was in Hawaii, but I dropped in at a local drugstore and asked the pharmacist if he could recommend some kind of a medication to relieve my discomfort. He looked at me, asked me, "Are you on any kind of a medication?" I told him that I was on a medication called Pravocol. His ears perked up, and his comment was, "Stop right now. This is a dangerous medication." The next day I accompanied the group to the Island of Maui for three days. My condition got worse. We spent three days on Maui. Our last night in Maui was on May 19. We had a big party on our 47th wedding anniversary. We flew early on the following morning from Maui to Los Angeles. Yet, nobody in the group ever found out that I was sick.

As soon as our plane landed at the Los Angeles airport, I called my physician at his home. He had prescribed the Pravocol to reduce my cholesterol which prior to taking the medication was high. I told him how I felt and his first response was, "Stop taking the Pravocol." which of course I already had done.

Since we were to return to Selinsgrove the following morning, he suggested that I should come and see him at the hospital as soon as I could the next morning. However, when I got to the hospital, he was not there, and I was examined by an intern who told Ilse that I was very tired and exhausted and that there was really nothing else wrong with me. He sent me home to rest. During that night I got really very sick. In the morning Ilse called our neighbor Dr. Joseph Smith who at the time was a physician at the ICU at the nearby Geisinger Medical Center. He came right over that Sunday morning to see me, examined me, and thought that I had a stroke. He had Ilse take me back to the hospital and called Dr. Jeffrey, the head of the Neurology Department for consultation. Dr. Jeffrey examined me and immediately asked me if I was on Pravacol. When I confirmed in the positive, he said that I had a violent reaction to this medication and immediately hospitalized me. I spent the next four weeks in the ICU at the hospital and saw about as many doctors as there were at Geisinger. Everyone came to ask me a million questions and poked at me, and took test upon test at all times of day and night. I was getting weaker and weaker. I had more delayed reactions from the Pravacol.

A Dr. Hadash whom I had never seen before at the hospital came with his entourage to see me early one Sunday morning and told me that they had found "the culprit." He told me that all the tests which were taken showed that I had cancer of the lymph node. He suggested that I should discuss with my family whether I wanted to go on chemotherapy or radiation treatment the next morning. He would not recommend which one, saying this was up to me. Needless to say I was devastated. I called Ilse and gave her the news. Ilse called Dr. Smith, and both came to the hospital to see me shortly thereafter. Dr. Smith told me that he would check my medical records because he was convinced that this was not true.

After what seemed like a long time, Dr. Smith came to my room and told Ilse that she should check me out of the hospital immediately. Ilse checked me out and took me home. The next day, Ilse took me to see Dr. Steckel, the family physician. When I told him what medication I had been given, his only comment was, "Glad that you are still alive." He asked Geisinger for a copy of my records, but Geisinger never gave one to him. About two weeks after I was home from the Geisinger, I suddenly passed out and fell on the kitchen floor. Ilse called Dr. Smith again who immediately called Dr. Steckel, and they had me hospitalized at the Evangelical Community Hospital in Lewisburg. After another week at the Lewisburg Evangelical Community Hospital's intensive care unit, Dr. Steckel got me back on my feet again. Five months later, in November of 1993, I was able to return to work at Liberty Travel.

I really enjoyed my 18 years working at Liberty Travel. It was truly and honestly the best time of my working days, not only for me, but also for Ilse. From the top management on down to the local level, everyone was just super nice to be together and work with. I had told my managers that I was willing to do all the escorting tours and travel with the groups, but only together with the love of my life, and never alone. They accepted my request, and I enjoyed traveling with Ilse as much as we could for many years. Over the years, Ilse and I managed to travel around the Caribbean, Europe and Asia, the Hawaiian Islands, and many other exotic places. We took cruises galore, had first class seats on airlines, outside cabins on the cruise ships, some with balconies, sometimes even Captain quarters. We were spoiled wherever we went, treated royally by the airlines and cruise lines, as well as by the hotels, usually paying just a token.

I was very happy until the infamous day of September 11, 2001 came along, and we lost 85% of all our bookings within a few hours. The rest is history.—I had lost most of my clients not only to that unhappy event, but also to the use of the Internet because many people did their own bookings. Like so many other travel agents, I decided to call it quits and end my second career. I retired from the working force after 66 years of work. The day that I retired on April 1, 2002, was a sad day for me which I will never forget.

# Moving to Ithaca, NY

Sometime in 1998, Claudia and Bruce visited us one day in Lewisburg and suggested that we should start thinking about the fact that we were getting older, and might no longer be able to take care of ourselves. Therefore, they came up with a suggestion that we should look into a retirement place in Ithaca, called Kendal which also had a nursing home. Should anything happen to either one of us, we would not be separated. The next time we visited Ithaca Ilse and I visited Kendal. We really did not like it; as far as we were concerned, "it was for old people," and we still felt too young. In addition, we could not financially afford the place. Moving to Kendal would have taken all our money and then there would have been nothing left for us to spend, or leave to our children at the end of our days. Many years before we had taken out a nursing home insurance policy to protect ourselves. This policy will pay about half of the nursing home's cost, and the other half would come from our investments, pensions, and social security, etc. So we felt we were well protected on this issue.

We continued to consider Kendal and checked it out further. After we moved to Ithaca, we spoke to some people who knew residents at Kendal. They said that it was not the greatest place. But Claudia and Bruce had put the idea into our heads and kept bringing up the subject every so often. We told Cliff and Maj-Lis that we were considering a move to Ithaca. They were very much concerned that we would burn all our bridges behind us, and we might not like living away from Lewisburg. Cliff suggested that we should first rent a place in Ithaca for a year to see how we would like living there before we sold our home and moved. He had a valid point, and we thought about the problem for a year.

We had witnessed some very sad experiences with people we knew who had no children or close family living in Lewisburg. The Freemonts and Mrs. Stiefel, for example, both were without their children or any family in Lewisburg, and when they got sick, they had to rely on neighbors or friends to look after them daily. Their own families had to make constant trips to Lewisburg, and when they finally were in nursing homes, only their friends in Lewisburg had the time to visit them. These tragedies made us decide finally that one day our time would come, and that something similar could happen to us. After years and years of deliberation, we decided to opt for selling our house and moving into a rental unit in Ithaca.

On the Internet we found a new development going up only about two miles from where Claudia, Bruce, and the children live in Ithaca. During a visit to Ithaca in April of 2001, we looked at the apartments. They were lovely and ready for occupancy, but we were not ready to move from Lewisburg yet and give up our home.

We had many good friends in Lewisburg and Sunbury, Connie and Bob Heyman, Phyllis and Norman Rich, Evelyn and Morty Hershman, Fran and Shelly Bernstein, Terrie and Herb Hyman and Renee and Phil Sosland. Our friends were very close to us, and many times we helped each other. We shared together the good and the bad times, happy hours, and the sad ones, especially with Connie and Bob Heyman. We were really sorry to move away from all of them.

On May 1, 2002, we decided to sell our house in Lewisburg and move to Ithaca, NY. We went to visit the apartment complex again and rented our unit as of August 15, 2002. Evelyn Hershman was our real estate agent and sold our house a month later to a very nice elderly couple who moved from Maine to Lewisburg to be closer to their daughter.

On August 29, 2002, we moved into Apartment 7 at 210 Summerhill Drive in Ithaca, New York. A week before we moved, Cliff came to Lewisburg to help us with the final move to Ithaca. We loaded a rented van with packed cartons, which Cliff then drove and unloaded in Ithaca. On the 29th of August, Claudia flew in from a visit to San Francisco to meet us in Ithaca and helped us move into the apartment.

# Reflections

When I look back at my life, I realize that together with Ilse and her mother at my side, and with their physical and moral support at all times, their understanding and love for me, we were able to accomplish together the impossible. Whatever Ilse and I did in our marriage we always discussed; neither one of us made any decisions without both of us fully agreeing. This included raising our children, managing our money, and most of all doing what we believed was right for all of us.

However, I also now realize that all my work at various jobs, both to earn a living and to improve our home, was at the expense of not spending enough time with my little family at home. Certainly I did not spend enough time with Cliff and Claudia while they grew up. I am forever sorry for that and regret it so much more now, when I see how my grandchildren are growing up, and how their parents have more time than I ever had to be with them.

On the more positive side, Ilse and I managed every year to go with our children as they grew up on vacation. Sometimes, I had to borrow money doing that, but I always felt that it was important. While Clifford and Claudia were still little, we always went as a family together with Omi Olga, Ilse's mother, to some hotel in the Catskill Mountains of New York.

When Cliff and Claudia grew up, we toured the White Mountains in New Hampshire. We went to the sea shore. We went to Niagara Falls. We went to the Poconos.

Over the years Ilse and I took many memorable trips:

March 1977, Israel to visit Claudia during her junior year in college
September 1982, France and Israel
July 1983, Hawaii to visit Cliff, Maj-Lis and Dani
November 1987, Cancun, Mexico
July 1988 Israel, during the Israel-Lebanese war
January 1988, Hong Kong, Macau and Canton, China
March 1989, Thailand and Japan
October 1990, London
February 1991, Hawaii
February 1992, Switzerland, Italy, and France
March 1993, Bahamas
February 1994, St. Lucia

*Bermuda, May 1996, our Golden Wedding Anniversary. Back, left to right: Maj-Lis, Clifford, Bruce, Ari, Claudia, Ilse, me, Daniel. Front: Joel, Gabriel, Stefan.*

July 1994, Alaska

February 1995, Hawaii

January 1996, St. Lucia

May of 1996, Bermuda, for our Golden wedding anniversary trip, together with our children and grandchildren

June 1996, 1997, 1998 and 1999, Alaska escorting groups

February 1997, Hawaii

February 1998, Panama Canal

August 1999, Canada

May 2000, Bahamas

January 2002, Jamaica

January 2003 and 2004, cruises through the Caribbean.

July 2007, London, to revisit where we met

May 2004, San Franciso, to see my parents' graves and visit Daniel and Diane

May 2008, California, to see Joel graduate from Stanford; we also had Daniel and Stef drive us to the cemetery to visit my parents' graves

In 1972, shortly after my mother's death, my brother Ed and his wife Lore got divorced. Because of this divorce, we eventually lost our contact not only with Lore, but more so with Bob, Ken and their children. I will forever be sorry about that.

One year later, Ed married Diane LaVoi. They were very happily married until October in 1991, when Ed passed away at the age of 78 years. Ed had suffered a bad heart attack in 1964, from which he had a tough time recuperating. His body had weakened over the years, and he needed several surgeries. However, his death was caused by bladder cancer.

# Concluding Note and
# Some Other Thoughts and Memories

In 1960 Elie Wiesel published the English translation of his first book, "Night." It was translated from the French "La Nuit." In his book Wiesel tells the story about his life as a ten year old prisoner of the Nazis in Auschwitz. During the next few years Wiesel continued to write the memoirs about his Holocaust experiences. His books are considered by many as the voice and conscience of the Jewish people.

In 1961 came the electrifying news that Israeli agents had captured the most wanted killer of the Nazi regime Adolph Eichmann in South America. He was taken to Israel to stand trial for mass murder. Several years later, when the Eichmann trial started in Jerusalem, the world learned more about the Nazi atrocities. The Eichmann trial started a period of reflection and recording of memories of the Holocaust.

During the following two decades Elie Wiesel and many other Holocaust survivors urged that the United States build a museum in memory of the six million Jews who were killed by the Nazis during the Holocaust. In 1978 President Jimmy Carter proposed to establish a Holocaust Memorial in Washington, DC.

Ilse and I immediately thought about getting involved. Having been survivors of the Nazi era ourselves, we recognized that this would be a perfect memorial to the six million Jews who died at the hands of the Nazis and specifically to both Ilse's father and younger brother who died in Auschwitz with no grave markers for them.

The Holocaust museum was to become a central force for shaping my activities for decades into the future.

In April of 1978, I volunteered to be a Hillel co-adviser along with Dr. David Finkel a professor of mathematics at Bucknell University in Lewisburg, PA. Together with the Bucknell University Hillel students, we arranged to have the university bring Elie Wiesel to Bucknell as a lecturer. The university was only willing to pay a certain amount towards his honorarium. However, we were able to find a donor in Sunbury, PA, to subsidize the remaining expenses. With his help, it was now possible to have Mr. Wiesel come to the university on April 27, 1978 to deliver his lecture. I was fascinated with the way he presented his experience of the Holocaust. For Ilse and me it was a great honor to be Mr. Wiesel's hosts. We were very fortunate to take him for coffee to a nearby restaurant after his lecture, and we had a long discussion with him about the

Holocaust, both our lives, and his life as well. There was no doubt that he had taken a liking to both Ilse and me. He is a very observant Chassidic Jew, and his meals in the evening consisted only of fruit and coffee (as well as chain smoking his cigarettes). The same was true again for his breakfast the following morning which we hosted. After breakfast we drove him to the Williamsport airport for his return flight to New York. In one of our discussions, he told us how important it would be to join the Holocaust Museum as Charter members. He also said many times that it was so important for us to speak out, most of all for tolerance. I remember his words, "When people suffer anywhere, and we don't speak out about it, eventually we all will suffer." Ever since that day, a friend-

ship developed between Elie Wiesel and us. We are exchanging Rosh Hasha-nah greetings every year, and personal letters during the year. Ilse and I met him again in 2011 when he vis-ited Ithaca.

Nine years after that evening and morning with Elie Wiesel, on October 7, 1987, the US Congress unanimously passed a law

*We meet Elie Wiesel again in Ithaca in 2011*

which established a "permanent living memorial to the Holocaust." Shortly thereafter, Ilse and I both got involved with the establishment of the Holocaust Memorial Museum in Washington DC. In 1990, we both became Charter Members of the Museum, and in 1996 we became members of the museum's "Circle Of Life."

The Holocaust Memorial Museum invited both Ilse and me to be at the opening ceremony which was held on a very rainy day, April 26, 1993. President Bill Clinton and Mrs. Hillary Clinton, as well as Vice President and Mrs. Gore, and many other dignitaries were pres-ent. It was a very emotional and somber opening ceremony which Elie Wiesel addressed. The Museum was dedicated as a "witness and as a living testament to the victims and survivors." It was a day that I will never forget. On that day I made a solemn decision that I would speak out against all kinds of hate and speak out for tolerance for oppressed people everywhere.

Around that time, Ilse and I were attending a dinner function for a Hillel Holocaust presentation at Bucknell University and met Chaim

Potok. He urged us both to start speaking about the Holocaust and educating the younger generations about the dangers of hate in society.

In the fall of 1993, the temple board of our synagogue of Temple Beth-El in Sunbury decided to lease a bus and take interested members to the Holocaust Museum in Washington, DC. One evening I got a telephone call from a Jedd Levinson who was a member of the temple and had volunteered to arrange such a trip. Jedd called me and asked me to come along on this trip and tell the group Ilse's and my personal experiences during the Nazi era. Up to that time I had never spoken about the Holocaust in public, and I told Jedd that I really had to think about it. I was not ready to speak openly on this subject. Jedd argued that I owed it not only to the membership of the temple, but to everyone concerned to tell every detail that I could remember. After a long deliberation with Ilse, our daughter Claudia, and our son Cliff, I finally agreed to go along with the group to the museum. I began writing a presentation starting with the first day that Hitler came into power and ending with the day we finally were able to flee from the Nazis six years later.

Unbeknownst to me, a local newspaper The Daily Item sent a reporter Mike Glacier along on the bus for a trip to the museum. It was a 50 seat tour bus with a TV screen for movies and a microphone. I spoke for close to one hour on our trip to the museum and then showed a PBS movie about the infamous Kristall Nacht. The following day, Mike Glacier's story about the trip appeared on the front page of the Daily Item.

It didn't take long before phone calls came pouring in, from schools, service clubs, and churches, to come to speak about the Holocaust. My first appearance was in the spring of 1994, when I was asked by the administration of Susquehanna University in Selinsgrove, PA to participate in a roundtable discussion with faculty and students about the Holocaust. The program was to start at 7 PM and last until 8:30 PM. Over 100 people attended, and the program finally ended at 9:30 PM. Again, it was covered by the press, and my name and quotes from my talk were reported in the local newspapers the following morning.

I was invited to speak at the Harrisburg campus of Penn State University, at Susquehanna University, Bloomsburg University, and Bucknell University, as well as to all high schools in our area. I lectured especially around the time of Kristall Nacht, the night of the broken glass, and various yearly memorial services remembering the death of the six million Jews.

In 1979, Dr. Finkel and I approached the Bucknell administration to discuss establishing a residence for the Jewish students at Bucknell. The other two major religions had already homes for their students. At first

the administration gave the excuse that there was not a sufficient enroll-
ment of Jewish students at Bucknell to have a residence exclusively for
them. We found an ally in Father Martin the Catholic campus chaplain
who agreed with Finkel and me. The Jewish students circulated a petition and together with Father Martin we presented the petition to the
administration. At about the same time, a house known as the Martin
House was standing idle,and the university finally agreed that this should
become the residence for the Jewish students. We were able to house
eight students at the Martin House which we unofficially referred to as
the "Hillel House." This was a major breakthrough for the Jewish students at Bucknell and for the town's Jewish residents.

In October 2001, Bucknell University's newspaper "The Bucknell-
ian" had printed an advertisement from a group headed by David Irving,
the notorious Holocaust denier. The university was embarrassed that this
advertisement had appeared in their paper. I got a call from the President's office asking me to speak in memory of Kristall Nacht on November 2001 at the university and address David Irving's advertisement.
With close to 300 people present, I ripped Mr. Irving to pieces. I also
praised the university for their tremendous tolerance towards all people,
students and faculty alike. This event was covered widely by the press.

On many church sponsored bus trips to the Holocaust museum in
Washington, DC, I have spoken about the Holocaust, with my emphasis
against hate and asking for tolerance. I have spoken at many universities,
schools, churches, social clubs and temples. Most of my presentations
were covered by the press. I became known regionally as a speaker on
hate and tolerance issues. In 2002 I moved to Ithaca NY, and soon again
found my way to speak to many audiences from Cornell University to
the local middle and high school. Again, the press featured my talks in
the local newspaper.

*I speak at Lansing High School, near our home in Ithaca, NY, in 2008. (Photo courtesy of* www.LansingStar.com*)*

Over the years I must have spoken to several thousand people about the Holocaust. I have received hundreds of letters from school children and from people from all walks of life who heard me speak and urged me to keep on speaking so that the hor-rible events which led to the Holocaust and the Holocaust itself would never be forgot-

*November 9, 2001. Left to right: Captain George Elliot, me, General Unger-leider, Lt. Colonel Boehnien.*

ten in history. I have never failed to mention the fate of Ilse's father and her twelve year old brother at the hands of the Nazi killers. It is my way of assuring that their names will never be forgotten.

Before we moved from Lewisburg, PA to Ithaca NY, the Milton, PA school board decided to honor me for my years of speaking to their school about the Holocaust. They established a yearly award for the student who scores the highest marks in the Holocaust studies unit. To make the award more important, Ilse and I set up a little scholarship fund for the student so honored. The name of the fund is "The Ignatz and Kurt Machauf Memorial Achievement Award."

Another opportunity for spreading knowledge about the Holocaust as well as memorializing Ilse's family arose in the summer of 2001. Unexpectedly I found myself in the possession of over one hundred photos taken by General Eisenhower's personal photographer during World War II. These original photos belonged to this gentleman who by now was up in his eighties, who happened to meet and speak to my good friend Bernard Greenberg in Mexico. He confessed to Budd that he taken and owned historic photos and that they had never been published. He was afraid that one day after his death, somebody in Mexico would find these photos, and not knowing what they are, would discard and destroy them. The photos documented the American liberation of the Ohrdruf and Buchenwald Concentration Camps. Many of them show General Eisenhower and other generals inspecting these camps after their liberation. He asked Budd for advice about what he should do with them now. Budd told him about my involvement with the Holocaust Museum and that I would put them to good use. Shortly thereafter, I received these most valuable photos.

On November 9, 2001, on the 63rd anniversary of Kristall Nacht, Ilse and I presented the set of photographs to the Bucknell University Art Department to be a traveling memorial to universities and schools across the United States. We dedicated the exhibit "In memory of Ignatz and Kurt Machauf who lost their lives at the hands of the Nazis during the Holocaust." The evening when these photos were exhibited for the first time at Bucknell was a major event. Retired Lt. General of the United States Army, Alvin Ungerleider, was invited to dedicate these photos. General Ungerleider himself, when he was a Major in the army, led his troops during the liberation of the Buchenwald concentration camp. Coincidentally, Buchenwald was the Concentration Camp where my late father was sent by the Nazis as an aftermath of Kristall Nacht on November 9, 1938, and was finally freed in 1939.

That night, as I stood next to General Ungerleiter, I was struck by how my life had come "full circle." There was an emotion within me which I cannot express. While I was introducing General Ungerleiter, I suddenly had a flashback to the night of November 10, 1938, and all its horrors and destruction and to when as a young boy I had watched as my Dad was taken by the Gestapo and sent to the Buchenwald concentration camp. The fear of that night, that we might never see my father again, was more than my mother and I could bear. I would have never thought that sixty three years later I would stand in my adopted hometown in the United States, an honored speaker at a major university, educating the public on the horrors of the Holocaust. I was introducing young American students (and the Bucknell community) to an American general who helped liberate that very same concentration camp where my father had been imprisoned. General Ungerleiter's presentation and the photos of the atrocities were the evidence of what my father and others in my family had suffered at the hands of the Nazis.

I must not close this particular subject without thanking Ilse for her total support in my speaking career. She never failed to accompany me whenever and wherever I spoke regardless of how she felt physically. She has always been by my side listening to every word I said and was and is my only honest critic. Without her support, I could never have succeeded in my efforts to fight hate and plea for tolerance. Ilse has allowed me to follow my conscience and heed the words of Elie Wiesel, "When people suffer, no matter where or when, and we don't speak out about it, sooner or later, we all will suffer in one form or the other."

# How I Would Like To Be Remembered

I have often been asked how I would like to be remembered. I have given the answer to this question a lot of thought.

- I would like to be remembered as a man who loved only one woman all his life, the girl he met and adored when we both were only in our teens.
- I would like to be remembered by my family as a man who loved every single one of them including those who entered my family by marriage, and a man who always was there when needed, who always listened to their problems and tried to help.
- I would like to be remembered as having answered the call to serve my adopted country during the second World War.
- I would like to be remembered as a man who spent the later years of his life as an activist for human rights, pleading for tolerance and understanding for all people.
- I would like to be remembered as a proud Jew, with great love for Israel and ready to support Israel whenever called upon.
- I would like to be remembered as a man who helped others wherever he could, especially those who could not help themselves.
- I would like to be remembered as a law abiding citizen who never got in trouble with the law.
- I would like to be remembered as a man who would rather help and care for others, than have others help and care for him.
- I have learned that nothing is impossible to do if one puts his mind, energy and ambition into achieving the goal. I have always tried to succeed and do the best I could possibly do to reach my goals in life.

Of course, I could not end writing my memoirs without paying a special tribute to the love of my life. Ilse has lived a noble and totally unselfish life with a willingness to help others and to deny herself many things in life, as long as they would benefit our family. Never have I heard her complain about anything; never ever have I heard her say a nasty or bad comment about another human being. Ilse is always happy as long as everyone else is happy. In all of our almost 59 years of married life we never ever had a major disagreement or argument. We never ever went to bed at night angry at each other. There was never a night which didn't end with a kiss, and with telling each other, "I love you."

Ilse's life as a child and teenager was so similar to my life. The major difference was that my immediate family survived the Holocaust intact. Unfortunately, her father and brother became victims of the Nazi murders. She missed them all her life.

Ilse and her mother, Olga, having survived the Holocaust together, had a very close and special relationship. Ilse worshipped her mother and took care of her all of her life. In her mother's later years there wasn't a day that she wouldn't go to the nursing home, not only sit with her for hours, but also feed her and make sure that she was well taken care of. She was a wonderful daughter to her mother and is a great, loving wife to me. Ilse is the best friend I ever had. She is the love of my life.

I always wished that we both had more than one life on earth to live together.

I do want to add a final word on a subject that I have thought about many times, the hereafter. I do not believe in it. I think that almost all religions that promise the followers various after-life have invented these stories as the best way to "sell" religion to the believers to make them behave well while they are on earth. Only recently I listened to a speaker on television who said that he was a professor of astrophysics. He assured his listeners that he has spent years listening to outer space for some word of some other life somewhere which he failed to hear. I also read a quote by Francis Crick, the winner of the Nobel Prize for his co-discovery of DNA, the double helix, the so-called blueprint of life. Here is what he wrote. "In the fullness of time, educated people will believe there is no soul independent of the body, and hence no life after death." This is what I believe as well. However, just in case that I should be wrong—I will see the readers again.

Until then,

So Long, Adios, Au revoir, Arriverderci, Auf Wiedersehen, Shalom.

# Postscript

Today is August 4, 2011. For a summer holiday, our family rented a beautiful house for one week at the gorgeous Owasco Lake, near Auburn, NY. I am using part of our time at the lake to write this Postscript.

At the end of 2004 I finished writing my book. On the day of my 85th birthday in 2005, I presented my book to my family and friends. The book was originally written as a family biography and I thought it would be kept as such. But because so many people asked for copies, it was published, and by now people have read the book not only in the United States, but also in Germany, Israel and France.

The purpose of this Postscript is to review the past six years since the book was first printed and update all the happy family events as well as the sad ones which have occurred since then. I am writing about what has changed in the lives of my children and grandchildren, and I hope that future generations will from time to time bring it up to date, so that the family history will be kept alive. I have received many, many comments from people congratulating me for writing this book and for giving them the idea to write their own family histories. Others wrote to me that they would wish that such a family history book would be available for their family.

A number of readers have asked me for more details about both Ilse's and my lives in the past, for stories which are not in the book. So hopefully this Postscript will help not only to record the changes within our family, but also to tell some forgotten stories. So, here we go....

\*\*\*

On May 19 this year, Ilse and I celebrated our 65th wedding anniversary. It was a lovely occasion, where we invited our friends and relatives to the Ginny Lee Restaurant along the

*We celebrated our 65th anniversary with the original "cake topper," saved all these years*

*On May 19, 2011, we celebrated our 65th wedding anniversary. Three days later, many of our Lewisburg and Ithaca friends, along with Claudia, Bruce, & Ari, joined us at one of our favorite restaurants, the Ginny Lee on Seneca Lake, NY, to celebrate.*

shore of Seneca Lake, one of the beautiful Finger Lakes in the wine region of upstate New York. The guests, the weather and the food were all delightful.

Being married for a very happy 65 years is one of the many blessings we have and are still enjoying. It is just too bad how quickly the years have gone by. During the five years that we were separated because of World War II, we exchanged a total of close to 2000 letters. We still have and cherish reading them so very often and realize how much in love we were then, and are even more so today

Our oldest grandson Daniel flew the family coop in 1999, at age 19, to pursue his interest in sound design at Expressions Media in Emeryville, CA. He was happy to escape the hot and humid summer weather in Virginia and settled in Oakland, CA. Daniel has worked with many music groups, and also worked for several years for Lionel Trains as a Sound Designer.

The next oldest grandson, Joel, graduated from the Ithaca High School in 2004 and was accepted at Stanford University in Palo Alto, CA. He spent the next four years there, studying Symbolic Systems, a mix of computer science and psychology. He was also a photographer for the school newspaper, the *Stanford Daily*. Upon graduating, he moved to San Francisco, and has been working as a web designer for two Internet startups, first GoodGuide.com, and now Quora.com.

Stefan, the next grandson, had decided that finishing at his science and technology high school was not worthwhile for him, so he completed his high-school diploma by taking courses at the local community college. Then he began college studies in Richmond, VA, but was not happy there. He moved to Sweden (Gothenburg) to assert his Swedish citizenship, to study, and possibly to stay there. But after intensive activities and learning some Japanese from a new friend there, he came back to the USA. Stefan stayed for a short while at home in Virginia before moving in with his brother in Oakland, CA. To date, Stefan has remained in California, mixing times of studies to finish his college degree and work in various professional jobs.

Gabriel, who follows next, will soon start his senior year at Tufts University in Boston, MA. He has studied International Relations, focusing on environmental issues. Through Tufts, and especially Tufts Hillel, Gabriel has traveled a great deal. He spent 10 days in Rwanda, learning about the 1994 genocide from a Jewish perspective. Between June and August, 2010, he lived in Mumbai, India, conducting research on urban environmental issues. Finally, in 2011, Gabriel studied abroad in Quito,

*Our five grandsons. Front row, left to right: Daniel and Stefan Voss, Ari Lewenstein. Back row, left to right: Gabriel and Joel Lewenstein. Photo taken June 2004, Ithaca, NY.*

*Our five grandsons at the time of Ari's bar mitzvah: Stefan, Gabriel, Ari, Daniel, and Joel. Photo taken June 2008, Ithaca, NY. Copyright © Julie Magura/www.jonreis.com, reprinted with permission.*

*...and two more years after that: August 2010, Owasco Lake, NY. Stefan, Daniel, Ari, Gabriel, Joel.*

*In August 2010, we celebrated our 70th year of knowing each other with a family gathering at Owasco Lake, NY. Top row: Claudia, Maj-Lis, Cliff, Bruce, Ilse, me, Daniel. Bottom row: Ari, Stefan, Gabriel, Joel*

Ecuador. Throughout college, Gabriel has been very active in Hillel, and will be President for his senior year.

The youngest of our grandsons is Ari, who will be a senior this year at the Ithaca, NY, high school. Since his freshman year, Ari has been a member of the Ithaca cross country team and has been a member at the varsity level for the past two years. This fall Ari will be a captain of the team and one of its top runners. Ari also will be applying to college in the fall, and hopes to attend a small liberal arts college after high school.

Our son-in-law's father Harry Lewenstein passed away on February 3, 2010, in Palo Alto, CA. He had had an unfortunate bicycle accident some 13 year earlier which left him totally paralyzed, yet in the end it was a blood cancer which led to his death.

In November 2010, our son Clifford and our daughter-in-law Maj-Lis sold their house in Reston, VA, to move to Moss Beach, CA. They drove by car all the way from Reston to Oakland, where Daniel lives. Clifford changed offices from the USGS office in Reston to the office in Menlo Park, CA For a long time it had been Clifford and Maj-Lis's dream to move to California to be together with their sons Daniel and Stefan. They revel in both the absence of winter and in the blue clarity of the Pacific Ocean.

In the Spring of 2011, our daughter-in-law's father passed away in Sweden. The losses of both Bruce's and Maj-Lis's fathers saddened us. The deaths were close to home.

Unfortunately, in November of 2010, I was diagnosed with stenosis of the heart (a thickening of one of my heart valves). I am happy to say that my condition since then has been stabilized, and I am doing well enough to do everything I enjoy doing.

\*\*\*

For me personally, I had a great and a happy surprise in 2009, when some regional historians from Aachen and Bielefeld in Germany made contact with me. One of them had found my book at a local bookstore in the city of my birth, Aachen. There are three of them, whom I have met only through the Internet: Iris Gedig (Dueren), Peter Bruecken (Aachen), and Stefan Kahlen (Bielefeld). These three people had established a "family book" which they call "Familienbuch Euregio," which now includes my family They also have a website, www.familienbuch-euregio.de. They are documenting the life and the stories of people who lived in the region of the "three connecting corners" – where Germany, Holland, and Belgium meet. This area includes my hometown of Aachen. They are very much trying to reestablish and to remember the culture of those people of the past and preserve the contribution of those people who are no longer alive.

These three people have the objective of keeping the past alive to warn new generations to avoid the mistakes of the past. They represent the new German generation and I have bonded with them. We have become friends, even though I have never met them personally. (Once, Ilse and I did "meet" Iris and Peter by using Skype. We had a great time introducing and seeing each other.) These historians have a great deal of knowledge about what happened to the Jewish people in the region during the "Shoah," the Holocaust. Their objective is that it will never happen again. Stefan Kahlen, Iris Gedig and Peter Bruecken and I are working very closely together trying to find out what happened to many of the families, and finding their offspring when we can. We have found, alive all over the world, many people who once lived in Aachen and its suburbs, as well as the children of those people.

On Thanksgiving Day 2009, I received from this group a beautiful book, which really is a family tree about Ilse's and my family, with many stories about our lives then and now. They established my family roots on my father's side going back to 1729, and on my father's mother's side

*Among the information my German historian colleagues have sent me are these 2009 photos of a group of Catholic teenagers cleaning and replanting the Würselen cemetery where my ancestors are buried. Mrs. Ella Shvemmer (top photo, far left), a Russian immigrant as are many of the Jews in Aachen today, helped organize the cleaning. Present at the rejuvenation of the cemetery were Catholic priest Huu Duc Tran and Rabbi Mordechai Bohrer, the leader of the rebuilt Jewish community in Aachen. Photos provided by kind courtesy of Mr. Vladimir Shvemmer.*

they found records dating back to 1806. For my mother's family they found records about her father going back to 1746, and on her mother's family going back to 1807. On Ilse's father's side they established a family tree going back to 1843, and on Ilse's mother side they found records going back to 1862.

\*\*\*

Over the years many people have asked me to tell them more about some of what I have written. I will do so with a few words so that the book will not be increased by too many more pages. To answer all the questions is impossible to do in this Postscript, because each answer leads to even more stories, as you will see below:

For example, I've been asked about the aftermath of the pogrom on Kristall Night on November 9, 1938. The next evening, November 10, 1938, my father was arrested by the Gestapo in our home, under the pretense "that it would be for his own safety." He was driven handcuffed from our house in a Gestapo car, first to the local prison which was located on the Albertsetinweg. Because the prison was overcrowded, the Jews in the prison were then taken to a gym, which belonged to the Jewish Community, at the Oligsbendengasse in Aachen. He and 70 other Jewish men who were arrested that night in Aachen spent about two full days there. Anything they had carried with them, or were wearing, except their wedding rings, were confiscated and never returned. It was a windfall for the Gestapo and the SS. While they were in this gym, they received no food to eat or fluids to drink. On the morning of the third day they were paraded through the town of Aachen, before they were loaded on the train for the Buchenwald Concentration Camp. Some of these men, including my father, were beaten with sticks upon arrival -- some were even bitten by dogs.

Several of the questions I have been asked involve parts of my Army service in Europe. For example, I have been asked about the location of the St. Maur Prisoner of War (POW) camp that I discuss in the chapter on the "Liberation of Paris." To clarify this, there were actually two camps within two miles from each other. The second POW camp was in Bonneuil-sur-Marne. Both camps were under the command of Captain Kearns. I was a full time interpreter at the St. Maur POW camp. At the Bonneuil-sur-Marne camp, some of the prisoners, especially the German officers, spoke some English. However, when Captain Kearns was involved on a special issue, he would take me along as his personal interpreter.

As an interpreter who spoke German, English, and French, it was not unusual for me to be deployed to various areas within France and Germany. Looking back today, I must say that both the French as well as the German population were always cooperative with us. These trips brought me several times to Aachen, especially shortly after the city was entered by the American army during October 1944. It was the first city in Germany that the army entered. Other cities I visited included Heidelberg, Cologne, Bad Ems, and Koblenz.

These travels for the Army also gave me an opportunity to spent several days in Brussels, Belgium, with some members of my family who survived the concentration camps and with those who had returned from hiding places within France.

Another Army story: In the book, I wrote that "From General Larkin I never heard again. I was told that he had returned home sometime in April of 1946 and retired from the army." But now, through information which is available on the Internet, I have learned that this is not correct. In March 1946, General Larkin returned to the United States and was promoted from Brigadier General (1 Star) to Major General (2 Stars). After his service in the European Theater of Operations he was named by President Truman as Quartermaster General of the Army. He served in that capacity until March 1949. His next assignment was as the Army's Director of Logistics (later called Assistant Chief of Staff for Logistics) for which he was promoted to the rank of Lieutenant General (3 Stars). He served this post until his retirement on December 31, 1952. General Larkin died at the Walter Reed General Hospital in Washington, DC, on October 17, 1968. He was buried with full military honors at the Arlington National Cemetery. He was one of the finest officers and gentlemen which I met during my military service.

In my book I wrote the story of how our lives were saved in Aachen by an old lady, Mrs. Leroy, who at that time was close to 80 years of age. She was a neighbor of ours and had a grocery and vegetable store, which she operated with her son Willie. During the nights from sometime in November 1938 until April 1939, she put herself in mortal danger by leaving sufficient food in front of our door to sustain ourselves. Through Stefan Kahlen, one of the local historians I mentioned above, a contact was made with Willie Leroy, who was named after his grandfather. His great-grandmother was a heroine. I was able to let him read the story of how his great-grandmother saved four lives: my grandmother, my parents and myself. He still lived in Aachen until about a year ago when he moved to Ulm on the Donau.

\*\*\*

I cannot close this Postscript, without thanking my son–in-law, Bruce Lewenstein, for all the help he has given me developing the book as it is now. Bruce has spent as much time, or even more so, on the completion of the revised versions, as I have spent writing the book. Hopefully, he will be the one who will carry on with the history of the book, so that those who come after Ilse and me need not search for our stories. Simply said: thank you, Bruce, for your work to make the book the success it is, and by providing part of the royalties to organizations dedicated to preserving the memory of the Holocaust through living actions.

Fred Voss

# Another Miracle After 77 Years

On June 22, 2012, I became the beneficiary of the American dream. I was honored by the Lansing Central School District, in Lansing, New York, to receive an accredited high school diploma after satisfactorily completing the requirements prescribed by the Board of Education and New York State.

Mrs. June Martin, a teacher of English at Lansing High School, introduced me that early summer evening during the outdoor commencement ceremony to a group of gathered students, parents and grandparents by saying:

> For the past ten years, Fred Voss has enriched and empowered the lives of thousands of Lansing students and, by extension their parents and an entire community, by sharing his knowledge of history and personal experience of being a World War II Holocaust survivor and an American war veteran. Fred shares his mission of fighting against hatred and prejudice, and promoting tolerance and diversity, with young people so that they will cultivate a better future for us all....
>
> Tonight, through a unique collaboration of the US military and NY State, at the spry age of 92, Fred is receiving his high school diploma....
>
> It is one of the crowning achievements of my career to have the honor to introduce you to Fred Voss.

*June Martin holds the Golden Apple*
*I received after my commencement*
*speech at Lansing High School*

As I stood among my fellow Lansing High School graduates of the class of 2012 and their guests, school staff, and the larger community, I explained briefly my 77-year journey that eventually led me to the commencement podium. Here are some of my words as I accepted my high school diploma that evening:

> From the bottom of my heart, I wish to thank you for bestowing upon me this great honor, and I am proud to accept an accredited diploma from the Lansing High School....

*I acknowledge applause after my Lansing High School*
*commencement speech*

As part of the Nazi campaign of anti-Semitism and racism, the Nazis took away my right to an education, so this is my first opportunity after 77 years for me to receive a high school diploma.

I, Fred Voss, am accepting this great honor not only in my name, but also in the names of the one and a half million Jewish children, from tiny babies to early teenagers, whose innocent lives perished during the Holocaust in Nazi-occupied Europe. May they never be forgotten.

We must continue to reject all kinds of hate wherever it takes place....

The world will never know how many future brilliant scholars were lost, how many of those children might have contributed to all of us to live in a better world. It was my fate that I was able to escape the killers by being legally permitted to live in the United States of America – or I, too, would have become one of the Nazis' victims.

In my appreciation for being allowed to come to the United States legally, I volunteered for the United States Armed Forces, shortly after my adopted country was attacked by our enemies on December 7, 1941....

My final words to the graduation class were those by which I lived my entire life: "Always remember, one of the greatest pleasures in life is actually doing what some people say that you cannot accomplish."

By coincidence my youngest grandson, Ari Lewenstein, graduated from the Ithaca High School just one day before I graduated from the Lansing High School.

*Ari and I share our diplomas,*
*awarded one day apart*

*Editor's note:*

*This edition is being prepared in May 2016 to celebrate Fred and Ilse's 70th wedding anniversary.*

*After open-heart surgery in early 2013 to replace the worn-out valve he mentions in the Postcript, Fred continues to live an active life. He and Ilse live independently, eat out regularly, and visit with friends and family. For several years, they worked out at the gym several times a week -- in their 90s! In May 2015, Fred fractured his hip and spent a couple of weeks in the hospital and rehab. Within a few months, he was back to walking (though with a cane) and riding his stationery bicycle. All this time, Ilse just keeps gliding along, looking 15-20 years younger than she is. Fred consults regularly with the German historians he mentions in the Postscript, and has been interviewed several times for German television. On the occasion of his receiving a high school diploma in 2012, newspaper and television stories about him appeared around the United States and in Aachen.*

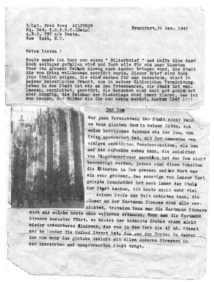

The first page of Fred's 1945 letter to his family

*In 2014, Fred rediscovered a letter he had written to his parents from Aachen in December 1945, which included photographs. Though the paper was crumbling away, Fred managed to transcribe and translate the letter. His German historian colleagues arranged for a copy of the letter, including "before and after" photographs, to be deposited in the Aachen city archives. For his contribution, Fred received a formal certificate of recognition from the Mayor of Aachen.*

*Through the fourth edition of this book, Fred had listed his cousin Heinz Stiel among those killed in the Holocaust. But in 2013, through the German historians, Fred discovered that his cousin was still living, having built a successful life in the United States. They have corresponded by e-mail and phone.*

*Although Fred no longer speaks regularly at schools, he and Ilse remain connected to Holocaust education. In 2016, the Ithaca Area United Jewish Community produced short video interviews of Fred and Ilse to show to local schools; this will help children see people from their own community affected by the Holocaust. On Yom Ha-Shoah (Holocaust Remembrance Day) in early May 2016, Fred and Ilse were honored at an IAUJC event, lighting candles in memory of the relatives they lost.*

Ilse and Fred at Yom HaShoah event at Temple Beth El, Ithaca, NY May 5, 2016

*In 2015, the district of Liesing (now part of the city of Vienna) dedicated a memorial stone in front of the house where Ilse grew up. The stone acknowledges that Ignatz and Kurt Machauf who had lived in that house were murdered in 1942. Ilse and Fred's daughter Claudia and her son Gabriel attended the dedication, which they found very moving. They found that young Austrians are acknowledging that Austria was a perpetrator of the Holocaust, not just a victim of the Nazis.*

Claudia Lewenstein at the dedication of the memorial stone in front of Ilse's family house in Liesing, June 13, 2015

January 2015: Fred and Ilse celebrate the 75th anniversary of their meeting on New Year's Day 1940

*Fred and Ilse continue to enjoy following the lives of their children and grandchildren. Daniel Voss has moved to Sweden to continue his career. Stefan Voss completed his undergraduate degree at Sacramento State University in California and is working for the U.S. Geological Survey there while waiting to begin a graduate program. He recently bought a house with friends in Sacramento. Joel Lewenstein still works for a Silicon Valley startup, Quora.com. Gabriel Lewenstein graduated from Tufts in 2012; after working for a non-profit in New York City that specializes in international transportation and development policy, he recently became a community liaison in the office of the Public Advocate of New York City. Ari Lewenstein will graduate from Wesleyan University three days after Fred and Ilse's 70th anniversary, and take up a job in Boston as a health care policy analyst.*

*An anecdote to close this story: More than 75 years after meeting, Ilse and Fred are still flirting. In January 2016, they had gone to lunch at a deli near their home. They sat across from each other at a small table, sharing a Reuben sandwich. They didn't talk much, because of the crowd and noise. When they finished, Ilse took the plates and utensils to throw away, while Fred stood up.*

*At that moment, a man at the next table spoke up. "I was looking at you and your wife," he said. "I assume that was your wife? Can I ask: How long have you been married?"*

*"Come this May, 70 years!" said Fred.*

Ilse and Fred celebrate their 68th wedding anniversary with Claudia and Cliff

*"Oh my god," the man said. "I'm only 68. You've been married longer than I've been alive! It was just so obvious that the two of you are in love."*

*Just then, a young woman at the table on the other side of Fred spoke up. "I was watching you flirt with each other, too," she said. "I'm a high school senior. You were just looking in each other's eyes."*

*So, after all these years, Ilse and Fred's love still shines.*

*July 2007, Ilse and I revisit our wartime walk on Oxford Street in London.*

*(see page 150 for the original photo)*

Printed in Germany
by Amazon Distribution
GmbH, Leipzig